Corvix

Poems of Love, Sex and Death

Expanded Edition

Valentin Per Lind

First paperback edition 2022
Book design by PublishingPush

ISBNs:
978-1-80541-040-9 (paperback)
978-1-80541-041-6 (hardback)
978-1-80227-215-4 (ebook)

Published by
Per Lind Publishing
Eastbourne
United Kingdom

To Fatna
beloved of my heart,
companion of my life,
who alone understands me.

To Adam
who has the talents of a true artist.
(more than he knows!)

To my dearest lifelong friend,
Rosina Marquez.

And to Maxine Sanders,
the wisest of wise women.

Birth and death belong
To Nature;
All experience in between
Belongs to Man.

Contents

Middle Period 2000–2009

Late Period 2010 – 2021

Poems of 2022

A Poem for Christmas

Liturgical Poems and Prayers

Additional Poem by Adam Holland

A Candle Before the Sun

Preface to Second Edition

It is now the summer of 2022, some 8 months after the first edition of *Corvix* came out. At the time, I thought, wrongly, that I had written all I would ever be likely to write, but my Unconscious continued to excite me with lines and images for new poems. The choice was to wait another few years until I had written sufficient for a second volume, or work them into an expanded edition of *Corvix*. Bearing in mind that I could only afford to publish once more, I chose the latter, because I really wanted to get these poems out.

As I said in the foreword to the first edition, *all poetry is autobiography*, and that is certainly true of this collection, which has been expanded to include several new works. Additionally, minor improvements have been made to some of the original poems, and accompanying notes have been revised for readability, with some of the longer notes being hived off into separate discursive essays. I sincerely hope the reader finds something to interest them, and hopefully inspire them... or at least something that resonates with their own feelings. As it developed, the book became less of a volume of poetry and more of a philosophy of Life and Being, the poems becoming boards from which to dive into meditations on mysticism, philosophy and politics, but the reader is free to enjoy the poems for their own sake.

My experience of poetry published by mainstream publishers has been decidedly underwhelming. They are frequently churned out in cheap-looking paperbacks (often titchy 'pocket size' editions) with tiny fonts that strain the eyes and insufficient white space to set off the poems. By contrast, some of the most beautifully produced books of poetry are by independent authors, exquisitely tailored in bespoke editions. I have taken especial care in producing this book to choose fonts that are elegant but easy on the eye, offset by lots of white space. Thus, I chose Century Schoolbook for the poems, which, although a serif font, is pleasantly rounded with nice spacing (kerning) between the characters; and for the notes I chose Baskerville, whose serifs are sufficiently low key that the text doesn't look cramped at a low font size.

These are not poems about daffodils: they are poems of terror and magnificence that lay bare the human soul; they are voices vying for attention and demanding to be heard: voices of lovers and rogues, of witches and necromancers, of the betrayed and the murdered, and those left behind by the ongoing propulsion of life. I hope my book finds a loving home on your bookshelf, and that you derive as much pleasure in reading it as I have enjoyed in the writing of it.

Foreword: The Purpose of Poetry

Some time ago, I received the finest compliment I have ever been paid when a lady said to me, "Mr Lind! You are the most dysfunctional, maladapted person I have ever met!" It was a compliment because there are many things in this world, gentle reader, to which I would not want to be adapted in my wildest dreams; but it also reminded me that we live in insecure times, when people gravitate to celebrities and other icons of positivity, preferring the overtures of revolting motivational speakers and oily evangelicals to deep thinkers and truth-tellers, among whom I number poets. We prefer the assurance of cheap certainties rather than to ask the difficult questions. The tormented alcoholic poet does not exactly fit the definition of an icon of positivity, but at least they have something interesting to say about the human condition; and they remind us that suffering is a shared human experience, but also one that deepens us. The Greeks, as usual, had a word for it: *pathei mathos*, the gaining of wisdom through adversity. Would John Milton have written such sweeping poetry if he had not lost his sight, and would Dylan Thomas have attained such sublimity if he had not had a relationship with the bottle? Would Byron have been the poet he was if had not been 'mad, bad and dangerous to know', and would Sylvia Plath have written such emotionally deep poetry if it were not for the depression that took her life? Social conformists don't write poetry; poetry is the voice of the untamed heart, the gravelly drawl of the hard-won life. So, the volume I offer you is not a 'feel good' book; it is not intended to be inspirational, but it *is* intended to evoke thought and feeling.

Poetry is the art of painting with words; encapsulating emotion, meaning and imagery into extreme economy of phrasing and line. Poetry is the shot glass next to the pint glass that is the novel. We write novels, but we *compose* poetry, which implies that poetry possesses a musicality that prose does not. To say it is 'composed', in the same way as an architect designs a house or a draughtsman designs a car, is a misapprehension. It is rather a process of self-creation in which the poet acts both as mother and midwife. The poet gives shape and form to something that composes *itself*; he or she lends economy and discipline to the Promethean stream of consciousness. A poem, ultimately, is something that pushes itself up unbidden from the rich soil of the Deep Self where it has been quietly germinating even while we sleep and go about our daily business, blissfully unaware of its existence until we get 'contractions'. We write poetry because *poetry is in us* and we can't stop writing poetry. It is a voice that forces itself up from the depths, demanding to be expressed.

Any creative act demands an open line to the Unconscious or Deep Self, and this occurs mostly when the mind is in an abstracted state that allows the imagination to wander, as, for example, drifting in the state between waking and sleep, walking in beautiful countryside[1], luxuriating in a hot bath, or relaxing with a warming coffee beside a fire, such that one enters a dreamy state of consciousness

---

[1] The rhythm of walking stimulates thought and refreshes the mind, creating a pleasant diversion while the subconscious processes ideas.

– anything but sitting behind a desk waiting for inspiration to happen (it won't); the desk part comes when you organise the stream of imagery and nascent lines of text into a coherent flowing tapestry. I composed much of my poetry walking from door to door delivering mail; miraculously, the right letters ended up in the right boxes – mostly.

In retrospect, the Unconscious was misrepresented by Freud as the source of our most primitive impulses, a wellspring of atavistic violence, of monsters and demons (and this is because Freud saw it as a threat to the civilised order), but it is also the source of all creativity and beauty. I liken it to a poison garden, full of beautiful flowers, some rich and perfumed, others dark and deadly; some will inspire you; others will give you a bad trip. Think of it this way: there is a door to the Unconscious. Open it a little and you get art and genius, but open it completely or remove it altogether, and you get psychosis. It is important, I think, to understand that no one can control the Unconscious. It is its own realm with its own sun, moon and stars, and although one can inhibit it, it is beyond our purview. I can go for weeks or months with no inspiration at all, and then suddenly my

Unconscious gears into action and starts throwing up streams of imagery which my conscious mind translates into fragmentary lines, which in turn become the nucleus of a poem built around them. But I need to be clear that a poem is not just a succession of images strung together: it has to flow, and while it does not have to conform rigidly to the requirements of meter, it does need to have cadence and flow with the breath.

When inspiration comes, one needs to write in the white heat of creativity. If one puts it off, the inspiration may dry up and the original genius of the poem will be lost. The more one writes, the more one stimulates one's Unconscious to keep writing. I always remind would-be writers that they need to have a relationship of trust with their Unconscious, that the inspiration will come even if one has to wrestle mentally with a concept before the solution begins to flow. The writing of poetry always comes easier when it is approached as pleasure rather than as work.

What makes a poet is the ability to observe acutely and experience intensely. Poetry, like faith, is a means of looking beneath the surface of things. It is the revealing of the hidden beyond the outward appearance of form, be that the presence of the numinous behind the veil of existence, as in nature poetry, or the lies and propaganda that society unquestioningly accepts, as in radical social poetry (which I call the 'social realist' form). To perceive reality through new eyes... *that* is poetry.

A poem works with reality as it is experienced rather than the reality which is objectively observed. For example, a scientist will describe hail as frozen water, but to the poet, it is 'Heaven's scorn, bane of Man', a rainstorm is 'bleak sheets of pain', trees are 'homes for rooks', the ocean is 'the whale road'[2], a sword is a 'shield biter'. When we write of the beauty of a woman, it is of her Mystery, not of the rouged model on the cover of *Cosmopolitan*, and thus in poetry, we attempt to capture the concealed light that shines through the paper shade that covers it. I cite as an example, *Valentine*, an exceptional poem by Carol Ann Duffy[3], whose opening lines read:

---

[2] Seanus Heany *trans.* (1999) *Beowulf.* Faber & Faber. Line 10

[3] Carol Ann Duffy (1993) 'Valentine', *Mean Time*, Anvil Press Poetry (1993)

Not a red rose or a satin heart.
I give you an onion.
It is a moon wrapped in brown paper.
It promises light
Like the careful undressing of love.

Why give a Valentine card when you can give the moon and the luminescence it represents? So here we have a physical object which, when lit by the imagination, is transfigured into something more than itself. A further example, from Sylvia Plath[4]:

The night sky is only a sort of carbon paper,
Blue-black, with the much-poked periods of
    stars
Letting in the light, peephole after peephole –
A bone-white light, like death, behind all
    things.

An astronomer will tell you that the stars are not holes shone through by an otherworldly light, but the poem is making a statement about the

---

[4] Sylvia Plath, 'Insomniac', *Crossing the Water*, ASH 813 PLA CRO

'otherness' of reality: the numinous that underlies physical reality that is so alien from physical reality that it would dissolve the universe back into itself. Imagination is integral to the ability to experience reality through Mind; to read and write poetry is to feel and experience intensely and that is why poetry is the exact antithesis of banality, the bovine half-light which the masses have been conditioned to accept as 'life'.

A poem is not written to entertain but to provoke a response. It is not intended to be pretty, or, to coin a phrase, as 'wallpaper for the middle classes'. As such, it should explore, not merely that which is bright, but that which is dark in the human experience: racism, war, murder, rape, suicide, teenage pregnancy... all are fair game. Poetry is intended to storm the battlements of the senses, to overwhelm one's defences. If it awakens the sensual memory through the power of shared experience, it has served its aim. If it makes you cry, if it revolts you, if it makes you angry, it has achieved its purpose. It is above all intended to evoke feeling in a world that is averse to feeling: a hyper-masculinised world that perceives feeling as weakness, and where to feel anything, frankly, is to be perceived as 'gay' or effeminate, an aberration and distraction from the process of making money and fighting over dominance.[5] It is an electric cattle prod applied to the skin of a numbed world.

Poetry also offers us the solace of shared experience. It reminds us that there is very little that has happened to us that has not happened to someone else. We don't read poetry to make us feel better; we read poetry that resonates with what we're feeling. To chance upon a poem and say, "That's exactly how I feel!" is testament to how similarly most of us think and emotionally experience life. The poet (who is part of that shared empathy) articulates that experience for the rest of humanity.

A poet writes predominantly for him or herself: it is about finding one's voice and articulating one's imagination in language, and whether anyone else derives pleasure from it is entirely coincidental.

---

[5] If one walked into a modern pub and told the assorted company that you wrote poetry, one would be laughed out of the door, and yet the 'battle poet' was inextricably a part of ancient warrior societies such as the Celts and Norse. Even a nation like modern Russia (whose people are renowned for hard living) reveres its poets. Poetry can start wars or end them: there is no weapon so powerful as the word.

I think of composition as having an intimate conversation with myself. Unlike fine art, which is firmly rooted in the commercialism of the 'collector's market', or the professional novelist who earns lucrative book contracts, poetry and poverty have traditionally gone hand in hand, and a poet never gives up the day job. A poet, unlike a novelist, does not write for a 'target audience' or a 'niche market', and because poetry cannot be written in industrial quantities, the idea of 'commercial poetry' is an oxymoron. There is some truth to the adage that 'the only famous poet is a dead poet', not that a poet would ever write for fame. As William Blake remarked, "Damn braces, bless relaxes", in other words, when we become too comfortable, we cease to strive to create. In truth, fame is the judgement of posterity on the quality of our work and not something we aspire to for its own sake.

To write a poem for one's own delight is a process of self-discovery and self-unfoldment, underpinned by the richness of a life well-lived. That doesn't mean that poetry is written by 'old men looking back': if one is a teenager growing up in an impoverished ghetto or on a farm, then one already has ample life experience on which to draw. But it isn't just life experience that is needed to write poetry: one also needs a good vocabulary and the ability to look at familiar things in a different light... to inject 'the unusual into the usual'. One reason why young would-be writers come up short is that they have the imagination and imagery but they don't have the rich vocabulary necessary to articulate it. I always advise young writers to read as much poetry as they can, in that way unconsciously absorbing both style and vocabulary. But it isn't just vocabulary, imagination and life experience that are needed, however. There is a fourth quality, and that is an appreciation of how language flows: the cadence and modulation of speech, which is to say, its musicality. To compose poetry of any merit, learn to think of poetry as music... not the music of instruments, but the music of words. *Poetry is the music of love, life and death.* I will speak further of this in the Introduction.

Poetry is written to be recited, either to oneself or to others, and when one recites poetry one should feel the words in one's mouth. In that sense, words are like food: every word has its own flavour, each phrase its own scent, and just as flavours fight so we must choose the correct blend of flavours when we write poetry. There is a difference between reading and reciting. Recite with passion and emotion, joy and sadness.

There will come a time, however, when one wants to share one's poetry with a wider audience, and that can evoke feelings of insecurity: 'Is it good enough?' 'Am I going to be laughed at?' I liken the experience to this: to share one's poetry with people one has never met is to have a layer of skin torn off, exposing the sensitive nerves beneath. It is like the betrayal of a confidence, and that is why these poems have been published under a *nom de plume*, also known as a 'pen name'. There are many reasons why authors do this: if the poem isn't kindly received there is less damage to one's self-esteem and no one is going to point at you and say, 'Ah, failed poet'. But a more positive reason is that I consider it healthy to separate one's creative persona from one's mundane everyday identity. Another reason, however, is that the poem transcends the poet. Once it is 'out there', it becomes part of the cultural consciousness of the age; it acquires its own life, separate from the person who wrote it. Certainly, it has a name that can be pinned to it, but the poem is now itself. People recite it softly as they walk through parks on late summer evenings or amid the jostle of rush hour, even if they cannot remember who wrote it, and that is really as it should be. A poem is the cultural heritage of us all.

Every poet leaves something of their own mind in every poem they write, and, contrary to T. S. Elliot, in this sense all poetry is autobiography. So, I offer up my own skin to be applauded, derided, banned or ignored as it may be, in the knowledge that it will outlive me, and if it brings pleasure to someone on the underground or subway, or in a park a generation down the line, I shall have died happy.

Introduction

I write poetry that is intense, visceral and emotive. My poems have been described as 'a grey sky flecked with rain', punctuated by an occasional beam of sunlight. They are the children of dissonance, penned by a dreamer and an outcast, and as such they render my mind in oils.

I have never thrived in this world. If you believe in the idea that not all of us are born fully into life, then that would be me. From the earliest age, I lacked physical build, could never put on weight and was always getting ill. Moreover, I had an extreme shyness and reticence about engaging with life. As a young man, I was gauche; I didn't know how to make friends or communicate with people. I had difficulty forming close relationships, and intimacy was impossible. I was always on the side of the pitch but never played the game; I hid.

If truth be told, it probably goes back to the womb. My natural mother had an affair with a man she met in Canada in the 1950s. She got pregnant; her family called her home in shame and sent her away to avoid social embarrassment. My very existence was a threat to the family honour. They pressured her to have me aborted but it was too late, so they forced her to sign the adoption papers. On the very day I was born, I was taken away and put up for adoption with a new family who could not have children.[6] My mother had a mental breakdown and was institutionalised (albeit temporarily). I think that during this time I absorbed my mother's own fear and insecurity and it left me with a feeling of not entirely belonging in this world.

I grew up as a troubled, introspective teenager, never really feeling that I belonged; I was just a passenger passing through life with no connection to it. I was bullied at school; I had no friends and no girl would look at me. I became withdrawn and

---

[6] The prevalence of forced adoptions in the 1950s is becoming more widely known now. I call it the 'tyranny of morality' and it is what happens when religious-based public morality declares war on innocent people, and 'respectability' becomes more important than kindness and compassion. Single mothers need help, not punishment!

retreated into my own inner world. *The imagination was my panic room.* In retrospect, I didn't even really have the social instincts of a normal child, and to this day I have problems expressing affection and intimacy; there is probably something of the autistic in me. Certainly, there is a dissonance between my imaginative experience of intimacy and my ability to express it in real life. Eventually, I was pushed through university, more to please my parents than for myself; and although I gained immeasurably from the mental stimulus, I rebelled against my parents' attempts to push me into a 'professional' career, left home and joined a Rajneesh meditation commune. However, my pagan soul won out and I was later initiated into a Wiccan coven under Maxine Sanders in Bayswater, London – a profound experience that has informed many of my poems. I was now officially an outcast. Nonetheless, I look back fondly on my bedsit days in Bayswater. I was alone in the heart of the great city with the whole West End at my feet, and my beloved Kensington Gardens just down the road. Poor but free, the parks and the streets were mine to explore. By night, I would dine on a sandwich, a block of cheese and a bottle of wine, and compose poetry in my head with

Beethoven's Ninth thundering in the background on my antiquated gramophone.

I drifted through life doing low-paid dead-end jobs until I landed a long-term job with the mail service which at least gave me stability. I certainly fitted in there. But during all this time, the one thing that held me together was poetry. Delineating my feelings through poetic metaphor and imagery was a process of expiation and understanding that brought mental clarity. The sheer joy of writing and composing, of channelling all my pain and anguish into something beautiful, was the only thing that preserved my mental health and my faith in myself during the dark times in my life. "Art is a wound turned into light."[7]

While I might have slipped through the drain cover and become a social failure, my reticence conferred the abilities of an observer of nature, people and things, and an introspective understanding of my own mind, and of mind in general. In short, I discovered the secret garden of the imagination. While others were busy forming relationships, raising families, and working their bones off to

---

[7] Georges Braque.

survive, I could immerse myself in stories, books of history, mysticism and philosophy; and I had time alone to walk in nature, to still my thoughts and feel the immediacy of life. More importantly, it gave me the freedom to follow my imagination and see where it took me. All of this led me to the understanding that the poet is inherently rootless: they may have wild affairs occasionally, but they are always essentially alone, and they do not fit tidily into the 'normal' stereotype of a family with two children, a car and a dog. The poet lives and experiences life intensely, and it is the ability to translate this intensity – of imagery, thought and feeling – into language that defines poetry. Words are like muscles straining to pull into language intimations of truth and apparitions of feeling that resist form. Poetry, then, in its very intensity, is sharply juxtaposed with what we would define as 'normality', which I equate with banality: existing for the sake of existing; life as a permanent subroutine, lived without thought or feeling; to be so focussed outwardly into the world that we lose the ability to introspect, wonder, imagine and ask questions of life. I study faces and I see so many people walking the streets whose spark has gone out, prematurely aged, their eyes dull, rolled over and crushed by life, their imaginations stunted, their horizons permanently constrained. What do they live for? What keeps them going? Devoid of the light of the mind, what is the meaning of life?

Banality terrifies me: the crushing mundanity of everyday life with its deadening of the imagination. Truly, banality is the nadir of the human spirit. Our mental health is dependent on moments of peak experience, and it is those peak experiences which build us... those images and events that burn themselves into memory with the intensity of light. Banality is the antithesis of peak experience and reduces everything to a single shade of grey. The feeling of energy from driving a sports car, the rushing of air as one parachutes out of a plane, the first time someone makes your heart glow, holding one's new-born baby, a fiery unset on a late summer evening or the singing of birds in the wet trees after a fall of rain... these are the experiences that give meaning to life, and which sustain us.

Any society that sacrifices quality of mind (and indeed life) to the economic machine is on the royal highway to cultural collapse. A civilisation is not defined by productivity: it is defined by the quality of its thought and the way people treat each other. Yet, such is the pernicious relationship between government and industry, that education has been hijacked as a tool of the economy to breed a generation of mindless, unthinking technocrats, and bang goes Renaissance Man. Already, we are seeing music, art, history and literature (including poetry) being dropped from school curricula because they are perceived as 'not relevant' to economic activity, and with them goes creativity and the ability to imagine, which is the basis of all invention and scientific discovery. So, I take enormous pleasure in being 'irrelevant' to economic production.

Imagination is the light of the mind and it turns to gold everything it touches. It is the hidden light of the soul; it is what makes us human. To imagine is to create: to create art, to design a car, to make a quantum leap in scientific understanding, to create a more just society; and yet the very subjects that stimulate imaginative engagement with the world are under attack. Worse, our culture of Rationalism has divorced us from the higher emotions like love, compassion and empathy which drive our moral sense. Anything and everything, no matter how horrific, can be justified by Reason.

So why do I write poetry? To write poetry is to live, feel and connect. It is an inner impulse, an unfolding of the Self. Images push themselves up from the depths like a scream and I have no choice but to ride the crest of inspiration. The imagination is a drinking horn that ever refills itself, and I am drunk on words. It is an imagination filled by the supernatural, of seductive *femmes fatales,* of heroes and monsters, of love and loss, of bitterness and regret, and the horror of a solitary man watching the slow settling of the dust of time, the inexorable weakening of the bonds of matter by the forces of entropy, for is it not the fate of the greatest of men to die an old fool, a Lear where once was king, ignored and patronised by the world? And yet, as Dylan Thomas adjured, I shall not "go gently into that good night." On the last day, there will be two glasses of scotch set out: one for me and one for God, so we can both get drunk together.

Corvix is a product of the oppositional tension between Life and Death, a love-hate relationship with Existence. In *Corvix*, I explore how the themes of love, sex and death interweave to form a complex anatomy of the human experience, in which eroticism is inextricably meshed with silent longing, but probably Death occupies the premier seat: ruminations of impending death, contemplation of suicide; elegies to the loss of youth, vigour and sensual experience; of absorption back into nature... and looking back over the collection, I don't think I have glorified Death, but I *have* humanised it. My poems are replete with anger, violence, sadness and emotional pain, and there is much that is confessional, but the exploration of the darker emotions of the human soul is an act of expiation in which something *beautiful* rises out of the ashes; terror and magnificence are never far away. Much of what I write explores the themes of regret and opportunities missed; of growing old, of not experiencing the world with the same vividness and intensity as in one's youth; of the loss of vitality and sensual awareness; and of the stunning realisation that one has become an ageing irrelevance: no one gives a damn about you, no one listens to a word you say, and in front of you is a yawning black hole that one day you will walk into. Hands up, anyone who has felt this! There are, however, spiritual themes within my poetry, as exploring spirituality was also a major component in my life. I write of the spirituality of the soul, but also the spirituality of the gutter: the commonality of the invisible and forgotten. The saint and the rogue speak through me and I am their voice. Spirituality, after all, is not focussed exclusively on life or what follows life, *but on what we are rooted in and what we are connected with*. There are also poems dedicated to the joy of love, as well as those bending to humour, but even love takes us out of the zone of innocence into the world of adult complexity: we long for love, but when we find it, it is never what we expected. *Corvix* is a map of the human soul: a masquerade ball of love, folly, cruelty and madness, the whole procession hobbling inexorably toward the gates of death wherein all is extinguished.

I have divided the collection into 'Early', Middle' and 'Late' periods, with a fourth section for poems written after the first edition. Doing this was a revelation to me, as the early poems are, for the most part, melancholic reflections on Nature, the loss of youth and the approach of death, written predominantly as prose poems, in which Nature often assumes a metaphor for the phases of life, e.g. Spring as youth, Summer as the height of one's powers, Autumn as one's declining years (an age of maturity and calm reflection as well as a little sadness for opportunities missed) and Winter as the approach of Death. The reader will also find a strong mystical element in the poems of this period: themes of the Goddess, pre-Christian religion and Jewish mysticism which date to my involvement in the Craft during the late '80s and '90s.

The middle section shows increasing experiment-ation. Poems emerge with darker supernatural themes, and we see some examples of social realist poetry. I begin to experiment with regular rhyming meter, but also with a form that is midway between prose and rhyme. This is continued into the late period where I deal with a wide range of themes such as obsessive love, stalking, suicide, abuse, social change, authoritarianism, social isolation and neglect. I experiment with odes, ballads and Norse poems. Still, there are poems given over to love (*To His Dark Mistress, An Oxford Professor, Lovers in Chains, Bartholomew Fair, The Storm that Blows the Rose, Love at Midnight*) as well as doomed love (*Pompeii, The Mummers' Play, 1913*), and, as always, there are the dark supernatural poems, which run through the anthology as a connecting thread.

Some years ago, when I was setting out on this path, I asked myself the question: why can't a poem rise and fall like a song? Why can't it have changes of key like music? There are instances where a poem benefits from a regular meter, and there are instances when it doesn't, so the question was a liberating one. A song is, of course, lyrics set to music. The difference between a song and a poem is that a poem is not set to music but *is* the music: the musical flow of words, where words are essentially notes.

Regular verse is good for poems requiring a strong driving meter, such as action (Tennyson's *Charge of the Light Brigade* being an example) or satire. Dreamy evocations of mood and landscape such as Keats' *Ode to Autumn* and *Ode to a Nightingale* (which rely on evoking dreamy images in the reader's mind) can also comfortably be expressed through rhyming meter, as can complex emotions like love and desire, as per the sonnets of John Donne and William Shakespeare. In verse poetry, though, there is a danger of a triumph of style over emotional force, which limits imaginative flow: a poem can be technically perfect but lifeless... and very often, rhyming can feel trite and forced. Repetitive meter is also better suited to short poems for the simple reason that it is, well, repetitive. Prose poetry allows more imaginative and descriptive leeway and is perfectly suited to contemplative 'rhetorical' poems but depends on a rhythmic cadence that mirrors the natural rhythm of thought as opposed to externally enforced meter. It is heavy with symbolism and metaphor and will also use techniques such as repetition and alliteration; it likewise requires considerably more discipline than rhyming meter... and prose poems are also harder to round off. In between the prose poem and rhyming verse, I found myself drawn to a third form which is intermediate between the two. I call it irregular rhyme or 'chaotic rhyming', where rhymes are inserted into the poem at irregular intervals and sometimes in the middle of lines. Doing so can add to the dramatic tension in a poem by introducing a sort of psychic shock or jolt, but its main advantage is to add momentum to a poem without confining it to a rhyming straitjacket. It works like this: regular rhyming meter conditions the mind to anticipate where the next rhyme will fall, but irregular rhyming breaks the pattern by displacing the rhyme to one or several lines down, confusing the mind but allowing the pleasure of discovery. So, breaking up the rhyming pattern keeps the poem fresh and exciting by introducing an element of unpredictability. I have found it ideally suited to poems of a rhetorical or discursive nature. Remember this when you write: the lines of your poem should flow like a river and soar like a symphony.

I have restrained myself to short*ish* poems: long poems are prone to suffer from loss of momentum. A classic example of this is John Milton's *Paradise Lost*; his later books lost the power and drive of the first. The only really long poem is *The Story of Gunnar and Hallgerður* which is written in the epic format. Going back over my collection and reviewing poems I wrote thirty years ago has been an eye-opener. Poems I once thought brilliant seemed flawed, requiring extensive re-editing, and some have had to be re-written altogether. In this anthology, the reader will find otherworldly descriptions of nature, ruminations on age and impending death, of war, of suicide, of cruelty, of sorrow and loss, of intrusions by the supernatural into waking life, and of madness. You will encounter experimentation with style from odes and elegies to Norse poems and Jewish erotic poetry, to ballads and roaring anthems. Hopefully, you will find something in the collection to 'strike a chord' but as with every good meal, there is always one course that disagrees with the eater.

THIS IS MY VOICE THAT I LEAVE BEHIND ME

Early Period
1985–1999

Autumn Leaves

Now in this autumn of repose,
When Nature draws her breath
Afore the fall of winter's leaden weight,
And the shadow of the Friend[8] hangs close,
When furtive breezes stir the papers on my desk
And the ivy at my open casement licks,
It is my pleasure to step abroad
Amid the richly tinted world
Of golden lights and blushes deep,
And fall amidst
The cornflake crispness of yellow leaves,
Curled conch-like,
Chrysalid graveyard racked by autumn's
    freshsome gusts,
That swoop like carrion among the hollows
To waltz and whirl the scabrous skins
Of new-shed trees; mournful marionettes
That jig and jerk on withered wire,
Or tremble with the fretful flutter
Of a broken wing.

---

[8] Euphemism for death.

Even now, my love, the ivy flames,
Like unto the blood-red flares that streak the sky
At eventide,
When birds wing silent to southern lands
And clip the edge of night,
And the cries of children echo far away
In the ringing silence of the ashen dusk.
Rapt in my 'loneness,
I tread the wanderer's unended quest
Through russet realms,
Silent witness to the year's long breathing out,
Footfalls muffled in seas of burnished tears
Wept in expiation of some unspoken deed,
Settling like the dust of Time...
A calendar's crumpled sheets scattered in the
    wind;
There is forgiveness
In the falling of a leaf.
Oh Nature!
With what infernal beauty dost thou grace the
    ageing year!
What rest the heart, what sweetness breathe
'Pon souls who more clamorous times
Hath known?
And oft I gaze 'pon silvered hair and faces etched,

In whom the flame of youth is long
Burnt dim,
And see in them a deeper glow,
Like unto lanterns softly raying the night;
Youth's sharp angles smoothed away
Like pebbles rolled long upon the bed
Of some swift stream;
Love claims the space desire hath fled
And peace fills up the mansions of the soul.
Then take me, dark angel,
For I hath lived
And filled my saddlebags with spices rich.
Now in this time of rain,
With kindly fingers draw close my lids,
And clasp me to thy satin robe
That I may quit this shattered bowl
And walk in beauty
In the forest of the soul.

Notes

In *Autumn Leaves*, the narrator draws a comparison between the mellowness of autumn and the mellowness of his own declining years that have rounded him '*like pebbles rolled long upon the bed of some swift stream'.* I often reflect on how, even after our reproductive days are over and Nature relinquishes its grip, we become more fully ourselves and continue to grow and develop in wisdom and experience right up until the moment of our death, proof to me that Humanity is not merely a creature of Nature.

Children of the Poppy

We lay about the room
That night before we took our leave
Of old Seville,
And talked and drank and loved
And laid our heads upon our women's folds;
Breathed the bitter perfume of orange groves,
And the musty scents of bodies close.
Set upon the floor,
One lonely candle yet remained
In that room of shadows.
Dissipated,
Dwarfed by the creeping dark,
Its substance spent and overspilled,
As a man's seed in summer's restless heat,
Still it burned;
One small bright quill of flame,
Bending like the meadow grass,
Fanned by summer's soft silk airs,
Emptying its life to the inky dark
Like a whisper swallowed in silence.
Loud the cricket's chirp,
Living heartbeat of the close confiding night;

A ceaseless scissor song
That pulsed the dreaming hills
And beat like steady rain
Upon the casements of our sleep.
Sweet the night birds' call,
That filled the air with fever dreams
Of pale women.
Fitful thus we slept,
'Til wine and love bought deeper rest
And blackness girt us round
With heavy wings
Like unto coins that weigh the eyelids of the dead.
So remained,
'Til dawn's young light
Forged the rigid lines of day,
And the gates of Time slid shut.
There stood she, the town -
Proud upon her plain,
Ancient, bleached and fair
Like some celestial city,
Twinkling
In the azure sky.
Long lingered we and drank the sight,
And knew it was our last

'Til winter's rains had earthed the dust of
    summer,
And the days once more grew long.
Then should we return
To eat of lotuses in the Spanish night,
And love amid the poppies tall.

Notes

In 1816, Lord Byron, Percy Bysshe Shelley, his
wife Mary Shelley and Dr John Polidori rented the
Villa Diodati, near Lake Geneva in Switzerland.
Housebound by bad weather, they composed stories
together and the result was John Polidori's *The Vampyre*
and Mary Shelley's *Frankenstein*. In this poem I have
transposed the scene to Spain and conjured the image
of a group of young poets enjoying the Grand Tour of
Europe, which most aristocratic young men undertook
at that time, smoking opium in the warm Spanish
night. I don't think people realise just how much
opium use fuelled the intense imaginative imagery
of the Romantic-era poets, epitomised by Thomas
de Quincey's *Confessions of an English Opium-Eater*. It
did so by inducing a dream-like state of melancholia,

ideal for the composition of poetry. Unfortunately, our risk-averse paternalistic nanny state has chosen to downplay this aspect of literary history.

The Circle

"Where are they?" I said,
"The time has almost come".
"They are preparing," she said,
"Can you not hear them descend the stair?"
And on an instant,
White-clad forms shuffle in
On soft and silent feet,
And like marbled pillars
Stand about the room,
The hidden children of an ancient power
That calls them in their hearts,
Like the whistle that only a dog doth hear:
"Come home, come home,
Come to me."
And She is there among them,
In the nervous flicker of a candle flame,
In the lazy swing of a censor,
In the sweep of a robe about a dancer's legs,
In heads bent in devotion,
And voices wracked with love.
Time was when they danced 'mid wild olive,
Felt the prick of grass against their limbs

And washed their faces in the moon-charmed dew
Ere they melted to their homes.
Now they work in darkness
And keep her service
The old, old rites
That once blessed Man as he walked behind the
    plough;
Gather now in the furry gleam of lit tallow,
The lantern's lance-like beams rayed forth
From some high vault,
Shafting the torpid vapours
That cling and coil,
Moving fantastically
In the draughts of myriad secret forms.
Weird shadows loom and retreat
On soft-illumined walls,
And low murmurs fill the thickly perfumed air;
The circle cast, the mass begins.

Notes

This poem was written during my years in Bayswater,
London, in the late 80s and early 90s. I was fortunate
to meet Maxine Sanders, elder of a coven called

the Temple of the Mother, who then resided in Clanricarde Gardens. This poem is inspired by my experiences during that time. One would have to stand in a ritual circle to fully understand the feeling of intense expectation and sense of presence. One of the lessons I learned during this period is that if one expects something to happen, then it is more likely to happen. Successful ritual always works on this principle of expectation, which is why sceptics never experience anything. Faith really does open doors. I also talk a lot about 'presence' in the poem, and it describes the feeling of something condensing out of the ether in response to a group summoning, whether that 'something' is objectively real or an archetype within the Unconscious. One attracts to one the object of one's focus, so if one focuses on the goddess Hekate, or the Virgin Mary or the Holy Spirit, that is what one attracts towards one.

Corvix

Black are my lover's eyes
As wells of ink,
And black her hair,
So lustrous
That, startled in a sunbeam,
It flashes iridescent as a crow's wing
That beats the murd'rous air.
Black ravening whore
That scours the field grim
Through mist and marsh,
And plucks the sightless eyes
From sightless men,
I would make a fine meal, my sweet,
For *you* to peck at.
And in your passion
I am but carrion for your clever mouth
And quick, sharp fingers that rake and rack.
Ah, my love,
The morning dew sits like a pearl on your black
    wing,
Black as the coal in the hills of Merthyr,
Black as the mines where the miners toil

And black as the hearts of the men that send
   them down;
And I would drink the dew from thee
And give up my life in thy feathered bed.
Is that a skein of blood upon thy ruby lips?
Then thou hast drunk me dry
And ere the dawn delights the day,
I die.

Notes

One of the shorter poems in the collection, and its inspiration, *Corvix*, the Latin feminine of *corvus* meaning 'crow', is a poem about the predatory feminine, the woman who is beautiful, sensual and vampiric, and it serves as a companion piece to the longer *To His Dark Mistress* and *Lady of Crows*, which it predates by several years.

The Dispossessed

When we are no longer crazy diamonds, you and I,
What are we?
When we no longer fall carelessly among leaves,
Nor gladden at the lengthening of the day;
When the race is run,
When the metal wheel grinds in the rut of life,
And the mercury no longer breaks the glass
With passion o'erspilled,
What are we?
When our skin no longer thrills and burns to
    another's touch,
When we no longer tumble into bed
Drunk with the laughter of wine,
Turning in our sleep to seek our lover's mouth,
What becomes us?

What becomes us
When the cataract of age dulls the once bright eye,
And the world is warped through the misted glass
Of a broken window?
When the skin sags and the hair turns grey,
And the risen year is an enemy held at the door;

When image invades the house of fun,
And dignity is but a wreck to which we cling
As all around us sinks,
What hope is left for you and I, my love?
Live life and live it well!
For those who set aside the morrow, die today.

Notes

The Dispossessed belongs in the same vein as *On His Youth* and *Ode to Summer Lost*: a lament for the loss of the sensuality and vitality of youth.

Elegy

This I ask
When my time is come:
That I be taken to some quiet place
Where I may hear the music of the wind
In the trees.
No bugle call for me,
No organ sound,
But a rushing and a sighing
Like the whispered wisdom of a friendly confessor,
Teasing out the painful secrets of my soul.
No doleful liturgy of the cleric's art,
But a liturgy of the breath,
Shall transport me to the arms of God;
A mighty symphony of many movements:
The passionate gusting of the horn,
The soft tremble of the violin
Suspended on a single note;
An elegy of the air,
Paean of sweet repose.
Set me amongst these:
The hoary oaks and chestnuts,
Sturdy ruffians of the woods

With their mops of green,
Or upon a sunny bank,
Willow-swept,
Amongst whose weeping tendrils
The delicate breezes play
Like a harpist's fingers;
A sonnet's sylvan song.
I listen
And slowly float out upon the tide.
This is the music of Pan, my friend,
That drugs me in my hour of passion,
And pipes me to the Land of Youth.

Notes

Elegy visits a man in the autumn of his life, contemplating the approach of death, and describes how he would like to pass out of the world. I wanted to impart to the poem an air of melancholic wistfulness but which at the same time is very positive. This is a man who wants to end his life surrounded by the scents and sounds of Nature that bring peace to the soul.

Magna Mater

I

Man!
I am the Mother who brought thee forth,
And I am the Mother who gives thee suck
With the milk of Heaven.
Heavy are my breasts
Poured out to thee,
Pendulous as the apple bough
Laden with summer fruit.
Old am I, so old;
Old as Man,
Older still,
Yet youthful as the greenwood bride.
Many are the cities fallen to the sword,
Many the forests raped
And many the continents that hath groaned and
    sunk,
Yet hath I abode,
A silver star in the fathomless blue.
As gentle Isis am I known,
Mother of Souls,

Light-horned queen,

Secret Hecate,

Aradia fair.

Honour my heel, ye sons of men!

Lift up thine[9] eyes and gaze

Upon the radiance of my face!

Behold! I, who am the well of life,

Hath come among thee in this temple of flesh.

I am the altar at which thou makest thine offering.

I am the trembling bride who teases out thy heart
    with clever fingers.

Return unto me thy power of begetting, oh man,
    and I will give thee gifts.

Kneel, oh servant!

Raise up thine arms to receive;

Soft-sing my name with trembling lips.

Invoke me!

And thou shalt feel the silence form about thee

And I shall come to dwell therein;

Receive me and adore me,

Enfold me in thy heart!

And thou shalt feel the wind of my wings

---

[9] Both possessives meaning 'your', 'thy' is used before a conso-
nant and 'thine' before a vowel. 'Thine' is also used in the sense
of 'yours'.

And the firmament shall catch thee;
Unto Heaven itself wilt thou be borne
On winds of light.

II

I am the Mother of the Waters,
I am the living silence of the temple depth,
I am the vision palely shimmering
In the darkness of thy dreams.
I am the priceless jewel you kept hid
In a forgotten place:
Bring me forth into the day
And I will cast my lights upon thy face,
The cold brilliance of a thousand moons.
Weak and miserable is the man who has not
    known me,
For more faithful than any human love am I.
I passed into the world with thee
Through the same tunnel of pain;
But while you slept
I beheld all.
The reflected image of your thoughts I catch
As the rippling of water
Written in light upon a darkened wall;

Their babbling
As the congress of many voices
In a distant room.
And in the night I come to thee
And dress thy wounds,
And sing in thine ear of splendid things.
And though thou casteth not thy glance upon me,
Nor turnest in thy sleep
And stretchest out thy hand,
Yet am I eternally patient;
And if thou didst but know,
For a single vision of my beauty
Thou wouldst weep an ocean.

Notes

I composed this poem while I was a priest of the
Temple of the Mother, under the eldership of Maxine
Sanders, in Clanricarde Gardens, Kensington, London.
It attempts to reach to the heart of what 'the Goddess'
is by looking beyond the individual goddesses of
history and attempting to elucidate her essence. A
lot of feeling went into the poem and I still regard
it with fondness. Incidentally, the title *Magna Mater*,

meaning 'Great Mother', was the popular name of the goddess Kybele, a goddess from Anatolia whose cult was spread to the Greek mainland by Greek colonists and eventually into the Roman Empire, where she acquired the title Magna Mater. She was said to arrive at her rites in a lion-drawn chariot accompanied by a disorderly ecstatic following drunk on wine and music, not unlike the ecstatic rites of Dionysus. Her priesthood, however, were castrati, and during her festivals, new initiates would cut their genitals in sacrifice to the goddess and throw them to the crowd.

Oaks in Winter

Gaunt now stand the merry oaks
Who but a season past
Jested in their liveries of green,
Now bent and twisted,
Haunted by the rook,
Sad singer of winter's dirge,
Like dry-papped dowagers
Wed in black
To a memory frozen in sepia,
Bitter in the knowledge
Of a youth once full and vain,
Now sallow and collapsed,
Raising long fingers to the sky
As though to feel the lineaments
Of a face lost to blindness,
Stirred by a mournful sentience,
Twitching in the lonely madness of the year's end.
Barren is this place!
Unearthly quiet!
Only the glassy eye of winter doth record
The gibbet dance of summer's leaves,
The tattered rags of once-rich gowns,

While dark death-shapes wreath crowns of thorns
In their tangled hair.

Notes

I composed most of my nature poetry (including *Autumn Leaves*, *Snow* and *Elegy*) during the late 80s and early 90s when I lived in Prince's Square, Bayswater. Turning right out of my door would take me into the bustling heart of Queensway and Notting Hill, while turning left would take me down Orme Court and across Bayswater Road into Kensington Gardens. My favourite time for visiting was on early autumn and winter mornings when mist lay thick among the trees which loomed out, gnarled and tangled, and all sense of time and direction were lost, as though one had entered a gate into a faerie realm and left the ordinary world behind. During these walks, I would suspend thought and allow the imagery to fill my mind: the blackened, moss-covered trunks of the trees, the eerie cawing of crows and the occasional shriek of a child ringing on the air. This was a magical time for me!

Ode to Summer Lost

Now in this silvered age,
When the shadow of the horseman[10] falls long
Upon my years,
And the many milestones of my life
Are a storied journey
Ne'er to be retraced,
Nor unwise love pursued in haste,
I look back upon
The lost contentments of my youth
And in them find solace of a kind,
Of summers idly spent
In idylls far removed from madding crowd
And teeming cities with traffic loud,
But reclining shirtless in some whispering grove,
Or swimming in a sandy half-remembered cove,
Exulting in the gleaming smoothness of youth,
Skin like sun,
Limbs lithe and strong
As though forged in some Homeric song,
And then to sleep

---

[10] Death as 'the pale horseman', from the *Book of Revelation*.

43

Lulled by the pungent sweetness
Of cool grass
And drowsy buzz of nectar-laden bee.
Soft summer breezes brush my skin
Like the playful teasing of a lover's hair,
And suddenly I am there!
How the pages flick and fly!
Each scene lit as upon a stage,
Scenes from days gone by:
The dry click of willow on leather,
Crisp white shirts on village green
In endless days of sunny weather,
Plash of oar in light-spangled water,
Boating on the mill stream with the boss's daughter,
Weddings and regattas and village fairs,
Ribboned hats and envious stares,
The fragile *chink* of tall glasses
Raised in health,
Boring speeches taken in jest
Displays of wealth,
The easy, careless laughter of summer.
How I shall miss thee when I am gone,
Whose days were filled with love
And shadows long.
Oh summer!

Why in thy hour do I turn my thoughts to mortal
    things?
Mayhap the lassitude which steals my limbs,
Those heavy scents which drug my senses
Recall the repose of death,
Or is it that thy life, once freely lent,
Is soon so quickly spent?
A gossamer life
Turned to dust within the cycle of a moon,
A firefly's transience,
A youthful tree cut too soon.
Sad sweet summer!
No sooner hast thou lit the vale
And stroked the hills with warm caress,
Than winter in her jealous rage
Tears thy bridal dress,
And the light that lit my world
Shall never be as bright
Nor Nature so immense
As in my youth,
For old winter's violence.

Notes

In the same vein as *On His Youth, The Dispossessed* and *Autumn Leaves*, the narrator's experience of the joys of summer induces a reflection on the transience of life and what comes after. The phrase 'far removed from madding crowd' recalls the title of Thomas Hardy's novel *Far from the Madding Crowd* of 1874, although the phrase was already in currency, and I think its use in this poem is entirely appropriate.

O Where Art Thou, My Lady Dark?

O where art thou, my lady dark,
Whose bridle sang in autumn mists,
As wandered thou 'mong silver'd trees
In forests shadow brushed?

Wherefore my queen upon her pale horse,
Who rode the forest paths
And trod the turf 'mong terraced roots
That bank the sward,
And vein the ancient earth?

Shall I hear no more thy step
So light and fair?
The stealthy tread of Spanish shoes
Brittle 'pon the midnight frost,
Nor court thy sharp and secret smile
As taunted me in seasons past
When fields burned with yellow
And blossoms shower'd the grass?

Shall I kiss no more thy pale hand,

Caress thy ring?
Nor gaze upon thy sad and wild mien,
Thine eyes of jade and blood-red lips,
Thy furs and cloak of green?

Like the Summer thou art gone,
And in thy wake, the trees lay out their dead.
No comfort have I now in winter's chill,
No familiar laugh nor cry doth ring
Upon these cold stone walls;
No sound indeed,
But the yell of hounds in the grey fall
And the rain that beats like blood
Upon the glass.

Where walk thee now, my lady dark?
Cold is the bed where once didst wanly dream
And the memory of thee
Hovers 'pon the air in empty rooms,
And haunts the halls unseen.
For thou art gone, my lady dark,
And he who was thy lover once
Grows old within his castle dour,
Hears not thy laughter ring upon the air,
Nor hearkens more thy sad lament

That rose upon the chasing leaves
In winter's sullen hour.

The turning earth hath closed the lids of Summer
And silence and eternal snow doth weight
The coverlids of dusk.
In thy wake,
The frost doth blight the hay.
The black plum'd poplar sighs thy name
And the raven frights the winter day.
Gone away! Gone away!

She who troubles sleep,
Her tomb doth empty lie.
Four-wall'd, thy vault,
An eyeless socket, mocks
The stars,
And Heaven stares appall'd.
Crack'd the lintel, cleav'd the door,
The gate leers open to the dusk,
Old worn cross on lichened stone
Is all that doth remain,
And a weather'd name betrays the guest
Who liest not within her grave,
Though there wert laid to rest.

Notes

The principal inspiration for *Lady Dark* is from Cole-
ridge's *Christabel* (the prototype of the lesbian vampire
novel and a direct antecedent of Joseph Sheridan Le
Fanu's novel, *Carmilla*, which predated Bram Stoker's
Dracula), but there is also an influence from Edgar
Allan Poe's *Ligeia*.

In keeping with the Romantic tradition of landscape
reflecting mind and *vice versa*, the violent gusts of rain
and blizzards of leaves reflect the inner turmoil of the
protagonist's mental state. However, if one considers
the impact of the windswept and rain-soaked Scottish
Highlands on *Macbeth*, the idea evolved considerably
earlier. While the turbulent imagery of wind, snow and
rain reflects the barrenness of the surviving husband
who mourns his lost wife, there is no indication until
the final verse that she is not truly dead but somewhere
in between life and death.

Lady Dark is a prose poem with the introduction
of irregular rhyming, particularly in the final section
to increase the dramatic tension and bring the poem
to a climax.

On his Youth

I have forgotten
The warm wetness of a woman's kiss,
The pleasures of lips that yield
Like soft wax upon parchment,
A pas-de-deux of tongues that flicker and dart
Like asps,
The sensual mouth an Undine's cave
Wherein fragile fingered anemones probe
And twine.

Are they all passed,
These pleasures of a wilder youth?
Ne'er more to brush a burning cheek
'Gainst the downy softness of a woman's skin?
To glide glistening 'tween sappy thighs
And breathe the secret incense
Of hips heavy with the oils of love?
To fall 'mong breasts that pout
And press?
To tumble on furs in firelight
And gasp and cry in the
Foetal dark?

To be touched – just once,
Be gripped in love;
To be licked, bitten, kissed, caressed,
Drunk, sucked dry and bloodied lie;
Bound in the withies of a woman's hair,
Beswept by tresses dark and soft
That trail like moss 'bove tremoring skin,
And hips that silent' row the sheets
And brazen limbs that know no sin.

Gone now…
An old man locked in his cage of years,
Powdered with the dust of frozen stars,
All his knowing a white sound
That forbids sleep;
A mad king mouldering
In a castle of dust,
Joints that crack like frail buckram,
And skin yellowed
Like pages carelessly exposed to light.

'Twas not always so.
Once these livid arms were angel's wings
That knew the spires of Heaven…
A bright-feathered firebird,

Incendiary in the sun's light,
And from these haggard loins
Promethean seed sprayed forth
To paint the vault
With stars.
Such was I in youth,
And so in birth;
Tell me, pray,
What lights the soul
When love hath run to earth?

Notes

This poem, a companion piece with *The Dispossessed* and *Ode to Summer Lost*, and written around the same time, contrasts the sensuality of the narrator's life with the reality of ageing and eventual death.

Priapus

I am the flash that made the planets scream,
I am the voice that cleaved the primal stone,
With what shall ye compare my hideous strength,
Mere Man?
With the night-black bull that rears and spits
In its cloven lust?
With the fecund goat and the fiery ram?
With the sleek gazelle, fleet upon the plain?
Some do say
That when the earth was young
I walked the steaming slopes of glowing mounts,
And danced in sacred grove with nymph and faun:
Pan was I called by the children of men,
Great Pan!
My eyes were as the Bel fires set upon the hill,
Like unto burning coals were they,
And where ere I trod,
The earth smokest to my step;
As black fire are the letters of my name,
Burnt into thy heart in the light blaze of my rage.
Such is my terrible beauty, oh Man,
That the eye dilates in awe

And the hair doth stir upon the nape,
And having looked once upon my face
No more walk they in mortal ways;
Gone from them, mortality's dim light,
And in their eyes a feral gleam,
Nor cast their glance 'pon worldly things
But straight-ahead gaze
Like they who scan the sea for distant ships,
For I hath plucked them from the earth
And they feast on greater things,
And of such men say,
They have gone mad at the table of the gods
And walk at noon in gardens strange and wild,
Nor pass again the cherub's flaming sword
That bars the gate
'Tween gods and men,
But evermore
Alone and silent wander
The sleep-torn shore.

Notes

It is as if the current of some strong different life swept through them, different from our shallow current to-day; as if they drew their vitality from different depths that we are denied. ...

Behind all the Etruscan liveliness was a religion of life ... Behind all the dancing was a vision, and even a science of life, a conception of the universe and man's place in the universe which made men live to the depth of their capacity.

To the Etruscan all was alive; the whole universe lived; and the business of man was himself to live amid it all. He had to draw life into himself, out of the wandering huge vitalities of the world. The cosmos was alive, like a vast creature. The whole thing breathed and stirred ...

The Whole thing was alive, and had a great soul, or anima; and in spite of one great soul, there were myriad roving, lesser souls; every man, every creature every tree and lake and mountain and stream was animate, had its own peculiar consciousness. And has it to-day.

D. H. Lawrence, *Etruscan Studies*

In the late seventeenth century, with the dawning of the Age of Reason after two centuries of religious war, there evolved among the founding fathers of the scientific revolution a rationalist idea of God as Divine Geometer, Watchmaker or Architect, which basically envisaged God designing everything on a draughtsboard and then creating it. This is still pretty much the view among Christians today. The counterpoint to this belief in the rational nature of the universe is the Great God Pan, who represents the creative power in Nature as violent, erotic and amoral, though not without intelligence. I regard 'God' not as an entity, but rather as the expression of the 'Primal Will to Be'. I used *Priapus* as a title instead of 'Pan' because I wanted to emphasise the sexual nature of the creative act, of which our own sexuality is a lower analogue. The latter half of the poem works with the consequence of 'seeing' Pan, engendering 'divine madness'.

THE SANE ARE TOO RATIONAL TO COMPREHEND METAPHYSICAL TRUTH. THE INSANE COMPREHEND IT BUT LACK THE REASON TO TELL US.

In *The Birth of Tragedy* (1872), Nietzsche referred to two main traits in Greek culture and myth which he called the Apollonian and the Dionysian. The Apollonian was associated with the 'light' of reason, and the Dionysian with the atavistic. Today we can apply the same dichotomy to our ideas of what constitutes God or Spirit. On the one hand, the monotheistic religions focus on God or Divinity as 'light' and 'love' and emphasise the illumination of the mind that comes from the descent of the Holy Spirit upon the soul. Typically, it adopts a view of God or 'Monad' as an entity or being of which the Holy Spirit is an emanation. On the other hand, 'pagan' religions emphasise the primal and erotic nature of the life force, in which life or 'spirit' is perceived as a power or energy that flows through all things (also known by the Latin *numen*), but I have come to believe that these are really just two sides of the same coin: Spirit can be both, depending on how that power is channelled through the individual. Divinity encompasses the beauty of the Holy Spirit *and* the terror of Dionysus, and the way we experience Divinity is not Divinity itself. Similarly, the erotic is as much a part of Divinity as the illumination of grace, as D. H. Lawrence well understood.

For an actual invocation of Pan, I recommend Aleister Crowley's *Hymn to Pan*, which remains unsurpassed in its power and beauty. I speak from experience, as I was present at a Beltane rite in the woods at Alderley Edge where Maxine Sanders recited it. Absolute silence fell over everything and even the animals paused to listen!

ALL RELIGIOUS TRADITIONS CONTAIN WISDOM AND STUPIDITY IN EQUAL MEASURE AND THE ART OF UNDERSTANDING IS TO TEASE OUT THE ONE FROM THE OTHER.

Rite of Spring

I

Bright burning Child! Young Light
Whom Love hath kindled in Night's cold breast!
Infant god who yet, asleep, doth dream
Within the howling void:
From the bosom of winter we call thee forth!
Come, Fair One, on thy horse of white,
Over the land of ice and roaming deer,
Where the wolf stalks thru' the whispering pines
And the whale sings in the misty sea.
Come now, jewelled scimitar of Heaven!
Come now, brave warrior of the Dawn!
Over shadowy forest and grassy steppe,
Secret hill and sacred mount;
To thy temple of birth we bid thee speed.
Open are the portals of the North:
Boreas[11], their gloomy guardian, sleeps,
Hears not,
Nor sees the passing of a god,

---

[11] God of the North Wind in Greek myth.

Till seated on thy shining throne,
Thy flaming lance shall strike the East,
And thy face shall stamp the world with light!

II

He harkens! He awakes!
He breaks the chains of dark!
Even now he guides his barque upon the river of
    stars,
Through the halls of angels and the caverns of
    sleep,
Through the crystal spheres that ring and turn.
Like a star fallen to earth,
Thus he dwells:
A rose transfixed amid the thorns of time.

III

Herald of Light! Bright morning star!
Bring to us glad tidings of the new returnéd sun!
Our Lord Apollo is come among you
Though ye knowest him not,
For the nights are cold and the days short,
Yet doth he stir the inner sense.

He is the serpent that turns in the sleeping bud,
The hope that fills a virgin's dreams;
God of Life and Giver of Life,
He maketh the blood to course and the Soul to
    quicken,
And the fallow to run in the forest deep.

IV

Lord Apollo! Serpent-born Son of Night!
Who art Lord of Resurrection,
The sun behind the sun,
And even now doth sit enthroned in glory
In thy castle of the East.
Pass thou thy rod over the cold earth
Fulfilling the life of the seed;
Pierce with thy fiery spear our hearts
That we might know the passion of the gods!

V

Behold our Lord Apollo!
A mighty river in flood is he,
Whose voice is as the voice of thunder,
And whose laughter shakes the pillars of the earth!

His face is as the blue of summer skies,
And his mercy as the gentle rains
That kiss the land.
He descendeth the Heavens like the Northern
    Lights,
To walk the earth on silent feet
And move among the forms of men unseen;
A stealthy watcher of the naked soul, He,
Who knoweth the thoughts of all men.
He commandeth the winds and the secret tides,
The choirs of angels and the legions of Hell.
He weareth the fleece of purity,
And on his head the curling horns of the ram.

VI

The blessing of the God Apollo
I bestow upon all who worship in his presence,
By the power of his Name!
May he offer unto them the incense of wisdom
That they may be fertile in body and mind;
May he surround and protect his hidden children
As they tread the earth.
Blessed be.
Blessed be.

Notes

I wrote *Rite of Spring* as part of a Beltane ritual, celebrating the return of the Sun and the eruption of Spring with all its vitality, but the ritual was never performed and so I adapted the liturgy to a standalone poem. The title comes from Stravinsky's famous dance composition with its incredible use of motor rhythm.

Samhain – A Prose Poem

I

The wind that doth in autumn flay the trees
And moans among the mounds,
Now in winter chaps the once-soft earth
And blasts the rugged thorn.

The mournful low of pastured beasts
Who somnolent graze the sodden moor,
Echo through the drapes of rain
That sweep the gorse-clad fell.

Stoic, they shake their heavy horns,
Chew defiance at the storm,
And darkly fix the men and dogs
Come to bring them down.

And submissive stand in matted pelts,
And blink black eyes
Ere the shadow of the axe affrights the wall
And sings its bloody verse.

II

The black-shaped hills gather round the cloak of
    dusk
And a thousand torches spit and dance;
Strong men beat their chests in grief
And the wailing of the women haunts the stones.

Our Lord of Summer lies within his iron-cold tomb;
Even now they say
He cranes his tortured fingers to the sky,
Implores deliverance from his mother's black
    embrace.

Oh hard he lies!
Nailed in the frost-knit earth,
Thonged in ruddy roots that twist and twine,
And in his wake, fire doth lift the hearts of kin!

And thus they gather silent-ringed upon the plain,
Ready ere to share their victuals with the dead
Who leave their hills to stalk the fetid mists,
And dance with men.

Notes

Samhain is the Celtic Feast of the Dead held on October 31st and is said to be the time when the gates between the worlds are maximally open. It is also the time when the corn god dies and rests beneath the earth, to be reborn in the Spring. As the poem makes clear, at this time, the animals would be taken down from the hill pastures and some slaughtered, their meat being preserved for winter food.

Sementivae

Sator! Sator! Come Sator!

Farmer god! Lover god!

God of light and god of corn!

Come Sator! Come Sator!

Soft our lips that call thy name,

Wet from love and stained with wine,

And keen our bodies for thy god's touch!

Harness to the plough thy fiery ox

And drive thy furrow deep!

Give unto us thy hallowed seed,

The seed of light that flowers in truth:

To the belly of Earth,

To the womb of Woman

And the soul of Man!

Sator! Sator! Come Sator!

Farmer god! Lover god!

God of light and god of corn!

Come Sator! Come Sator!

Notes

The Sementivae, Feriae Sementivae or Sementivae Dies, was the Roman festival of sowing, held in honour of Ceres (goddess of agriculture) and Tellus (Mother Earth, equivalent to the Greek Gaia) and ran from January 24-26th. Sator was the Roman god of sowing (and hence fertility). Sementivae could be construed as the equivalent of the Celtic Beltane which occurred later on March 21. The poem is an invocation by the women of Rome to bestow his gifts of fertility upon them and upon the crops.

Snow

From somewhere high above it fell,
A livid sky bleached with pain,
The frozen tears of a murderess,
Confetti of silent death,
From a wedding where no guests remain.
A slow settling of feathers, floating
From some great snowbird,
Choking the life of the infant spring,
That from the smothered earth
No flowers shall bring.
Desultory drizzle of white rain,
Enfolding the land in a winding sheet,
A seamless shroud that bears no stain,
As beyond the wooded crest,
Like a bloodshot eye,
Bitter orange sun dies, dissolving
In the wind-washed west.
Sculpted into frozen dunes,
Broken by tracks of sledge,
Like white soot it lies,
Banked against fences
And covering the hedge,

Swept only by one who vaults
The old worn wicket gate, forlorn and
Blackly broken in the white waltz.
Silent, secret,
Landscape of imagined sounds
That tease the inner sense,
You move me now...
The soft cadence
Of wind among firs,
Whisp'rings of the dead
Who walk the furrowed way,
And bid the lonely traveller
To stop and stay;
Or, like faerie voice,
Phantasmal tinkle of icy shards
Showered from off a swaying bough,
Gently shaken as a limb gone to sleep,
As through the drifts you plough.
Shout,
Sing to the silence,
Whisper if you will,
And that ripe voice shall rise and ring
O'er downy fields blanketed and still,
Sound from trunks of timbers tall
That nod and sleep in leaden Fall,

Soon to ebb and melt away,
Eaten by the quietude
In the ghost light of the fading day.

Notes

When I lived in Bayswater in the late '80s and '90s,
I was fond of walking through Kensington Gardens
on early or late winter days when it was empty of the
usual tourists and I virtually had the park to myself.
I loved it when it was snowing because then the great
old trees stood out gaunt, skeletal and black against the
falling snow and I felt transported into another world.
What was special for me was the silence, because snow
absorbs sound, and the result was a depth of silence
that felt almost preternatural. At the same time, what
sound there was (children shouting, snow fights, dogs
barking) had a ringing quality and one could never
quite place where the sound was coming from, nor
even see who was making the sound. The sounds
were like ghostly, disembodied voices echoing from
some other parallel world. Like *Oaks in Winter*, this
dates from the same period and the same sojourns in
Kensington Gardens.

Snow can be beautiful or deadly. It can be robins and snowmen or Captain Scott dying in his tent. This is the nature of snow: beauty and terror, and in this poem I wanted to capture the ambivalence of a frozen landscape.

Song of the Shekhinah
(Inspired by the Song of Solomon)

O, my beautiful doe-eyed god!
Fruitful as the almond tree art Thou
That flowerest in the groves of Erech;
Thy odour is of kyphi[12]
And thy breath is as the cedars of Lebanon.
Gold is thy hair as the sands of Arabi,
And bright Thine eyes
As the rings on the hand of Solomon.
Thy body is powerful as the lion
The pharaohs hunt on the plains of Nubia;
Swift as the hawk that beats the wind
Before the disk of Ra.[13]

Come O fair one,
Let us love upon the sand,
For behold! The desert cools
And the stars burn bright as the eyes of Bast![14]

---

[12] A perfume made from mastic, pine resin (or wood) camel grass, mint, sweet flag, and cinnamon.

[13] Egyptian creator god who was the power behind the sun.

[14] Egyptian cat goddess (formerly lion goddess) and daughter of Ra.

Come with Thy women who dance and weep,
With pipe and lyre and cymbals shrill;
Come with Thy goats and gifts of gold,
Thy fragrant woods and jars of oil;
For my passions burn as arrows loosed
From ships of war,
And the song of the flute falls wild upon my ears.

No love is there so pure as woman's love
That moves the gods from their high watch,
Nor doth the rose's art compare
In scent and form.
Then come, O Mighty King, descend!
For ere the nets of night are cut
And cast away,
I will marry thee in the movements of my limbs
And bind Thee in the tresses of my hair.

Am I not lovely
Whom Thou mad'st for love?
Didst Thou not form me in beauty,
Declaring me fair among all the daughters of Israel?
For behold! I am cloven like the date,
And men draw succour from my shade;
My neck is comely,

And my breasts hang full like skins of wine.
Darksome are my thighs
As groves of terebinth,
Heavy with odours of spikenard and myrrh,
And the moistness thereof is as the resin of pines.

I have wandered among the tents of the women,
Who painted my hands with henna,
And put Thy mark upon my brow;
And my feet they bathed in balm of Gilead
And sewed jewels into my hair.
Am I not lovely?

O Thou secret hunter of the heart!
For how many moons didst Thou pursue me?
Thou stole my name from out my secret thoughts,
And like a dove set it forth upon the wind,
Beating soft against my tent flaps
As I fretted in sleep.
Thou sought me among the daughters of Shiloh,
But I dwelled not with them,
Nor by Gihon's fertile springs,
Nor in the fields of Heshbon beside the salt sea,

But in the land of the black earth[15] didst travail
In grief,
Mourning the love of my youth
And keeping vigil for my King.

I am tall and proud O ye daughters of Jerusalem!
And fragrant as the myrrh tree
Giving forth its odours to the night.
Black is my hair,
Black as the mines of Arabah;
My thighs are fertile as the reed beds of the Nile,
And the cleft therein is the dwelling
Of doves.
Bend Thy knee and weep, O mighty god,
For thou lookest on beauty!

O my handsome faun!
I stretched forth my hand to bathe Thy feet,
And the myrrh ran warm upon my wrists,
But Thou stayed my touch and anointed me,
And calling me 'Daughter',
Put a crown upon my head,
And Thy voice was as the laughter of silver bells;

---

[15] Egypt.

77

And I cast down my eyes,
And lo my belly was swollen with child,
And my breasts fat with milk.
Then didst we walk abroad
Upon the white and winding sand,
Beneath which ancient cities breathed in sleep,
For to keep the watches of the night,
Ere the sun rose up among the bloody waters of
    the moon,
And the dawn swelled forth beneath the bowl of
    stars,
Announcing with torches the fullness of the day.

Tonight the stars cascade like beads
Above the tents of Gerar,
And lovers sing of reachless love,
Of trysts thwarted and beauties unsurpassed,
While women laugh and curse the moon
Her gifts of blood.
Majestic moon!
The silver sandalled virgin walks the sky
And the lights of Heaven wash about her feet,
Ere she stoops to wreath with dew

The panting hills,
And turns to star-strewn surf
The clouds of day.

With reed song soft my soul is charmed,
Nor knows of speech.
But walks the columned halls of temples strange
Mid ancient symbols lost to Man.
O my Lord God!
I drink from Thy cup and fall among stars,
And a thousand years are but a thread of silk.
Is it life or is it death,
That thus I wander as a shade,
The ghostly ichor of the stillborn night?

Notes

The Song of the Shekhinah was my attempt to write
Jewish mystical poetry, in which the erotic and the
spiritual become intertwined. The Shekhinah, a term
derived not from the Bible but from Jewish rabbinic
literature, is the indwelling presence of God in the
world. In Kabbalah, she inhabits the lowest or tenth

sephirah[16], where she represents the daughter, or feminine aspect of God, and the power of Divinity flows down through the intervening sephiroth into and through her; but when Man turns away from God she is said to weep. She is analogous to the Holy Spirit in Judaism (*Ruach ha-Qodesh*), and to the *Parousia* or Divine Presence which descends upon the heads of the Apostles, and she anticipates the Gnostic Sophia. The *Song of Solomon* describes the search of the Shekhinah (as the Shulamite or 'Princess') for her love, and her abuse at the hands of the guards who send her away and block their meeting.

The observant reader will note the Egyptian imagery which was a cultural crossover into early Israelite civilisation down to the Kings. Indeed, the Egyptian imagery is entirely appropriate in the context of Jewish mystical tradition since the feminine soul (an aspect of the Shekhinah) is said to be 'in bondage' in the land of Egypt (the material world) and only when it unites with its bridegroom (the Spirit) is it said to enter Jerusalem, the City of God.

---

[16] The sephiroth (s. sephirah) are the ten emanations of the God-head, culminating in Earth.

In Christian mysticism, the Shekhinah is said to represent the Soul in relation to the Spirit, and thus the Bride of God. In St Francis of Assisi's *Canticle of the Sun and the Moon*, ostensibly a hymn to creation, we can detect the theme of the divine union in which the Spirit or God is symbolised by the Sun and the Soul by the Moon, in a mutually interdependent relationship with each other. The aspiration to divine union with God is perpetuated in the Christian mystics, St Teresa of Avila and St Thérèse of Lisieux, symbolised by St Teresa's account of being pierced through the heart by an angel with a fiery lance, and was also central to the Rosicrucians. Can we make a leap of intuition in suggesting that Mary Magdalene, Jesus' only female disciple, is a cipher for the Shekhinah?

The theme of the Sacred Marriage and the presence of its symbolism in the Christian Eucharist will be discussed in a short discursive essay at the end of the book.

Middle Period
2000–2009

Above the Pines

Sky burned to orange
Above the pines,
Burned to toffee along the ridge.
Toffee apple sky
Along the wide ridge above the pines.

Sky burned to black
Above the sand,
Above the mountains beyond the sand,
Smooth black pelt rolled in stars.
I stroke you. You sigh.

Notes

What I tried to achieve in this evocation of sunset is
a widening perspective as one zooms out from the
pine forest to a vista of mountains and from that to
an increasingly wider vista of mountains set back from
the shoreline. It is a very minimalist poem, designed
to encapsulate very intense imagery with extreme

economy of language. It concludes with an analogy between the night sky and a lover's hair.

By Saddleworth Moor

I met a man
Huddled in the Christmas snow,
In worn-out coat and cap to catch the coins
Of passers-by who paid no heed,
Nor desired to know,
The fate of this poor man
But chattered on at speed.

And something of his features made me stop,
For sure I knew him
From many years ago,
Though his cheeks were hollow
And stubble decked his chin,
And eyes that shone had lost their glow.

I proffered him a coin,
A shiny golden coin,
Which in his cap I laid,
But he stopped me, saying,
"Your coin I'll trade
For a minute of your time.
I was not always thus.

Hear me out and you will see."
And he lowered his eyes and said,
"I think this winter will be the death of me."

"Strange," he said, "there was a time
I stood so tall,
Had pride in my spine back then,
Kept me straight,
Never thought I'd have a fall,
Until that night and late,
I took my wife and daughters four
And lost them all on the M62
By Saddleworth Moor.

"I'd had a jar afore I left,
Small one mind, took the wheel,
Took it careful like I should.
One by one they fell asleep,
Never thought they'd sleep for good!
The bleak and barren moor,
Fog descending like a pall,
And me the last awake.
The night, the music and
The long dark road ahead,
And heavy rain withal;

Should have stopped to take a break.
Lulls the senses see, the endless miles, the
    monotony,
And all about, that dark and lonely peak –
Fills a man with dread;
Who could have known within an hour
My wife and daughters dead?"
Then a tear rolled down his cheek.
"I killed them all," he said,
"I killed them all.

"Now I see their faces in the rain,
Among the crowds that stop and stare
At windows brightly lit,
Or in dead of night
When papers flit along the street
As alone I sit,
And then it comes:
The anguish, torment and the pain.
And every time I see them there,
Though I close my eyes in vain,
They call my name through the sleet
And give me that accusing look,
And tell me we will meet."

"Poor wretch," said I,
"But sure I know you from a happier time.
Yet still you live though prosper not."
"Sir, I live," he said, "That no man can deny.
And folk will say I'm in my prime.
But of my soul?
My soul's been dead a year and more.
It died in that car on the M62
By Saddleworth Moor."

Notes

Having driven past Saddleworth Moor many times I can tell you what a wild and desolate place it is. It is famous (or rather infamous) as the moor upon which Brady and Hindley buried their child victims, but rather than focus on the Brady murders, I chose to focus on 'spirit of place', the tendency of a place where tragedy has occurred to attract more tragedy towards it (and living near Beachy Head, I should know). But the poem is also about the destructive effect of guilt in which the voice of conscience becomes an accusing angel drawing a man to his doom.

The Damned

Long have I dwelled by the ocean's boom
And walked the wind-wracked shore,
Transfigured by a dying sun
And deafened by the roar.

The bedlam cry of gulls
Haunts the sullen air,
Rings among the scudding clouds
And warns one to beware.

Behind the line of shingle
The banks of dunes skirt low,
The wild grass flickers in the wind,
Bears carrion for the crow.

Out to sea a steeple rises
Black against the sky,
And marks the ancient village
Whose souls were left to die.

Where now the vengeful waves
Crash down upon the sand,
Children played in muddy lanes
And farmers ploughed the land.

Then the sickness came
And took them all away,
And folk no more came nigh
The village in the bay.

The church bell sways upon the tide,
It tolls beneath the waves,
And summons unto evensong
The plague dead from their graves.

They rise up from the deep at night
And walk the moonlit sand,
Men and women dressed in rags
Standing hand in hand.

They stand upon the moonlit shore
And call on me to come,
But I'll ne'er join them 'neath the waves
Until my life is run.

Notes

The Damned is a supernatural poem that evokes the return of vengeful ghosts from a drowned village. It is based on the lost village of Dunwich off the Suffolk coast, which was the former capital of the Eastern Angles but succumbed to the encroachment of the sea in medieval times. One hot summer, I motored down with a group of friends for a long weekend, renting a cottage. We sunbathed naked among the sandy dunes from which tall spiky grasses sprouted and ate fish and chips: one of those enduring memories of my youth! But in winter it is a very different place, wild and forlorn and actually quite creepy.

Dead Can Dance

The seasons roll,
The wheel turns,
The snow that falls,
The sun that burns.

The days grow short
And darkness reigns,
And frost paints ghostly shapes
On window panes.

From spectral trees
The leaves do fall,
The gates are open,
The Dead do call

And walk among us
And tell their plight,
And dance with the Living
On Samhain night.

Some died in their beds,
Some drowned at sea,

Some buried alive,
'Neath mud and scree.

Some burned in their cars
Or at the stake,
Some died asleep
And some awake.

And their whispers
Strangely we do hear,
And faces see
When they draw near.

Livid skin
And lips of blue,
Dead black eyes
And mouths askew.

And all are come
By main and might,
To dance with the Living
On Samhain night.

Notes

Samhain is the Celtic Feast of the Dead held on October 31st and is said to be the time when the gates between the worlds are maximally open (see *Samhain–A Prose Poem*). The idea of a dance with Death, however, can be traced back to the Middle Ages and not specifically to any pagan festival. Between the Black Death and the Hundred Years War of the fourteenth century and the beginning of the Renaissance in the sixteenth, the Danse Macabre was a popular artistic meme with numerous church friezes in France and Italy, depicting alternate dead and living figures, arranged in hierarchical order of social importance, being led to the grave. The art form expressed the idea that Death was the great equaliser and no one was exempt from it: all are equal in Death. Alongside the art form, however, were very real ecstatic dance crazes. Beginning in the eleventh to twelfth centuries (and *preceding* the Black Death) St Vitus' Dance was a mass dance popular across the Low Countries, Germany and Italy, that took place in churchyards amid mounting hysteria with jerking convulsive movements (though there is some speculation as to whether consumption of ergot was involved), while from the fourteenth century the

Totentanz in Germany involved dances with the figure of Death randomly seizing people. Hans Holbein the Younger made a series of engravings of this dance. A further dance was Tarantism in Italy, possibly caused by the bite of a venomous spider, the tarantula or wolf spider, which had to be sweated out through dancing the Tarantella.

The Death Show

Roll up! Roll up! Come to the Death Show,
There's a weapon for everyone, don't y'know?

Microwave satellites that see from afar,
And pilotless drones that can blow up a car,
Napalm that burns and sticks to the skin
And a bomb full of shrapnel to do them all in.

Nuclear bombs, they'll level a city
Though the radiation sickness ain't too pretty,
The squares and the parks lie black in the rain,
And there's no one alive to build them again.

Let's fire up an African coup,
And hire ourselves a wrecking crew,
Rape a few women to build some fear,
And ride on a tank with a belly of beer.

The dealers are there, making their pitch,
By the end of the day, they'll be stinking rich,
"Burn a hole in their guts but not in your purse,
And kill them so quickly they won't need a nurse."

The President's there, his wife and his son,
He smiles for the camera as the deal is done,
How they'll be used he hasn't a clue,
But better dress smartly, there's killing to do.

The General, he's standing there dabbing his eye;
Is it just possible he's starting to cry?
But he's not mourning the dead and the dying,
No, Sir, he's thinking of the bombs he'll be buying.

The cowards' convention is drawing to a close,
Now every damn nation has arms to dispose,
Will they use them for good or for ill?
But there's only one thing a weapon does... **KILL**.

Notes

I temporarily moved away from the writing of
mystical and nature poetry into the realm of social
realist poetry to write his damning indictment of the
arms trade. What kick-started it was the now-famous
photograph of Phan Thi Kim Phúc OOnt, by AP
photographer Nick Ut, taken at Trảng Bàng, during
the Vietnam War on June 8, 1972, which depicts her

running naked away from her burning village after a napalm attack by South Vietnamese forces supported by the American Army. It was one of the iconic images that turned American popular opinion against the Vietnam War. But no one learns the lessons, and even today democratic governments supply arms and surveillance equipment to authoritarian governments as political allies, knowing they will be used against civilian populations and even, sometimes, against their own people. I have come to a realisation after many years that:

POWER DOES NOT UNDERSTAND MORALITY; POWER ONLY UNDERSTANDS POWER.

POWER DOESN'T RESPOND TO MORAL ARGUMENT; POWER ONLY RESPONDS TO PROTEST.

ONLY SOMEONE WITH POWER CAN INFLUENCE POWER.

Politics and international relations are extensions of the male ego, based on territory, power, dominance, suspicion and paranoia; and as long as the schism between Power and Morality persists, then international politics will always be corrupt.

Today, the cards are stacking up for another Great Power conflict, with Russia flexing its muscles in Eastern Europe, and China claiming the South China Sea as its own and poised to invade Taiwan. Meanwhile, Iran is starting proxy wars in the Middle East and North Korea is poised to invade the south, with nuclear missiles trained on the United States. One wrong move could start the Third World War, and unlike the previous two, this will be a nuclear conflict. Humanity is staring into the Abyss.

Let me lay my cards on the table. If every nation altogether at a single hour on a single day agreed to demilitarise, world leaders would be forced to resolve their differences by negotiation without resort to armies, and we would have world peace. This is why I am a proud supporter of

WORLD DEMILITARISATION

which demands a quantum leap of political imagination and will to bring it about. Who will be the statesman who has that breadth of vision to rise above the petty obsessions of national interest and act for the human good?

Evocation of a Spirit of Vengeance

Come from the graveyard,
Rise through the earth,
Cast off thy shroud,
For this is thy birth.

Rise from the mound,
Walk from the tomb,
Thou art not born
Of woman's womb.

Spirit of air,
Spirit of night,
Who haunteth the shadows
Twixt darkness and light.

Walk with the living,
Dance with the dead,
Visit the hangman,
The judge in his bed.

Thou walkest abroad
While the world is asleep,
Thou takest the unjust
Down through the deep.

Blood for the callow,
Blood for the knave,
Vengeance on them
For all that they gave.

Death to my enemy,
Blood to my foe,
Pain and suffering,
Travail and woe.

Stalk my accuser,
Fill him with dread,
Drain him of life,
For thou art undead.

Come from the graveyard,
Rise from the earth,
No power shall hold thee
In Heaven or Earth.

Notes

> Like one, that on a lonesome road
> Doth walk in fear and dread,
> And having once turned round walks on,
> And turns no more his head;
> Because he knows, a frightful fiend
> Doth close behind him tread.

Samuel Taylor Coleridge, *Rime of the Ancient Mariner*, VI, 37-42

These lines have always stuck in my mind as being particularly creepy. They evoke the feeling of something silent and invisible pursuing one... and getting closer. M.R. James used them as the basis for his classic ghost story *Casting the Runes*, and they were also the inspiration for this poem which depicts the conjuring of such a denizen from the depths of Hell to wreak vengeance on all those who have wronged the summoner.

The poem depicts a rite of necromancy whereby the dead are summoned to attack the living. If the dead have passed on, however, how can this be? It presumes that not everything *does* pass on. That part of the soul that belonged to Spirit maybe returns to Spirit, but those component parts of the personality that were never aligned with Spirit, or at odds with it, persist as chaotic fragments at war with each other, and which may also join up with other fragments of other souls; hence, that ominous phrase from the New Testament, *'My name is Legion for we are many'* (Mark 5:9).

This began to make sense to me when I read the Sorceress Cagliastro's *Blood Sorcery Bible Vol.1*, from which I would like to quote a short passage, not least because I think it is incredibly insightful and deserves to be heard:

A Demon is not simply an angry or disturbed disincarnate. A demon is an amalgam, a group creation derived from the collection of tortured energies of multiple people and occasionally animals and situations. The energy allows the tortured elements to bond and choose a leader among them. The leader can be one of the members from whom these destructive elements emerged, or it can be a new force fighting from within, wrestling amongst the ruffians in the group to emerge as a leader. Those are the most powerful because their internal conflict fuels them, keeping the heat within and churning it to develop stronger, more intense energies. Their powerful forces create EMP (Electro-Magnetic Pulses). These pulses attach to sound waves and push outward, getting trapped in metal objects, even moving the air itself. Those are the skills of the demons who have made aggressive physical contact with me. Those are the dangerous ones who can hold on to a physical place, inhabiting it with their hostility and causing grief for anyone who wishes to live there. Their hostility is viral. They spin and leave a thin coating of black dust. If any of my readers have ever lived in a house that seemed ripe with hostility of an unknown origin, you may think back and remember how dusty and grimy things seemed, how no amount of cleaning could make the environment fresh. The air was never quite clear and the lights were never quite bright. Joy and playfulness seemed clouded like an outdoor event that encountered a rainy day. If you have had those experiences, you have lived amongst them, among Demons.[17]

The attentive reader might recognise some of the features of poltergeist hauntings in this description, such as the notorious Enfield poltergeist where multiple personalities seemed to be involved. All of which begs the question, what is the nature of spiritual evil?[18]

Evil can be grouped into two sorts: human evil and spiritual evil. Human evil is basically an abuse of free will consequent on lack of self-awareness; it is often the result of unconscious motivations and prejudices, or identification with toxic ideologies. Diplomatically, one might call it an imbalance between the individual good and the public good, or a blindness to the public good. Most people who commit evil would never consider themselves to be evil.

---

[17] Sorceress Cagliastro, *Blood Sorcery Bible Vol. 1*, Original Falcon, 2011, p.133.

[18] Bearing in mind that good and evil are not absolute values but relative to the person experiencing them, they could, alternatively, simply be described as the forces of cohesion and dispersion.

Spiritual evil is another matter. Given that all things have their opposites, spiritual evil is the primal force opposed to Life and Being, which, in the Jewish Qabalah, is called the Qliphoth and in mainstream Judaism is termed *ruach tum'ah*, the Spirit of Impurity, being the opposite of the Holy Spirit (*ruach ha Kodesh)*. Just as the Holy Spirit can settle upon a person, so can the Spirit of Impurity, and who so turns from Life and Being the Spirit of Impurity shall take root in them. I prefer to call this primal force of spiritual evil 'Anti-Life', and it manifests as a spreading darkness and a pervasive sense of dread. It is that force that negates Being and desires to draw all things back into the primal void, in contrast with spiritual good which seeks to realise the potential of consciousness through Existence. You may think that the opposite of Life is Death but both Life and Death are phases of the natural order. Anti-Life is *opposed to the natural order*: it is opposed to Life, Light and Being. It is the force of Counter-Creation.

As soot falling from a chimney
Are they,
As black snow, charred embers void of life,

Black as the Night
Without moon or stars,
In darkness multiplied,
Shadow upon shadow
Descending through the lattices
Between the worlds,
Seeking the unguarded door,
The tormented mind that will admit them.

The common Christian view of spiritual evil is something that originates outside the Self. This goes back to First Temple Judaism when a goat 'for Azazel' was sent out into the desert to return sin to its source. Christians blamed the Fall of Man on an external entity (the serpent in the guise of Satan), and demons were considered to be fallen angels. St. Paul, in his *Letter to the Romans*, attributed sin to a malign force that entered the world at the Fall of Man. I take issue with the view that all evil comes from a force external to the self, for the principal reason that if we cannot admit our own potential for evil then we cannot take ownership of it, and that raises questions of moral responsibility; so, I am not responsible for beating my wife because "the devil made me do it". I offer an opposing view: that whatever force of Anti-Life exists, it can do nothing unless the soul itself turns away from Life and Being, and it is this very turning away from Life and Being that is the beginning of the demonic. Thus, the war for Existence is fought on the battleground of the individual soul. We have all seen the opportunist thief who does a bit of this and a bit of that and sometimes gets caught. That is human evil. Then there is the demonic personality: the psychopath, the serial killer, the torturer. *The demonic personality in life becomes a demonic force in death.* All that rage and aggression has to go somewhere and it joins up with other demonic fragments of souls that survive physical death until a composite entity is created that speaks sometimes in one voice, and sometimes in another, but has unified will and volition; I call such beings *quantum entities*. As beings of the Void, they invade places abandoned by human habitation such as attics, basements and wall spaces, which is where malicious hauntings often begin. In poltergeist hauntings, the counter-creational force of Anti-Life assimilates the intelligence of the dead souls it works through; the malicious and childish pranks played on the living are *the force testing its powers*. Similarly, the positive aspect of Divinity, Spirit, as it evolves through the consciousness of sentient beings and develops self-awareness through them, also assimilates the intelligence of the living faithful who have passed on from this world and becomes a positive force for human evolution. Evil learns, but so does Good.

However much we may turn away from Divinity or God or Spirit, or whatever one calls the basis of Life and Being, we can never not be a part of it. There is therefore a limitation on the power of spiritual evil. No soul, however fallen from its nature, can be cast into the outer darkness.

I don't subscribe to the Christian obsession with 'the Devil'. While there *is* a principle of spiritual evil in Judaism, the *shaitans* (from which Satan as a title derives), also known as the *ra'im* (from *ra* meaning 'evil'), were *a class* of devils and not a single entity, and they were adversaries of Man, not of God. The subsequent enthronement of Satan as Prince of Evil owes to Zoroastrianism which infected the Jewish apocalyptic cults in Babylon and through them Christianity; there is no Bond villain in Judaism. I also make a distinction between the demons found in the books of magic (grimoires) and the 'real' demons I have described here. The Goetic demons and their ilk are really egregores or thought forms derived from the 'demonisation' of pagans gods and goddesses (Hebrew *shedim*) by Judaism. Amoral rather than evil, they will appear if you summon them and you need to take precautions and show the proper respect, but they are fundamentally different from the demons responsible for terrorising people during poltergeist hauntings; these are the 'real' demons: the souls of the dead who have morphed into something much greater and more dangerous than they were. So, I believe in the demonic and respect its power, but ultimately, I believe demons have a very human origin, as tormented souls who have turned from the Light and become hosts of a miasmic counter-creational power, none of which bears any resemblance to the traditional 'hierarchy of Hell' promulgated by the Church, presided over by some Satanic 'Mr Big'.

JUST AS MAN CAN BECOME A PERFECT VESSEL FOR THE POWER OF LIFE AND SPIRIT, SO HE CAN ALSO BECOME THE PERFECT VESSEL OF THE POWER OF MALEVOLENCE

Hymn to Hekate

Hekate, Queen of Heaven and Hell,
Triform Goddess of Life and Death,
I call upon thy names and invoke thy presence
    this night,
Soteira, Chthonia, Trioditis, Klêidouchos,
Phosphoros, Propylaia, Enodia;[19]
By white and red and black,
By torch and knife,
By mirror and key,
I call upon thee, Hekate,
By blood, by honey and by rose,
Arise, arise, Hekate,
Light my path and come unto me.
Hail, Hekate, mighty goddess of creation and death,
Keeper of Boundaries, Guardian of Doors,
    Wanderer of the Ways,
Open thy gates before me.
Arise, Hekate and welcome.

---

[19] In order: 'Saviour', 'Of the Underworld', 'Of the Three Ways',
'Key Bearer', 'Light Bearer', 'Before the Gate', 'Wandering One'.

Notes

Take a good look at the Statue of Liberty, on Liberty Island in New York Harbour, and what you are really looking at is a statue of the goddess Hekate. Yes, right in the largest commercial city in the most Christian United States of America, she is there presiding over it. Look at the upraised torch and the rays extending from her head; it's her, Hekate in her aspect of *soteira*, thinly disguised as the Roman goddess Libertas.

Said to have originated from the Greek colony of Caria in Asia Minor, her cult became established in Greece between the 6th and 5th centuries B.C. Hesiod's Theogony of the 8th century lists her as a daughter of Titans, the primeval forces of Chaos in Greek myth, yet she fought on the side of the Olympians in their war with the Titans. A goddess of the heavens, earth and the underworld, she straddles all three realms and is thus a liminal goddess: one who guards the boundaries between the worlds. Hence, she is associated with the crossroads of three ways, and typically at crossroads one would find a Hekataeon, or pillar, where the goddess would stand looking three ways. Thus, also is she armed with torch and key to guard the entrances to temples and houses.

Originally known as soteira ('Saviour') and associated with light (her name has been suggested as an obscure epithet of Apollo meaning 'far reaching one'), her cult later took on a darker turn as Goddess of ghosts and witchcraft, and she acquired the epithet *Cthonia* ('Of the Underworld'), possibly due to her relationship with Persephone whom she searched for when Persephone was taken down into the Underworld by Hades. As such, she was central to the witch cult in Thessaly where she was known as *Enodia* ('the Wandering One') and she was depicted as accompanied by dogs which are traditionally guardians of the underworld, but also symbols of protection.

This poem imagines a hymn or invocation as it might have been intoned by a priestess of Hekate.

Lucifer Unbound

Lucifer, Prince of the Spirits of the Air,
Ruler of the powers of the mind,
Who art the bright and morning star,
Promethean fire
Who falleth as lightning from Heaven to smite the
    earth,
God of Witchcraft, Hekate's son,
Black sabbatic goat
About whose cloven form we weave and whirl
In the spirit-infested air.
Lucifer! Lucifer!
Come! Come!
Come unto us!
Old and young, cowled and cloaked,
We call thy name!
Come forth from thy realm of Chaos and pitiless
    Night
Where the Dead turn in sleep,
And bring nigh the Darkness to illumine the Day.
Drunk with hemlock,
Naked and free,
We celebrate thy rites of blasphemy!

Come, let us take fire from thy horns
As we dance and sing in arcane wood,
In forests where the wild things are.
Unbound spirit, thou canst not be confined in
    church of stone,
But on mountain top 'mid wind-stirred pine,
We sing thy rite and drink thy cup.
There, where the raven flies,
There, where the crow feeds,
There, where the serpent coils in the tall grass.
Come Daystar, Son of Dawn,
Come Sabazius, come Dionysus,
Come Azazel, come Lucifer,
Father of Lust and Angel of Light;
We recite thy barbarous names and invoke thy
    presence.
Thou art brother to the Sun and sister to the Moon.
Thou art pure being without attribute.
Thou art the ecstasy of life and the serenity of the
    spirit.
Thou art the raging fire and the cold brilliance of
    light.
Thou art the destroyer of falsehood and the
    initiator into truth.
In thee, all opposites are reconciled.

Through thee, all men and women shall become
    gods.
Hail Lucifer!
Hail my Prince!

Notes

Lucifer, whose name means Light Bearer, derives from the Greek god Eosphorus, who represented the planet Venus as Herald of the Dawn. Due to a mistranslation of Isaiah 14:12-15 in Jerome's composition of the Latin Vulgate, the words 'How art thou fallen *Helel ben Shahar?*' which were addressed to a *king*, were translated as 'How art thou fallen, Lucifer, Son of the Morning?' *Helel ben Shahar* literally translates as 'Daystar, Son of Dawn' and was a royal title, likening the king to the planet Venus, while Jerome's translation gave the impression that Lucifer was an angelic entity who had 'fallen' from Heaven, and with this, the whole legend of the battle in Heaven, and the Fall of the Angels commenced. It was in this way that the identities of Lucifer and Satan became merged in the theological mind and popular imagination. Satan had an entirely different origin, of course, as one of a class of accusing angels under the ultimate control of God (i.e. Adversary of Man, but *not* of God), but during and after the Babylonian Captivity in the sixth century B.C., Satan's identity became merged with that of Ahriman (the God of Darkness) under the influence of Zoroastrianism, and it was in this guise as Adversary of God that he was incorporated into Christian theology.

My interest is more in Lucifer as an archetypal principle of consciousness, however. On the one hand, he is a shadowy figure, since he represents the Other Side of Existence, and thus hidden knowledge. On the other hand, he represents the principle of the illumination of the mind, since he can open the gates of the mind to that knowledge. Thus he is very much a gatekeeper between the dayside realm of this universe and the other realm that lies behind the observable universe. There is also a palpable difference in emphasis between the Christian and pagan ideas of 'Spirit'. The Christian idea of Spirit is an emanation of the Divine 'Source' (God, Supreme Being or Monad) which not only 'makes' the world but also emanates through it to make itself known to Man and thereby achieve an 'alignment' of Man with the Source of his own being, whereas the pagan idea of Spirit is more akin to that of a vital force that flows through Existence that can be used for magic as well as illumination. It is to this second interpretation that Lucifer really belongs: as a 'trickster' god who reveals the secrets of spiritual power, but not necessarily spiritual love as in the Christological tradition. Decidedly amoral, in this, he is akin to the Yoruba Elegua or Elegbara, known in Vodou as Papa Legba.

However, in Christian Europe, the rebel label stuck. In Christian theology, both the natural order and the social order are reflections of the Divine order, so anything that contravenes the God-given order is *de facto* evil. Spiritual evil is therefore defined in Christianity as a transgression of the boundaries of the divine order. Lucifer is the transgressor of boundaries: he represents the intrusion of the shadow side of existence into the ordered universe, the numinous behind the veil of nature revealing itself through the deep Unconscious mind. He gives Man the choice: remain subordinate to Nature or achieve your spiritual potential.

That which is of Nature can never be more than it is. This is not to say it cannot adapt to its environment in Darwinian terms, but it can never transcend its own nature. That which is Luciferian is capable of being more than it is: it does not simply adapt to its environment but it can master its environment; it develops the capacity for free will; it acquires the capacity for abstract intellect and to free itself from the tyranny of social conditioning; it has a concept of time, and it possesses the capacity to imagine possibility; it is not a creature of instinct but is capable of self-mastery. Man is the perfect exemplar of the Luciferian ideal because, although originating in Nature, Man transcends Nature and has the capacity to become greater than itself and to control its own destiny. One might even say that the European Enlightenment of the eighteenth century was the apogee of the Luciferian spirit, and the framers of the American constitution were in perfect accord with Luciferian principles.

Luciferianism is not antithetical to Divinity (although it is antithetical to the idea of worship of deity external to the Self, that is, 'God'). Rather, it regards Man as the *fulfilment* of Divinity, perfectly expressing the power and beauty of Spirit through his own sentience. In expressing Spirit through his own self-aware consciousness, Man becomes a star, illumining others through his own light.

Lucifer also represents the 'visionary' faculty in Man that predates the growth of rationalism and the dominance of the pre-frontal cortex. That visionary faculty allowed us to make contact, not only with the Unconscious as it is defined today, but with the numinous 'Other Side' of existence and the quantum entities that dwelled therein. Even as little as two thousand years ago, when the 'veil' between the Conscious and Unconscious aspects of the *psyche* was not as opaque as it is in our own time, it was commonplace for people to see visions (such as angels and demons) and hear voices, and these formed the basis, not merely of the ancient soothsayer, but the entire prophetic tradition in the Bible: all the great religions of Judaism, Christianity and Islam were founded on this same visionary faculty of Man. With the growth of rationalism, the two-way communication between the Conscious and Unconscious during waking reality was slowly stifled as the veil between the two thickened, and thereafter, the Unconscious only made itself known through dreams. During the early modern period, as a product of rationalist theology, anyone outside the Church who had visions was condemned as a witch, and in our own hyper-rationalist culture, the visionary faculty is demonised as mental illness. Lucifer has been demonised twice: once by the Church and again by Rationalism. *The visionary faculty (the ability to see visions, hear voices, speak with supernatural entities and prophesy) is your birthright and older than reason.*

The challenge of Lucifer is to think outside the box, to expand the mind beyond the apparent order we take for granted, and this is what defines him as a revolutionary principle. We need to understand that Lucifer is not the adversary of order as such but the adversary of 'dead' order, by which is meant order that refuses to change or reform, and thus becomes corrupt; in other words, 'stupid authority'. Order of itself is not a social good. If one has an orderly society devoid of truth and justice, then it is a corrupt society however orderly it is (think of the Church in the Middle Ages or modern totalitarian states). Think about it: politicians always win elections by appealing to our fear of 'disorder', of crime and subversive minorities. They never win elections about injustice. They marginalise groups they don't like by presenting them as threats to children, threats to family life, threats to 'community', threats to 'society', threats to 'civilisation'. Latinx and persons of colour are 'criminals', gays and lesbians are 'perverted', Wiccans are 'Satanic', nudists are 'depraved'. The reason they do this is that threats to order evoke a visceral survival response while 'injustice' does not, and the reason is that we are programmed only to fear things that directly affect us.

In the seventeenth century, the poet John Milton, in his *Paradise Lost*, had portrayed Lucifer (in the guise of Satan) as the Byronic anti-hero who leads a rebellion against God but becomes corrupted by power. Even today, *Paradise Lost* remains the textbook on why revolutions fail. By the late eighteenth century, which saw the American and French revolutions, Lucifer had become the poster boy of radical politics and anticlericalism (decrying the pernicious alliance between Church and State and the Church's greed for power and money) in the cause of 'just rebellion'. With a resurgence of republicanism in the mid to late-nineteenth century, Lucifer (in his alter ego as Satan) once more became popular, as exemplified in Baudelaire's *Litanies of Satan*, and Giosue Carducci's *Hymn to Satan*.

Yet just as Lucifer represents political freedom, he also represents mental liberation: freedom from the strictures of cultural conditioning and religious and political indoctrination... and Lucifer reminds us that while culture and society can provide a framework for living, they can also be a prison of the mind, and a person is not truly free until they have transcended their own culture. The phrase 'small town societies breed small town minds' is particularly apt, and I am reminded of the phrase in Milton's *Paradise Lost*: 'The mind is its own place and in itself can make a heaven of hell or a hell of heaven,'[20] a phrase that should be inscribed on the desk of every practising therapist. To expand the boundaries of our minds, and become more than we are, is our right and our duty.

---

[20] Milton, John. *Paradise Lost*, Book 1, Lines 221-270

Mystae
(After Homer)

"Mystae! To the Sea!"
The old man cried,
Old Cleomenes, noble-born, vowed to Eleusis,
Swan-white hair bleached by Aegean sun,
Skin gnarled as the ancient olive,
Beaten like Spartan leather,
Burnished by eighty summers,
Hardened by eighty winters,
And we,
Yelping kouroi[21], lithe and lean,
Doffing simple robes, exulting
In the blessed unadorned nudity
Of gods made flesh,
Sporting naked in Helios'[22] harsh glare,
Racing down to where
The sea sucks,
Hissing among the fine sand,
Licks and laps
Round supple thighs,

---

[21] A *kouros* is a young man in Greek and *kouroi* the plural.
[22] Helios, the Greek god of the Sun.

127

Shining flanks, smooth of youth,

Chests like muscled cuirass[23],

Cocks quickened by smack of spray

Python-like, rearing,

Wicked daggers

Drawn but yet unbloodied,

The unabashed laughter of men at play,

Caressed by the soft-fingered wind,

Riding the heedless cataract,

The wild maenad[24] cry,

And on some stony field,

The hero's death still far away,

The warrior yet to come,

But now all care cast aside,

In pleasure's name,

To carouse the silver-tongued surf,

Ere the ember'd dusk sets afire

The singing sea,

Torches thread the temple gate

And for we

The solemn rite begins.

---

[23] Body armour covering the chest, i.e., chest plate.

[24] The maenads were the female followers of Dionysus who celebrated the god's epiphany with ecstatic rites (see *The Antlered Man*).

Notes

Intended as a homage to Homer, the poem is set in the Eleusinian Mysteries, one of the Greek Mystery Cults. Drawn largely from the aristocratic families, participation in the Mysteries of Eleusis was considered a rite of passage, and the poem concerns the reader, not with the rite itself, but with the ritualistic bathing in the sea that preceded the rite. Since all the celebrants are men, and the poem dwells on the aesthetic beauty of the male form, it would be easy to dismiss *Mystae* as a homoerotic poem, but this would be a mistake. What the poem shows us is the innocent pleasure of men abstracted from the theatre of politics and war and allowed, for that short span, *to be themselves*, freed from the stereotype that the hyper-masculine patriarchy imposes on them. Thus, they become sensual, playful beings and through this rediscover a kind of innocence that aristocratic society denies them. I have long lingered under the suspicion that many men find the expectations of manhood to be a burden they have no choice but to carry, so I wondered how they would behave once that burden was lifted, if only temporarily. *Mystae* is the result.

Passing

In my time of passing,
In wonder I can see
The doors of Spirit
Open unto me.

The Light of Lights
Doth fill my eyes,
And now I know
That nothing really dies.

By Heaven's grace
Vouchsafed to me,
Of all sights
This sight to see,

A thousand suns
As bright as bright can be,
And all about me and within,
The vast, eternal Mystery.

With heart of joy
My soul be free
Nor, born again, shall ever die,
The Lord of Lights is come to me.

Notes

Short, and beautiful in its economy, this is a poem about dying consciously, about entering death in a deeply meditative state. This is not always possible: sometimes we die in our sleep, sometimes our death comes with trauma, but it is an aspiration. I will explore some of the popular ideas of the soul and question what the various ideas of 'salvation' actually mean in the discursive essay *On the Idea of the Soul* at the end of this book.

The Pretty Magpie

Once I loved a pretty bird,
A black and white magpie;
They came and tore its wings off
And left it for to die.

Once I loved a little dog,
A golden spaniel bitch;
They came and shot it all to death
And left it in a ditch.

Once I loved a little cat,
Grey with stripes of brown;
They came round laughing in their car,
They came and ran it down.

Once I loved a pretty maid,
With skin the scent of musk;
They raped her till she died of shame,
I buried her at dusk.

Now I've nothing left to love,
My heart is turned to stone;
Hard as winter frost it is
And my soul they own.

Notes

One of my abiding memories is of Billie Holiday singing *Strange Fruit*, a howl of rage against the culture of lynching in the American South. Although recorded in 1939, it wasn't released until 1954, and popularised by Nina Simone just a few years before the Civil Rights movement got underway. I remember what a shock to the system it was, and I wonder how many consciences it pricked... if any.

Pretty Magpie, like *Strange Fruit,* isn't a 'nice' poem and it isn't intended to be nice; it is intended to shock and to repulse. Specifically, it is also a poem about the Jim Crow-era American South and its appalling history of lynching black people. The magpie symbolises the coming together of white and black into something beautiful, and tearing the wings off the magpie symbolises the white-dominant society's attempts to prevent the underclass from 'flying', i.e., to keep them down. More generally, however, the poem is a damning comment on the casual nature of male violence and 'toxic' masculinity, which, believing in nothing beautiful, seeks to destroy everything beautiful.

All of America's racial problems today go back to the failure of Reconstruction following the Civil War, specifically following the Compromise of 1877 which resolved the disputed election of 1876, under which Republican Rutherford Hayes removed federal troops from the southern states in return for the Presidency. The southern states' promises to protect the rights of the black population were reneged on, and the American South's culture of fear and repression began. Not only did the South never get over losing the Civil War, but it set out to claw back states' rights and use those to keep down the newly emancipated black underclass, which it regarded as a threat to its way of life. This created a culture so totally resistant to social change that, while the rest of America moved on, the South remained defiantly in its own time bubble. It wasn't that southern Americans were especially wicked: most southern whites regarded themselves as respectable citizens and most would have been found in (white) church on Sundays, for *evil is rarely committed by people who think of themselves as evil*. Rather, the Jim Crow system was driven by fear: fear of the black underclass their ancestors had themselves created.

To say that racial prejudice was the exclusive preserve of the American South, however, would be entirely wrong. Few know that the principle of segregation was actually legalised by the U.S. Supreme Court in *Plessy v. Ferguson* (1896), and lynchings occurred also in the nation's capital, Washington, as well as race massacres in Wilmington N.C. (1898), Tulsa, Oklahoma (1921) and in Redwood, Florida (1923), accelerated by the revival of the Ku Klux Klan in 1915. The American Army remained segregated until July 1948. In 1939, the Daughters of the American Revolution had even refused permission for Marian Anderson to sing to an integrated audience in Constitution Hall in Washington, D.C., so Eleanor Roosevelt intervened for her to give the concert at the Lincoln Memorial instead.

Although *Brown vs. Board of Education* in May 1954 had ruled segregated schooling as violating the Fourteenth Amendment, ironically it took the Civil Rights movement of the '60s to do what the federal government was incapable of doing on its own – ending segregation and discrimination on the basis of race in the Civil Rights Act of 1964, and allowing the right of black Americans to vote in 1965. The Civil Rights Act of 1968 prohibited discrimination in the housing market... on paper anyway, since 'redlining' continued for decades afterward. Much of the impetus for this was ordinary Americans' revulsion at seeing Sheriff Jim Clark's state troopers running down and beating peaceful protestors on the Edmund Pettus Bridge outside Selma in March 1965. However, as we know, changing the law doesn't change the culture, and systemic racism, police brutality and voter suppression, as well as housing discrimination and underfunded schools in minority areas, have continued to this day.

America is a nation of contradictions. It is a secular state that has as its motto 'In God we trust' (since 1955). Its founders Jefferson and Madison created a Bill of Rights that was the most enlightened in the world yet permitted the institution of slavery. Worse, Thomas Jefferson, had six children by his slave, Sally Hemings, of whom only four reached adulthood; he did not free her and only freed her children at the age of twenty-one. In 1941, the United States sent a *segregated* army to fight against the racial tyranny of Hitler. It seems strange to me that the citizens of 'the world's greatest democracy' should have to demand the very rights granted to them by the constitution, from a state that should have been the guarantor of those rights. But it also occurs to me that there has never been any real and open debate about the legacy of America's past. The culture of systemic racism and police brutality, of young black men locked up for ridiculous sentences for trivial offences and then beaten and abused in prison and denied medical attention, and of underfunded schools and services in black and Latin neighbourhoods, could have changed a long time ago if America's toxic history had been acknowledged, and there had been the political will to change. It could have changed a long time ago if Americans as a whole had looked their history squarely in the face and come to terms with it. America today is a nation that prefers to live on its myths than look its history in the eye.

The sum of American history is the difference between vision and reality, its trajectory diametrically at odds with the principles of its founding constitution, yet there is tremendous diffidence today about discussing issues of race. Instead, there is an impulse to retreat into a kind of romantic patriotism that blindsides debate about racial and economic unfairness. Partly, this is explained by the feeling that dwelling on the past is inherently divisive, and indeed,

Republican-dominated school boards have defunded the teaching of 'divisive' subjects like critical race theory and the Reconstruction Era, but if we cannot admit the past then we cannot mend the future. What I see in America today is not 'one nation under God' but a patchwork of constituencies living in fear of each other, unequal access to law and healthcare, decaying infrastructure, emasculated environmental laws (think Flint, Michigan) voracious self-serving corporations driving down wages and living standards, impoverished schools and communities and massive inequality of wealth and opportunity... and the one institution that could effect change – Congress – is so polarised as to be incapable of organising a children's tea party. True patriotism is not emotional flag-waving. It is celebrating what is good about one's nation while holding one's nation to account when it does wrong or refuses to act in the public interest. Put another way, one does not resolve one's country's endemic problems by wrapping oneself in the national flag.

A SOCIETY THAT REFUSES TO CHANGE WILL EVENTUALLY HAVE CHANGE FORCED UPON IT

Thou Shalt Not Rest But Think of Me
(From the medieval Scottish)

T'was at midnight, Hallow's Eve,
I gaz'd upon a mirror dark,
And called upon my love to-be,
"Come, my love, appear to me."

My love appear'd within the glass,
The fairest face I e'er did see,
And from that day I vow'd to thee,
Thou shalt not rest but think of me.

I tied a ribbon in my hair
And donned my gayest livery,
But my look of love thou didst not see,
Thou shalt not rest but think of me.

Thy husband took thee by the arm
And bore thee from the carriage door,
And still I had no glance from thee,
Thou shalt not rest but think of me.

I served thee meat so rare and pink
Its blood ran out upon the plate,
I cut it up and gave it thee,
Thou shalt not rest but think of me.

I made thee cup of honey wine
And in it put two drops of blood;
The honey wine I gave to thee,
Thou shalt not rest but think of me.

I made thee philtres, strong and sweet,
Of mandrake, herbs and bitter root,
And these I fed thee secretly,
Thou shalt not rest but think of me.

I took a dog and bitch in heat
And rutted them most merrily;
As they rutted, I'd rut with thee,
Thou shalt not rest but think of me.

I set the dog upon the bitch
And caught their lust in mirror fair,
The mirror fair I gave to thee,
Thou shalt not rest but think of me.

Of wax, I made a poppet small
That bore the likeness of thy face,
And for it plucked a hair from thee,
Thou shalt not rest but think of me.

I bound it 'bout with scarlet thread
And with my knife did prick its heart,
Forever bound and ne'er be free,
Thou shalt not rest but think of me.

Merry, merry, bright and fair,
I took a lock of my true love's hair,
No other man thine eyes shall see,
Thou shalt not rest but think of me.

I bought three silken cords of red
And plaited into them thy hair,
And wore it close where none could see,
Thou shalt not rest but think of me.

I tied nine knots about its length
And breath'd upon them, one, two, three...
For to bind my love to thee,
Thou shalt not rest but think of me.

I courted a maiden sweet and fair
And bore her thence on bonnie ship,
But my first love wilt thou always be,
Thou shalt not rest but think of me.

I took my young wife for to bed
And bairns she bore me, fair and three,
But none of these compare with thee,
Thou shalt not rest but think of me.

Though I cannot have thee now,
By Old Sow's name this I trow,
Though parted we shall always be,
Thou shalt not rest but think of me.

Thy body now is dead and cold,
But still thy spirit is not free,
Though thou rot and worms eat thee,
Thou shalt not rest but think of me.

Notes

There is something uncomfortable and disturbing about this poem of the manservant coveting his mistress and practising love sorcery to bind her to him, even beyond the grave.

To His Dark Mistress

You lit me,
Like an arc of fire from a sun
Your bright rim touched me
And set ablaze my soul
As though of tinder it were made,
That I now crackle and blaze
As might a lightning tree
From a mortal flash that seared its bark
And rent its heart in twain.

Not a second edges past its mark
But that your image slips into my mind unbidden,
As a lover slips between the sheets,
Loiters behind the curtain of my thoughts as
    might a thief,
While the master tosses in lustful sleep.
Comely assassin,
Would I die by your knife,
Or in passion raise my throat
To be torn by your lascivious mouth?
Sun, moon, moon, sun, all meld.
A washed-out addict, dark-eyed and wan,

Naught else exists for this poor wretch;
Cast from his throne,
The goblet rolls and the wine is spilled.
And my senses cry,
"Go to her! Leave all behind,"
And in retreat
Leave all the ships that were once a mighty navy[25]
Half-submerged and drown'd.

No match, I, thy coy deceits,
That, like Medea[26], hath witched my heart.
Oh beautiful devil
Who hath stolen into my chamber,
And even now standeth at my door,
Lips wrought in siren smile,
Eyes of black obsidian,
Sparked with fire,

---

[25] An oblique reference to the Battle of Actium on 2 September 31 B.C. when the fleet of Octavian (the future Emperor Augustus) defeated the fleet of his rival, and Cleopatra's lover, Mark Anthony.

[26] Medea, daughter of King Aeëtes of Colchis, sorceress and priestess of Hekate, who aids Jason in his search for the golden fleece (Apollonius Rhodius, *Argonautica*); but in Eurypides' play of the same name, Jason abandons her for the king's daughter, Glace, and in revenge, Medea murders his new wife and Jason's children, and her own children from Jason.

Thy wild high laughter rising
'Mid moonbeams in the limpid night,
And I, old Ahab,[27]
Drawn despairing to thy depths,
A hapless mariner shipwrecked and senseless
Upon thy shore.

Were you not born for lust?
Are you not that ancient goddess,
Full breasted and fecund,
Who takes a man to his doom
That I now lie wan and limp upon thine altar?
Oh dark art thou,
Dark haired and darkly beautiful,
Like a dark flower pungent in the night
Whose scent doth float upon the air at dusk,
And sweet,
So sweet,
That I feed upon your honey as might a bee,
In search of secret places.

---

[27] A reference to the sea captain in Herman Melville' s *Moby Dick*.

Oh, girl, you are but sixteen,
Yet know more of spells
Than she of Endor[28].
Can you alone do this?
Or is it She who stands behind you
Crowned with moon and stars?
And I transfixed
Like a sparrow by a dart,
Struck and brought to ground,
Uncomprehending of my fate.

I have but to submit and would be a man again,
And go forth and do manly things,
And I would bring treasure to my love,
For whom all heaven tilts,
My heart to gird in chains of gold
Whereon thy dusky breast it rests content
To sleep and dream.

---

[28] The Witch of Endor was consulted by the Israelite king Saul to summon the spirit of the prophet Samuel for advice on defeating the Philistines in battle.

Notes

Dark Mistress is a poem about the paralysing power a woman's sexuality can have over a man. It is about how love can derange the senses. Think of Anthony and Cleopatra, Abelard and Eloise or Paris and Helen, and you have the idea, but the familiar trope of a man attracted to a sensual woman who possesses him was also explored in W. Somerset Maugham's *Of Human Bondage*, and in real life in the relationship between W. B. Yeats and Maud Gonne. Once a beautiful woman has drawn a man into her orbit, it is very difficult for the man to break free.

The poem comes with a back-story. When I was in teacher training, I was assigned to a school in Sussex, and on one particular day, I was asked to participate in a staff v. pupils basketball tournament. The only problem was that I had never played basketball in my life. Things could have gone badly except that a particularly beautiful, open and friendly sixth form girl offered to coach me and show me the moves. I felt an incredible attraction to her, but not an overtly sexual sort: it was more in the sense of being 'lit up', of incredible joy in her presence and a lightness of being which she infused in me. I can honestly say she stole my heart. Common sense, however, told me just to accept her friendship and allow her to be herself. This was not going to be a Tristan and Isolde moment. I have a maxim that I live by - *beauty and innocence cannot be possessed; they can only be admired*, and sometimes we corrupt the innocence of the person we desire because we want them for *ourselves* and not *themselves*. So, I just acknowledged that she'd touched my heart and enjoyed the experience of having my heart touched. I doubt she would have been happy with a crusty, whiskey-sodden English teacher anyway. But my Unconscious never threw in the towel and over a matter of days, the poem you have just read virtually wrote itself. I seem to remember I fell over a few times during the match and gained a certain notoriety: every time I walked past the sports hall, the girls used to hang out of the changing room window saying, "You're a legend, Mr Lind!" I never saw my lovely basketball teacher again.

Witches' Chant
(Sixteenth century)

Oh thou spirits, come to me,
Across the mountains,
Across the sea,
Upon the wind flyeth thee,
And join me in my revelry.

Born of storm, born of rain,
Born of torment, born of pain,
Come thou demon,
Come thou sprite,
Aid me in my work this night.

Come thou Old Ones, through the door,
Through the keyhole, through the floor,
Fly unseen on wings of night,
And dance about my circle bright,
At the place where two roads cross,
Where gibbet creaks and branches toss.

Cow shall die and milk shall sour,
Foe drop dead within the hour,

Babe lie cold within the cot,
Blighted corn shall die and rot,
No love hath I for man nor maid,
But for the darkness Satan made.

Notes

Before all the Wiccans in the country start sending
me hate mail, no, I didn't set out to portray Wicca
in a negative way, and yes, I am aware that Satan
and Lucifer are different divinities originating from
totally different cultures. Lucifer originated in Europe
as the Greek Eosphorus, literally, the planet Venus as
the Morning Star, Son of the Morning, Day Star Son
of Dawn, Light Bearer, etc., while Satan is a Semitic
divinity, a persecuting angel, and is not actually a
name at all but a title that means 'Adversary'. While
Lucifer appears in medieval accounts of witchcraft,
Satan does not seem to have figured in Craft rites,
and Witchcraft and Satanism as practised today are
fundamentally different streams, the one derived
from a pre-Christian animistic religion and the
other a Judeo-Christian heresy. However, for most
of Christian history, Lucifer and Satan have been

regarded as interchangeable names for the Devil (at least by Christians), and there is a historical reason for this (See notes to *Lucifer Unbound*).

Witchcraft began in Palaeolithic times as a set of practices derived from shamanism, which was a way of 'seeing' beyond the boundaries of conventional existence, and a means of travelling between the worlds and communing with spirits – so-called 'soul travel' – and it is because of this common antecedent that traditional African religion bears such close similarity with European witchcraft. Central to its praxis was the belief that Nature possesses a numinous existential aspect, a shadow side behind the appearance of form, which can be accessed through ritual, mantras and the use of entheogens. Shamanism was originally an integral part of primitive animistic religion – a belief that everything is imbued with 'spirit' and essentially alive. This is not to say it was a worship *of* Nature, but rather that *through* Nature one might commune with spirits and intelligences on the other side of Existence. It is vital to understand that in shamanism there is no clear distinction between magic and religion: they are two sides of the same coin. Around 7,000 years ago, the rise of city-states, and then empires, resulted in kings taking control of religious expression and using it to legitimise their own rulerships. The result was the growth of temple-based religions based on mass worship of powerful divinities, overseen by state-approved priesthoods. The former shamanistic practices, however, endured at the periphery of these religions and, divorced from their original animistic context, were either absorbed into cults of religious mysticism existing on the fringes of orthodoxy[29] or assumed an antinomian persona and became witchcraft.[30] The state religions of the

---

[29] Sufism inherited techniques of shamanism from pre-Islamic times, as did the Bon religion of Tibet which was absorbed into Tibetan Buddhism. We can also mention *Hekhalot* or 'Palace' mysticism (also known as the *Merkabah* or 'Chariot') which comprised a visionary journey through the heavenly spheres, likening the soul to a chariot, and constituted an early form of proto-Qabalah or Jewish mysticism. Today, in West African religions (from which Haitian Vodou is derived), mysticism and witchcraft exist pretty much side by side as different facets of the same tradition.

[30] There is hint of when this split occurred in the story of Qayin (Cain) and Abel in the book of *Genesis* (*Gen.4:1-16*). Qayin refuses to offer a blood sacrifice to God, thereby symbolically refusing to return life to its source. The significance of this act is a statement: *non serviam*, 'I shall not serve'. Having killed his brother Abel, the favourite of God, he is exiled and has the mark of Qayin placed upon him. His descendants become witches and necromancers (such that, even today, witches are known as 'the children of Qayin'). A new child is born to Adam and Eve who is named Seth. From Seth stems a line of prophets and seers that passes through Enoch and Melchizidek who serve

time disapproved of these practices that they could not control, perceiving them as a threat. Witchcraft, indeed, was banned in the Roman Empire long before the advent of Christianity[31]. It is likely that witchcraft practices persisted for many centuries in Europe into the Christian era, long after heretical 'pagan' religions had been stamped out. But when we speak of a 'witch-cult', a problem arises, because shamanism was never 'cultic' (as in an organised religious expression) and its practitioners, for the most part, were solitary mystics and seers. Nor was shamanism concerned with the worship of gods but rather with mastery of the spirit realm, and this clearly distinguishes it from religion in our modern understanding of the word. Quite simply, there is no historical precedent for a witch-cult.

So, we need to ask the question, was the witch-cult a creation and who created it? To say that it was a creation of the Church (as in a figment of the Inquisitors' imaginations) is less likely than the

---

(the Jewish) God. However, *it is the same power of psychism that flows through them*! It is how the power is used and whom they serve that differentiates them. They are both plugged into the quantum universe. Sadly, one still finds ignorant priests and nuns dismissing people with 'the Sight' as 'children of the Devil'.

[31] As early as 81 B.C. under Sulla.

possibility that it was a vestigial remnant of European shamanic practices which the Church misinterpreted through the veil of its own theology and then embellished. It is noteworthy that the spike in witch hunts occurred during the height of the religious wars of the Reformation and Counter-Reformation, with each side outdoing itself to portray itself as the true custodian of Christianity. The universality of the Church was broken and evil could enter through the cracks. There were also precedents for the witch hunts in the anti-heresy crusades such as the Albigensian crusades, and the crusades against the Wends in the Baltic lands. This coincided with a theological transition within the Church against the *Canon Episcopi* tradition of the Middle Ages which held that witchcraft was a delusion of the Devil; that is, it didn't actually exist. In the new theology, God had licensed the Devil to test people's faith; now witchcraft was a reality and witches were agents of the Devil. Moreover, to lay claim to supernatural power was to transgress the boundaries of the Divinely ordained order, and if that power didn't come from God then it had to come from the Devil.

The alternative question asks, was there an actual witch-cult whose covens were run by disaffected priests and minor sons of the nobility? The identification of the Earl of Bothwell as the 'witch master' of the Berwick witches, who, in 1590, were accused of trying to sink James I of England's ship, lends credence to this, although no witch master is mentioned in the Pendle witch trials. True also is that the biggest practitioners of black magic in the Middle Ages and Renaissance were the clergy themselves, hence the term 'clerical underground', as indeed they were the only class capable of reading and writing books of magic. The universities of the Middle Ages routinely churned out more priests than there were benefices for, so it is not beyond the bounds of possibility that some of these men organised witch covens around themselves, carving out their own personal niche and exercising power that was denied them by the Church.[32] It is particularly noteworthy how much medieval witchcraft was influenced by Solomonic (and particularly Goetic magic), which clearly points to a clerical influence.[33]

---

[32] Rose, Elliott (1962, 1989), *A Razor for a Goat*, University of Toronto Press.

[33] Goetia was a system of Solomonic magic written to summon demons, the name 'goetia' derived from the Greek for 'howling'. A *goes* was originally a singer of lamentations at Greek funeral

The standard images associated with the witch-cult were the coven of thirteen, the Sabbat with its wild dancing by mostly women, the animal 'familiar', the pact with the Devil, and the central figure of the 'black man' of the Sabbat. We can ask, did these happen (organised by someone) or were they visions associated with 'out-of-body' experiences and astral shapeshifting, as the visions of the Scottish witch, Isobel Gowdie (tried in 1662), suggest?[34] There is evidence among the records of the Inquisition that women who claimed to be flying to the Sabbat were in reality observed to be unconscious in a state of catatonic trance the whole time, and a similar instance is reported by Abraham of Worms in his classic work *The Book of the Sacred Magic of Abramelin, the Mage*.[35] The similarity between accounts of flying witches and recorded shamanistic practices of soul travel (another word for astral projection) are too close to be coincidental, as are the reports of spirit familiars

---

rites but, over time, came to mean one who summoned the dead, i.e., a necromancer.

[34] Wilby, Emma (2020) *The Visions of Isobel Gowdie*, Sussex Academic Press.

[35] Dehn, Greg (trans.), Abraham of Worms (2006) *The Book of the Sacred Magic of Abramelin the Mage*, Ibis Press, Lake Worth, Florida.

who appeared as animals. The Sabbat flight and the infamous 'black man' of continental demonology are conspicuously missing from the Pendle witch trials of 1612, but animal familiars feature prominently. There was, however, a historical precedent for the dances: in the Classical period, the rites of Dionysus involved the ecstatic dancing of women, banned by most of the Greek states, and the Middle Ages also witnessed outbreaks of hysterical dancing such as the *Danse Macabre* where celebrants danced to exhaustion in graveyards, stimulated by folk memory of the Black Death of the fourteenth century. Then there are the folkloric accounts of the licentious revels atop the Brocken in Germany which may relate to the celebration of pre-Christian fertility rites. Did such dances by women continue into the Christian era as a kind of proto-feminist rebellion against the strictures of Christian morality, or were they imported from antiquity into a newly created cult?

Finally, we can ask what witches themselves understood by their practices. Did they regard themselves as Devil worshippers, or as latter-day 'pagans'? Did they have any historical understanding of their practices? Did they see witchcraft as a religious expression, or as a cult of rebellion against the Church and the social order that repressed women? Medieval Europe was a male-dominated society governed by strong codes of Christian morality. A young woman who wanted to go out dancing was a threat to male-controlled society and an old woman who was no longer reproductive was perceived as sinister. Conceivably, the powerless resorted to the supernatural to give them the power that the social elites deprived them of, and the witches of the 16th and 17th centuries appear likely to be confraternities of women using inherited practices to tip the scales of justice in their favour. In this way, Satan and Lucifer became antinomian entities and the witches' counterweights to the God of the Church and the culture of privilege.

I think it is useful here to state that the visionary experience is always determined by the prevailing religious and mythic context of the society. Thus, a shaman operating within the context of animistic religion would have a different set of experiences from that of a witch operating in the Christian Middle Ages. Therefore, a witch in Christian Europe may well have had the experience of attending a Sabbat presided over by Lucifer or the Devil since the dominant paradigm was one of theological dualism... all of which raises the tantalising prospect that witchcraft allowed itself to be shaped by the same Christian paradigm it was rebelling against!

The roles of Hekate and Lucifer (who figure prominently in Southern European medieval witchcraft) had virtually nothing to do with the nature religion that is modern Wicca. By late pagan times, Hekate had become a chthonic goddess of ghosts and spirits. Although she was never truly an underworld goddess like Persephone, she was formerly a Titan who had fought on the side of the Olympians, and her dominion extended through all three spheres of existence: the heavens, the earth and the underworld. Her true identity is not as a goddess of nature but as a 'gatekeeper' between the worlds, hence her titles *Enodia* ('of the streets' or 'wandering one'), *Kthonia* ('of the underworld'), *Kleidouchos* ('keyholder'), *Propylaia* ('before the gate'), etc. While Hekate is the gatekeeper, her son Lucifer (an amalgam of the Greek Eosphorus and Phosphorus – Venus as the morning and evening star), is the messenger and initiator into the realm of Spirit. He represents the illumination of the mind or 'gnosis' that is the reward for parting the veils of visible reality; psychologically, he also represents wisdom brought forth from the Unconscious. Lucifer is the emissary of the numinous 'other side' of existence, awakening Man to spiritual power. Although this sounds a lot like the Neoplatonic/Christian idea of the *Logos*, Lucifer is not concerned with the forgiveness of sin but rather with self-knowledge and spiritual awakening. While Christ is the path of spiritual love and divine union, Lucifer is the path of magical power and altered perception. He is the trickster god who transgresses the boundaries of the ordered universe (in some similarity with Satan), and, in this respect, has many similarities with the Prometheus myth and the Watcher myths.[36] Put it this way: if you are a marginalised woman locked in a fight for social justice, spiritual love is not a priority but magic will provide a powerful ally.[37]

---

[36] The trickster god is a feature of witchcraft traditions worldwide. For instance, Elegua or Elegbara, the trickster god of the Yoruba, became Papa Legba of Haitian Vodou. In the Norse tradition, Loki is another example of a trickster god, as are the Weird Sisters in *Macbeth*. The Trickster is also a Jungian archetype.

[37] Hekate and Lucifer are represented in the star and crescent motif which, after the Christianisation of the Roman Empire, became the symbol of the eastern (Byzantine) empire. The symbol came to represent variously Jesus as the Morning Star, symbol of spiritual illumination, and the Virgin Mary as the 'woman clothed with the sun, standing on the moon with twelve stars about her head' described in the *Book of Revelation*, in which form she asserts the dominion of Spirit over Nature and Time, and icons of the Virgin standing on the crescent moon were

While wild dances of women featured strongly in Southern European witchcraft, in the form of the sabbat and the mysterious 'black man' (Lucifer as the Black Light or Sun at Midnight) who presided over it, so much so that it is referred to as a 'cult', Northern European witchcraft was typified by the solitary practitioner. The solitary female witch was not part of any cult. She was a vestigial remnant of the 'wise woman' or seeress of Norse and Germanic tradition who was skilled in trancework and divination and could behold the threads of fate by which a person's life was woven. In Saxon religion, she was known as a *wicce* (*wicca* for a man). In Norse mysticism, she was termed a *völva* and would travel from village to village holding seated meditation practices (*seiðr*) with other women using chant (*galdr*), entheogens and the casting

---

commonplace. References to Jesus as the Morning Star abound in the New Testament: 2 *Peter* 1:19, *Revelation* 2:28, *Revelation* 22:16. Following the Ottoman conquest of Constantinople in 1453, the star and crescent was appropriated to confirm Ottoman dominion over the former Byzantine Empire, being first adopted as a symbol of the Ottoman navy from the Battle of Lepanto in 1571 (formalised in a decree of 1793, and probably deriving from Mary's role as protector of sailors as *Stella Maris*, 'Star of the Sea') and later incorporated in the Turkish flag in 1844. Ottoman influence spread the symbol across the Islamic world and it is often mistakenly considered to be Islamic – which it is not!

of runes. The fairy tale image of the old witch living in a house in the woods (as in *Hansel and Gretel*) is a folk memory of such seeresses. This being the case, curiously, those accused of witchcraft in Scandinavia were overwhelmingly men, many of whom were Sami shamans. It is important to understand that Germanic and Norse pre-Christian religion had not assumed the institutionalised state-controlled forms that pre-Christian religions had in the Mediterranean area, and one reason was the absence, not only of the city-state, but of any form of nation-state or centralised kingship.[38] As a result, Norse, Baltic and Germanic pre-Christian religions were closer in nature to the primitive animism of shamanic religion and correspondingly, witchcraft was not marginalised to the fringes as it was in Southern Europe. Add to this the relatively late Christianisation of Northern Europe, and the survival of witchcraft practices endured in a more coherent form into the Christian era. The fact remains, however, that the seeresses of the pre-Christian Germanic and Norse age were firmly rooted in pagan shamanic tradition and had nothing to do

---

[38] The role of Christianity in state formation and the consolidation of centralised power in Europe is a fascinating topic which is beyond our remit.

with the Devil or any of the Romano-Greek divinities that feature in Southern European witchcraft. Indeed, the idea of 'the Devil' was completely alien to the Germanic mind.

Commentators on witchcraft have consistently misinterpreted its history and nature. The Church projected its own dualistic theology onto the Craft, viewing the witch as the servant of the Devil and the Craft as part of a metaphysical conspiracy of evil. The anthropologist Margaret Murray[39] saw witchcraft as the survival of a pre-Christian pagan religion, when, in reality, it was never a religion in the way we understand a religion today, as an institutionalised system of worship of a god with a distinct priesthood and orthodoxy. Ethnologists studying the pagan animistic Baltic tribes in the Middle Ages recorded that they worshipped trees and stones when, in reality, these were merely gateways to the numinous 'other' side of existence and the spirit intelligences that dwelt therein. Even Wiccans today, who celebrate the rhythms and tides of Nature, personified as 'the God' and 'the Goddess', have mistakenly confused witchcraft

---

[39] Murray, Margaret (1921) *The Witch Cult in Western Europe.* Oxford at the Clarendon Press.

with the animistic religion it was once a part of, and have recreated witchcraft as a 'nature religion' that never actually existed.

By now, it should have become clear that medieval witchcraft had very little to do with 'nature worship' and a lot to do with visionary experiences that were shaped by the prevailing religious assumptions of Christianity. In whatever form it took (solitary or collective), it was also a cult of rebellion against the moral strictures of Christian society; that is, it was antinomian in nature. In short, medieval witchcraft had about as much to do with modern Wicca as a chicken tikka masala has to do with macaroni cheese. Thus, we are greeted in this poem with a wild dance of women, not celebrating nature, but instead, invoking the powers of Hell against a society that denigrated and exploited them. So, I make no apology for using the name 'Satan' in the poem as the Adversary of the Christian God, which is what he would have been to witches in the Middle Ages.

Wriggle, Wriggle
(Inspired by William Blake)

Wriggle, wriggle, little fly,
I've fixed thee with my beady eye,
From my web thou can't break free,
I am a spider and I'm coming for thee.

Pretty fly of bottle green,
Caught in a web you wish you'd seen,
Wings that flash all silver blue,
I am a spider and I'm coming for you.

I'll suck your fluids, I'll suck your blood,
I'll tear your life out in a flood,
And reduce you to an empty husk;
Another life snuffed out by dusk.

I'll run across my web so fast,
Then we'll see how long you last.
The web will bounce, the web will sway,
And there'll be no fly left to buzz away.

Though I'm battered by wind and rain,
By break of day I'll spin again,
And wait so still and patiently,
For a hapless fly to visit me.

Wriggle, wriggle, little fly,
Certain it is that you will die,
To feed me and my family,
I am a spider and I'm coming for thee!

Here I come!

Notes

I wrote this as a nursery rhyme for my partner's son, Adam. At the conclusion, I used to run my fingers up his arm like a spider. He screamed! The inspiration is from William Blake whose simple rhyming poems (such as *The Tyger* and *Poems of Innocence and Experience*), almost nursery rhyme-like, conveyed an extreme depth of thought.

Late Period
2010 – 2021

An Oxford Professor of Classics Contemplates His Wife

Did I ever say you are a goddess?
No?
I must have told you as many times
As there are leaves in a book.
The sun arcs around the window,
Falling into bright sequestered blotches,
Making of our plainly papered walls
A canvas for Renoir,
And yet your light is bright and unchanging
As though you inhabit your own sun,
And you blaze from room to room,
Subtly stirring the air as you pass.
Nor have you seasons,
But in you are spring, summer, autumn, winter,
All combined, merged and melded
In one temperate clime.

And yet (the question torments me),
What manner of goddess be thee,
That you appeared in my life like a poem,
Unbidden from some unconscious pool?

Not the dread Magna Mater,

In whose honour eunuch priests

Tore themselves with rusted knife,

Nor wild, bloody Artemis

Before whose altar the flower of Spartan youth

    were flayed[40].

A goddess of love? Ah yes,

And without compare,

As though your very nature impels you

To that high station.

Gentle Aphrodite,

A goddess of shells and the wide, roiling sea,

You rise from out the froth and foam

That crashes upon some Cypriot shore,

(Annoying cherubs buzzing about your head

Unfurling scrolls extolling your divine virtues),

Or walking barefoot upon the wave-washed sands

Of white-painted Crete.

I lay my head between your conch-like folds

And imagine I can hear the somnolent stirring

Of the salt sea

Booming in your womb.

Even Botticelli could not do you justice,

---

[40] Artemis Lycurgus.

And *there* was a man who could paint a goddess!

But surely *you* belong not to Olympian mount
Nor wine-dark sea,
But to skin and blood,
Whose being pulses deep in cathedrals of bone,
As though you had descended to the earth
From some empyrean realm,
And assumed the guise of woman,
Whose small intimacies
Wrapped in the fondness of years
Punctuate the exquisite sentences of life.
A goddess who sips of sweet red wine,
Drawn from deep vats,
Fixing me with the steady eye of a huntress
Over the rim of your glass,
A lustrous Diana of the Woods,
Dark and dangerous by moonlight.
A goddess of cheap paperbacks
Devoured on lazy Sunday afternoons
In dappled light of cherry,
Or perched upon a cushion in some picture window,
Wrapped in a sunbeam,
Picking out the warm chestnut reds and browns
Of your beautiful hair,

Mellow like the burnished wood of a violin
Whorled and streaked in autumn hues.

Spooned in companionable silence
In the flickering nimbus of a dying candle,
I brush your pale cheek,
Warm and peach-like in the summer night,
After the last bird has sung,
And experience divinity
In the most transient of things.
This old bald pate grows
Balder and patier,
And old white legs thin with age
Like the broken pillars of ruinéd Rome,
And yet mortality's cold hand
Stems not the course of love,
But rather in its shadow do *we* love more.
For even gods must stoop to love,
And in loving, accept mortality's fatal dart;
Their tattered rags cannot hold back the cold
Of a dying sun.
And in silent hour at fall of dusk,
As sleep skulks about my eyes,
I hold you tight and softly sing,
Bright goddess of my bed,

Of the joy your life has given me;
Better to love and die
Than immortal be.

Notes

This is a poem about an educated, sensitive man attempting to reconcile his idealised image of the woman he loves with her real flesh and blood personality. When we fall in love, our imagination projects an idealised image onto the person we are attracted to. To call it desire would be wrong; it isn't really sexual at all, but a pulling on one's heartstrings and a sudden expansive joy. A Jungian psychologist would say that we are projecting our own anima or animus onto the other, and we fall in love when our archetypal image of the opposite gender strikes a close match with the person we meet. Of course, this imaginative projection doesn't last, and sooner or later one has to accommodate to the real-life personality of the other; that is when the arguments start and compromises are struck. Occasionally, however, idealisation can be replaced by contempt and the relationship goes downhill very fast. Our professor has fallen in love with his wife's anima or feminine archetype, which is the goddess aspect of a woman, but he must come to terms with the fact that his goddess has definitely come down to earth! A Jungian therapist once told me, "You can fall in love with the Anima, but you can't have a relationship with it, you can't have children with it, and it won't make you soup when you're ill." I think that by the end of the poem, our professor has achieved the reconciliation he sought.

The Anima in the Goddesses of Ancient Greece

When we speak of the Anima and Animus (the feminine and masculine archetypes respectively), we would be mistaken to think of each as a single monolithic archetype but rather a spectrum of sub-types that shade towards and away from their opposites. Thus, the Anima shades into the Animus and *vice versa*. The Anima (feminine) archetype shades from the soft and sensual to the wild and warlike, represented in Greek mythology by Aphrodite and Artemis (Diana) respectively. Artemis, the she-wolf, is closest to Ares, the god of war, and thus begins to shade into the Animus, the male archetype. Between them stands

Athena, the goddess of wisdom, holding the balance, but Athena is also clad in armour and her mother, Metis, was a Titan, the primeval giants who pre-dated the Olympian pantheon. When Zeus swallows Metis, Athena is born from her mother and erupts fully armed from the head of Zeus, which is a metaphor for the sublimation of a woman's instinctual drives through the higher mind, and yet her armour reminds us of her primal force. Her totem animal, the owl, is a symbol of wisdom (because it can see in the dark) but is also a bird of prey. Athena presents an enigma because the Greeks were horrified at the idea of a fighting woman and yet Athena was the patron goddess of Athens. For the Athenians, Athena represented the woman as 'civiliser' (mediating between the extremes of the seductive woman, Aphrodite, and the wild woman, Artemis), but her armour was a symbol that Wisdom must ever be vigilant and always ready to defend itself against tyranny. It was also a reminder that a civilisation is historically carved out through war. The Britannia figure, which became a symbol of the British Empire, is an expropriated version of the goddess Athena.

Bring Me Your Oaks and Lindens Green

Bring me your oaks
And lindens green,
The fairest trees in England
I have seen,

That built the fleets of kings
And did battles win;
Stout wood makes stout ships
For stout men to sail in.

Bring me your maples
With leaves of fire,
That ring the white church
And flame the white spire.

Bring me your May Queen
Garlanded with flowers,
The dew of youth upon her lips,
And all her woman's powers.

Bring me the village boys
Who dance away the hours
Until the lanterns glow
Beneath the bowers.

Bring me the willow
Whose wanton hair
Drapes the village pond
And weeps with despair.

For the May Queen is dead,
And the branches are bare,
And snow decks the forest
That once was green and fair.

The singers are silent,
The dancers are still,
Barren are the fields
That fed the old mill.

The lanterns are dark now
And sway upon the wind
That soughs among the sycamores,
And whistles down the mynd.

179

Who will replace her
Ere the year is drawn out,
And the buds start to open
And the leaves to come out?

For a Queen shall rise
Ere the spring returns,
And bluebells sprout up
Among the ferns.

So blessed be this pleasant land,
And bless its forests green,
And blessed be the folk that walk its paths,
The kin that are now and the kin that have been.

Notes

I really wanted to write an unashamedly traditional English poem that celebrates our countryside, trees and forests, something that could be banged out at rural celebrations, and this is it.

On the origins of 'mynd'

In the poem, I employ the word *mynd*, which some may not be familiar with. I wished to convey the idea of the wind whistling down a mountain, and so chose *mynd*, primarily because it resonated with the pagan Celtic theme I was seeking to convey. *Mynd*, however, is not a generic word; moreover, as far as I know, it is confined to Shropshire. The Long Mynd is a moorland plateau that forms part of the Shropshire Hills, running seven miles from the Stiperstones range to the west and the Stretton Hills and Wenlock Edge to the east. A literal translation of the name is 'Long Mountain', *long* being Anglo-Norman and *mynd* being Brittonic/Brythonic (referring to the patchwork of Celtic languages spoken in the British Isles as opposed to the Goidelic languages of Ireland). The question arises, though, as to whether *mynd* was ever an actual word for 'mountain' in any of the Brittonic group of languages. The Welsh for mountain is *mynydd,* not *mynd*, and since the word is specific to Shropshire, it is reasonable to assume that it is a dialect word. A dialect is a local language variant created by the interface between two cultures and ethnicities, taking elements from both; in this instance, the Welsh Marches forming the interface between the Anglo-Norman kingdom of England and the Welsh tribes. In the Middle Ages, the Welsh borders had been ruled by the Marcher Lords. Centuries earlier, they had formed the border with the Anglo-Saxon kingdom of Mercia (think of Offa's Dyke). One possibility is that *mynd* is a contraction of *mynydd,* and thus an anglicised dialect version. However, interestingly, there is also a Welsh irregular verb *i mynd,* meaning 'to go' or 'to travel to'. *Mynd* also exists as a word in Faroese and Icelandic (both derived from Norse) meaning 'image' or 'picture', which, in the case of the Long Mynd, might be contextualised as 'panoramic view', but Wales lay outside the sphere of Viking settlement and is overwhelmingly Celtic in culture and language, so the influence of Norse can be discounted. The presence of the verb *i mynd*, with its identical spelling to the noun, is intriguing because it raises the possibility that *mynd* borrowed from the verb to express not only the idea of 'mountain' but the idea of 'a mountain that is walked along', essentially a ridgeway, which is precisely what the Long Mynd is. In prehistory until medieval times, such ridgeways acted as Palaeolithic 'superhighways', rapid transit zones that avoided the meandering river valleys (and provided safety from ambushes), a prime example being the

Ridgeway Path which runs from Avebury in Wiltshire to Ivinghoe Beacon in Buckinghamshire. This is, of course, not intended to be authoritative, but more in the way of a working hypothesis, and I invite local historians with more knowledge and experience than myself to submit their own interpretations.

Dear Leader

It's the cunts who rule the world,
They've sown up all the power,
The secret police break down your door
No matter what the hour.

You didn't praise the leader,
You didn't lick his shoes,
Now you're in a prison cell,
How can you refuse?

They ever make it to the top
And kept there by the mob,
They're there because the decent people
Didn't want the job.

They always look so kindly,
The dad you never had,
But if you vote against them
Things turn really bad.

They pretend to be respectable
But that's not what they are;

If it bought them popularity,
They'd sell their own grandma.

You need re-education
Then you'll see they're right,
So they'll put you in a cage with rats
And then turn off the light.

They're there to save the nation,
Make it great again.
Don't want saving? Never mind,
Here's a stick to cause more pain.

There are jobs, you know, for comrades,
You'll be secure for life,
Poison the opposition's lunch
Then arrest his wife.

Scratch their backs and they'll scratch yours,
You'll be rich beyond your dreams,
Siphon off a few state funds
Till it's bleeding at the seams.

They want to teach your children,
There are lots of things to choose,

Like how to do the goose step
And how to spit at Jews.[41]

And always look the other way,
No prison camps round here,
The barbed wire's really just for show,
Move on or disappear.

It's the cunts who rule the world,
They're in it for the power,

---

[41] I want to talk about Mr Carvalho, sadly deceased, to whose
care I was assigned back in the 1980s. Mr Carvalho was a retired
Jewish solicitor of huge intellect, but also irascible temperament,
who didn't suffer fools gladly. Descended from Sephardic Jews
who had migrated to Portugal from Spain to escape the anti-
Semitism of Ferdinand and Isabella in the 1490s, he kept the
faith but was also surprisingly liberal (and even counselled me
against ever getting married). He also had a rather old and
grumpy cat that slept on the landing and refused to move for the
wheelchair, so one had to carefully position the wheels on either
side of the animal and go over the top of it. We became good
friends, to the extent that one day he asked me to be a family
guest at Yom Kippur, the Jewish New Year, even though I was
not Jewish by ancestry. So, I donned the yarmulke (the Jewish
prayer cap), partook of the ritual meal and read my portion of
the liturgy (fortunately from a prayer book in English). This man
was so gracious that he took someone who was not Jewish and
'adopted' me into his family, and I have never forgotten this act
of kindness. So, when unthinking fools speak ill of the Jews, I
feel both sad and angry.

They've never heard of morals,
They're just a crooked shower.

So remember when you cast your vote
For the man whose heart is on his sleeve,
Once you've put him where he wants to be
Is he ever going to leave?

Notes

> Why, I can smile, and murder whiles I smile,
> And cry 'Content' to that which grieves my
> heart,
> And wet my cheeks with artificial tears,
> And frame my face to all occasions.
> I'll drown more sailors than the mermaid
> shall;
> I'll slay more gazers than the basilisk;
> I'll play the orator as well as Nestor,
> Deceive more slily than Ulysses could,
> And, like a Sinon, take another Troy.
> I can add colours to the chameleon,
> Change shapes with Proteus for advantages,
> And set the murderous Machiavel to school.

Can I do this, and cannot get a crown?

Tut, were it farther off, I'll pluck it down.

Richard of Gloucester (future Richard III) in
Shakespeare's *Henry VI* Pt. 3, Act 3: Scene 2

Poetry isn't always beautiful; sometimes it's angry, and a spade needs to be called a spade. *Dear Leader* is an indictment of Power and its abuse. This is protest poetry.[42] The word 'cunt' is a pejorative for a despicable person, with connotations of 'slippery' and 'slimy'. That's a pretty accurate description of many of our world leaders; the rogue ones certainly. A cunt is as a cunt does. A political leader who presides over an authoritarian police state is a cunt. A president who has critics arrested on phoney espionage and tax evasion charges, or worse, has dissidents assassinated, is a cunt.[43] Governments that lock up journalists for reporting the truth are cunts. Regimes that arrest

---

[42] My own rule for using an expletive in a poem is that it should be intrinsic to the context, and not used for the sake of vulgarity. As an example, Philip Larkin employs the 'f' word perfectly properly and within context in his poem *This Be the Verse*.

[43] One example among hundreds stands out: the dismembering of Saudi dissident and journalist Jamal Khashoggi in the Saudi consulate in Istanbul on October 2nd, 2018. How ironic that after Putin's invasion of Ukraine, nations are rushing to buy Saudi oil!

innocent foreign nationals, take them from their families and lock them up as political hostages are cunts. A tyrant who authorises ethnic cleansing and forced assimilation is a cunt. A regime that withholds food and medicine from its people because they are the 'wrong' tribe are cunts. A head of state that uses chemical weapons or barrel bombs against civilian populations is a cunt. A ruler who targets hospitals and schools and apartment blocks for air raids is a cunt. A person who kidnaps aid workers is a cunt. A government that sentences gay and transsexual people to thirty years in prison (just for being who they are) are cunts.[44] A governor of a city who sends police to beat up peaceful protesters and fire into crowds is a cunt. Angry? You should be!

People do not commit ethnic violence and atrocities until they are incited to do so by governments and political leaders. It is governments who are the criminals – the same governments that sit at the UN and talk about world peace!

All of these people pretend to be respectable members of society. They travel in private aircraft

---

[44] Law should be grounded in rational ethics, not cultural and religious prejudice.

and blacked-out limousines with police escorts and live a charmed life remote from ordinary people. They dress in smart suits in a pretence of decency, but their souls are rotten. They are the 'respectable' face of governments that arrest journalists and torture opponents, extort businesses, and repress their own people, all the while preaching 'traditional values'. They manufacture 'threats' and 'Western conspiracies' from external enemies to justify their own hold on power and thrive in a climate of paranoia.[45] They siphon off funds from state-controlled companies and sequester them on off-shore accounts (as revealed by the Panama papers). They award business contracts to family and political supporters. Anyone who criticises them is deemed a 'terrorist', yet it is they who commit acts of terror, only it is called 'state policy'.[46] They even

---

[45] "The welfare of the people has always been the alibi of tyrants..." – Albert Camus, *Resistance, Rebellion and Death*, 1960.

[46] In September 1999, Russian FSB agents exploded bombs in four apartment blocks in the Russian cities of Buynaksk, Moscow and Volgodonsk, to create a *cassus belli* for the second Chechen war, killing more than 300 and injuring more than 1,000. The Russian government refused to co-operate with the Independent Public Commission and two of its key members were assassinated. Former FSB agent Alexander Litvinenko, who defected and blamed the FSB for the bombings, was poisoned and killed in London in 2006.

want to rewrite history, just as China has written the Tiananmen Square massacre out of its history books and Turkey the Armenian Massacre. They are accorded respect as foreign 'dignitaries' (I love that word!), and because they are governments, they can't be brought to justice. The worst thing is, at least until Russia's atrocities in Ukraine became too egregious to ignore, whatever these people do is just greeted with hot air by western democracies, and why? Because western corporations are the biggest investors in authoritarian regimes, and western democracies don't want to spoil the party. Why do western corporations invest in repressive regimes? Because for them, making money and 'business as usual' is more important than human rights and international law.[47] Capitalism is morally bankrupt. Indeed, the crisis in western democracy is precisely an absence of moral leadership. Having

---

[47] After Russia's Putin annexed Crimea in 2014, Chancellor Angela Merkel of Germany actually deepened German (and European) dependence on Russian oil and gas, to the point of commissioning the Nord Stream 2 pipeline. The West's response to Putin's invasion of Ukraine in 2022 has been piecemeal and bumbling, and if Ukraine falls to Russia, the blood of Ukrainians will be on the West's hands. Major American corporations continue to trade (and have a physical presence in) China despite the imprisonment of ethnic Uighurs in detention camps in Xinjiang, and their use as slave labour in Chinese factories.

principles assumes that one is prepared to defend them; if one is not prepared to defend one's principles, why have them?

TO SPEAK THE TRUTH
IS A REVOLUTIONARY ACT

In reality, these despots and tyrants are merely symptoms of a political culture of authoritarianism that stretches back centuries before the present regime. Modern Russia harks back to the Soviets and the rule of the Czars, and modern China to the rule of the Emperors, while the antisemitism of the Third Reich reached all the way back to the Christianising policies of Charlemagne and the Holy Roman Empire; the political culture of a nation transcends the regime of the time and a regime always reverts to its political culture. Many of the worst regimes today are nations that have a history of ethnic and religious division, compounded by extreme poverty and corruption; they literally require a 'strongman' to hold them together. The Middle East, for example, is divided by tribal and religious factions (Sunni vs. Shiite), and culturally by modernism versus conservatism, and the tragedy of that part of the world is that there is no middle ground between the authoritarianism of religion and the authoritarianism of the state. Other nations, such as Russia, China and Iran, have succumbed to virulent forms of nationalism in response to historical humiliation and a perceived state of insecurity, while yet others (such as Latin American countries) are beset by a wealthy landowning class with the power to undermine populist governments. Eastern Europe, in particular, has endured centuries of oppression from the Mongols to the Ottomans followed in turn by decades under the Soviet Union, compounded by a landed nobility that exploited the peasantry and prevented the growth of a middle class; by the late Middle Ages, as the grip of feudalism was loosening in the West, the landed boyars and junkers were tightening their grip on the peasant class, and feudalism wasn't abolished in Russia until 1861. It was as though, in Eastern Europe, civil society had been suffocated by a pillow. It was this absence of civil society and institutions independent of the state compounded by centuries of despotism, poverty and corruption that explains why Eastern Europe has veered between autocracy and revolution for most of its history. Yet, in the greater scheme of history, it was this same Eastern Europe that absorbed the invasions that would have overrun the West, and it is no understatement to say that the West prospered at the expense of the East.

Western-style democracy simply cannot take root in such divided nations, and the sad reality is that the peoples of these nations make a calculated trade-off between security and freedom. Russia is an example of this. After the chaos following the collapse of the Soviet Union in the 1990s, the security provided by the Putin regime under the thin guise of 'illiberal democracy' was welcomed, in a not-dissimilar way to which Hitler was welcomed by the German people after the chaos of the 1920's. So, whatever the Russian government does, like invade Crimea and Ukraine[48], close down

---

[48] During the late dark ages, Kiev and Novgorod existed as independent principalities before being absorbed into the Muscovan state. In 882, Kiev was absorbed into Novgorod, and Novgorod in turn was conquered by Muscovy in 1478. The Ukraine always had its own distinct identity, however, and it seized the opportunity of the 1917 revolution to break away from Russia, before being forcibly reincorporated into the Soviet Union at the end of the civil war in 1921. In 1932, Stalin engineered a mass famine called the Holodomor to break the spirit of the Ukrainian people. After the Soviet Union collapsed in 1991, Ukraine declared independence. However, Russia continued to attempt to influence Ukrainian politics through political stooges such as Viktor Yanukovych, elected President in 2004 and unseated by the Orange Revolution in 2014. Putin, Russian President from 1999, believing that the breakup of the Soviet

independent newspapers, news channels, and jail dissidents, the Russian people will always support their president because the alternative is internal dissolution and chaos... until, that is, they get conscripted into a war none of them wanted. Another example is China whose state is based on the Confucian principles of hierarchy and obedience and for whom chaos (*weiji*) is anathema. The result is a social order based on surveillance, coercion and control where spontaneity and initiative cannot flourish.[49] Sometimes, a people can have lived for so long under authoritarianism that freedom can feel like chaos; it becomes the 'habit of tyranny'. After all, the safest, most familiar, place to be is one's cage.

Union had been a catastrophe for Russia, sought to re-create the Russian state, seizing Crimea in 2014 (which, ironically, had been transferred to Ukraine SSR by Nikita Khrushchev after Stalin's' death) and invading Ukraine in 2022 in defiance of the Budapest Memorandum of 1994, which offered 'assurances' to Ukraine in return for giving up its share of the post-Soviet nuclear arsenal.

[49] Deng Xiaoping liberalised the Chinese economy during the 1980s and 1990s but failed to liberalise its institutions of government and the judiciary, not realising that democracy and rule of law were fundamental to the development of Western capitalism. The resulting rise of corruption in the Chinese Communist Party led to the determination of Xi Jinping to restore the moral authority of the party.

One can make some generalisations in respect of a nation's propensity to slide into tyranny:

1. Nations that are riven by internal division and nations that have suffered historical humiliation in the past are more likely to embrace militaristic nationalism under authoritarian governments.
2. Cultures that have never fostered a tradition of critical thought, a culture of individualism, a tradition of protest, strong independent institutions, and respect for rule of law are more likely to succumb to political and religious tyranny.
3. Nations that have what the nineteenth century French political scientist Alexis de Tocqueville referred to as "the spirit of provincial liberty", that is, strong bonds of community and democratic decision-making at local level that cut across ideological, religious and ethnic divides, are inoculated against the centralising impulses of authoritarianism. A healthy civil society was ever an inoculation against tyranny. Further, the role of the police in pluralistic democracies is – or should be – as defenders of community, not as agents of the state.

4. The political culture of a nation influences its ability to adapt to democratic government. Democracy is ultimately protected not by constitutions (for these can be rewritten by pliant parliaments) but rather by a political culture or 'habit' of democracy and just as there is a habit of democracy, so there is a 'habit of tyranny'. The longer a people have lived under autocracy, the more difficult it is for them to embrace democracy. And what is this 'habit' of democracy? It is surely a consensus that, however much we disagree, we are bound by a moral vision to move society toward a greater good, and the pursuit of power without conscience serves only to fracture the consensus on which society is built.

5. As Lenin observed, it is the apathy of the masses that allows a tyrannical regime to survive, which is why a strong ethic of political participation is so important in protecting democracy. Even so, people rarely rise up against tyranny over abstract principles like freedom and human rights; they will only rise up if their own self-interest and survival is threatened. People don't fight for freedom and democracy any

longer: they fight for jobs and living standards. However, no people will forgive a ruler who loses a war, and wars notoriously rebound on those who start them; leaders who lose wars of their own making are judged harshly by those who sons died in them. Consider how the loss of the Russo-Japanese war of 1905 and poor performance in the First World War facilitated the demise of Tsarist Russia, the Second World War hastened the demise of Hitler, loss of the Afghan war hastened the demise of the Soviet Union, loss of the Falklands war unseated the Argentinian junta, and loss of the First Iraq war set the stage for the demise of Saddam Hussein. This lesson was lost on Putin.

Important also, however, are cultural assumptions about masculinity. Brutal societies breed brutalised men, and it should not surprise us that the leaders of the world's most brutal authoritarian states are sociopaths. These internally divided nations, with a long political history of repression, are the perfect breeding ground for sociopathic alpha males to murder and assassinate their way to power. Alpha males always gravitate towards power, which means they always end up at the top of the food chain. The alpha male is engineered for aggression and competition, so the paradox is that, although they pursue power, they are the least qualified to wield it responsibly. What one gets are adrenalized military types, corrupt politicians and anal-retentive dictators propped up by a cadre of career men invested in the regime. Together, they suck the oxygen out of the room. Life is so tightly controlled that nothing spontaneous is allowed to happen; order becomes dead order. These people have clawed their way to the top and stitched the system up in their own interests and they have created an inverted value system based on money, power and greed (a.k.a. crony capitalism). Truly, as poet Philip Larkin writes in *This Be the Verse*, "Man hands on misery to Man / It deepens like a coastal shelf."

This is not just peculiar to authoritarian regimes. Even democratic governments veil themselves in secrecy, and the political class has become remote from the people it serves, mostly churned out by the same elite schools and universities, unresponsive and immune to public opinion and totally out of touch with the everyday concerns of ordinary folk, habitually appeasing business at the expense of the public good and eviscerating once great public institutions that took our forebears generations to build. They have not learned that ideology doesn't solve anyone's problems. Politics is now a partisan game of point-scoring to the detriment of people's real-life needs, and western leaders are not above lying to their own people as per the Iraq War, waged on the false pretext that Iraq possessed weapons of mass destruction. The modern state (whether 'democratic' or authoritarian) is not an ethical entity: it has no moral direction, dedicated solely to its own survival and expansion. It will use fear (fear of disorder, terrorism, crime and moral deviance) to expand its own powers, and its *raison d'être* is to control its own population and reduce it to a state of unthinking conformity. It is shocking to see so-called democracies, in our own time, framing draconian laws to crush the power of trade unions and unleashing militarised thugs to beat up unarmed protesters and shower them with rubber bullets and tear gas. Mortgaged to the lie that what is good for business is good for society, passing tax cuts for the rich that never translate into investment or jobs, while holding down wages for the poor that are deemed 'inflationary', the modern state has abandoned its role as arbiter of the public good to cosy up with the vested interests that fund political leaders' election campaigns. Anyone who protests is a 'militant' and a 'threat to democracy', but as Martin Luther King Jnr. said, "Every man of humane convictions must decide on the protest that best suits his convictions, but we must all protest." Divided societies slide into tyranny, democratic societies sleepwalk into it.

THE GREATEST THREAT TO INDIVIDUAL LIBERTY IS THE STATE ITSELF

To cede allegiance to an authoritarian regime is to deny one's own sense of Self with the moral autonomy that is core to it, and to live in constant fear of saying anything that will jeopardise one's own security and the safety of family. The net loss is to the richness of that nation's culture: all the intelligent, creative people leave and all that's left is a nation of nationalist thugs, gangsters, corrupt politicians, spies and hackers. True art and literature die, to be replaced by propaganda. No one uses initiative in case they are criticised for it.

Some of the worst abusers of freedom are so-called revolutionaries. Men like Julius Caesar, Cromwell, Robespierre, Napoleon, Lenin, Stalin, Mao, Pol Pot, Castro and Mugabe are really a single personality type: ideologues with no humanity. They see revolution as an opportunity to advance their own ambitions and are prepared to see the world burn to achieve them; and historically, they kill more of their own people than anyone else. *"Better to reign in Hell than serve in Heaven."*[50] Revolutions always attract psychopaths because psychopaths are attracted to causes as witnessed by the number of young, marginalised Muslim men who joined ISIS. No matter how noble the cause, if the person fighting for it is a psychopath, it is already lost. The international order is an expression of the male psyche writ large: the idea that a strong man can do anything he thinks he can get away with, pursuing the idea of 'greatness' through wars of aggression, empire building and carving out 'spheres of influence'. To make a bold statement, most of the problems in the world are caused by toxic masculinity, and world leadership is skewed by a gender imbalance favouring men. If we had more female leaders, with their natural gifts of empathy and interpersonal communication, the world would be a better place for everyone.

---

[50] Milton, John (1667) *Paradise Lost* (1.263).

WHEN POWER IS DIVORCED FROM CONSCIENCE AND LAW FROM ETHICS, IT IS THE BEGINNING OF CORRUPTION.

There also needs to be a set of internationally agreed standards for the behaviour of world leaders. When Russia invaded Ukraine in 2022, I was appalled to watch China, and many other nations, cynically refuse to sanction the aggressor because their trading relationships with Russia – and contempt for the West – were more important to them than international law and human rights, although for many the cost of sanctions would have devastated their economies. I was even more appalled that Russia and China (who hold seats on the UN Security Council) are in a position to veto any investigation into war crimes and human rights abuses committed by them or their allies, as happened in 2014 when both these nations' representatives used their veto to block the referral of atrocities by the Assad regime in Syria to the International Criminal Court, and it is a certainty that Russia will use its same power of veto to block investigation of its own human rights abuses in Ukraine. So, the criminal can sit in judgement on himself! As Volodymyr Zelensky has said, what is the point of a Security Council that doesn't guarantee security? In truth, the Security Council is a throwback to the world order created at Yalta in 1945, dominated by the Great Powers, and has no place in the modern world; its members' power of veto should be removed and an inability to agree should be referred to the UN General Assembly as court of world opinion. More worrying, however, is that we live in a world where strategic alliances and national interest matter more than international law and common human morality... and this is the beginning of the moral corruption that will destroy civilisation.

Personally, I think there is a hair's difference between an alpha male and a sociopath, which is what most authoritarian types are. Unfortunately, history has shown that, in times of uncertainty, people will elect strongmen instead of statesmen, not least because political types are adept at exploiting the fears of the masses.

EVIL IS ALWAYS AT ITS MOST DANGEROUS WHEN IT MASQUERADES AS THE PUBLIC GOOD

Empires of Iron

I

Black-faced crew hack and hew,
Under the mountain toiling true,
Crawling through darkness in lantern's beam,
Crack the black coal and bruise the black seam.

Ripping and rending the guts of the ground,
Gouging the heart of the worm-run mound,
Coal for power and coal for steam,
Coal for the empire and the national dream.

Furnace glowing in the fading light,
Smelters of ore, molten and bright,
Who hammer and hone, and melt and mould
Until the iron is smooth and cold.

Engines thundering through the night,
Pistons pounding with all their might,
Red sparks dancing in the frozen air,
Fireman shovelling in furnace' glare.

II

Papers blowing through shuttered pit,
Abandoned since the closures hit,
Young men shuffling in employment queues,
Big Coal and Iron are yesterday's news.

Furnace no longer blasts and booms,
But silent lies like empty tombs,
No more to glow at close of day,
But rots in the rain, shrouded and grey.

Cold wind croons 'neath winter skies,
Through the old scrapyard where old iron dies,
Steam train rusting on its side,
That, gaily painted, puffed with pride.

Empires of iron rise and rage,
Become the giants of the age,
But every empire has its day,
And in its turn shall fade away.

Notes

When the lines of this poem first started to surface in my mind, I had never thought of working with industrial imagery – landscapes are more my thing. However, the lure was irresistible, and I found the poem assuming a symmetrical 'mirror' in which the industrial age of Britain's past was sharply juxtaposed with the post-industrial present, which conveniently worked out at four verses per section. Each section cycles through the production process: coal is mined for the blast furnaces that make steel, from which the great steam locomotives were made, which in turn burned coal for steam. Technically, of course, blast furnaces use coke which is a refined form of coal baked in a coke oven with the smoke-producing constituents burned off, and, having a higher carbon content, burns hotter than coal. I also use the word 'iron' throughout the poem, when, in fact, most iron output is in the form of steel.

The pit closures following the miners' strike of 1984-5 are a historical sore point. Although the United Kingdom's coal industry was in terminal decline (beset by cheaper imports from abroad and a rising environmental movement at home, although climate change had not yet become an issue) and was only propped up by government subsidies, the systematic assault on the industry, on the unions and on the communities that had grown up around the pits, motivated by a purely economic agenda, and replacing the lost jobs with nothing, was unconscionable, and many of those communities (particularly in Wales and the North of England) have still not recovered to this day. The irony is that Britain was still dependent on coal for its coal-fired power stations but chose to import cheaper coal from abroad rather than preserve jobs and communities at home. So, this poem is really a paean to the loss of British heavy industry, and the lie that those jobs would be replaced by a 'service sector' which never materialised or was 'outsourced' overseas.

The First and the Last

Thus passes the glory of the world
In the dying of the day.
Petroleum sun drops like a burning plane,
Quenched in the sea
That forgives all things,
Self-immolating barque of Ra,[51]
Bale-eyed, bleeding into crevasses of cloud,
Flaying red the penitent sky at eventide.

Old man dying alone
In gloomy garret, groaning,
Ground to dust by mill of age,
Old, crooked body, medalled with moles,
Paper skin inked with scripture of toil and pain,
Passion play written in verses of vein.[52]
Gravity wins as he knew it would,
As it always does.
Who shall mourn such one

---

[51] The sun god Ra in Egyptian myth was said to travel across the heavens in a boat ('barque') and to travel through the underworld at night.

[52] The body as the book of a person's life, veins likened to ink.

Betrayed by lie of life,
Who slips like a shadow unremarked,
Known only to the cockroach and the rat?
Who shall sing the dirge of one
Sieved through the mesh of reckoning?
The last song played on the radio,
The last scotch sipped,
The book put down
And the light put out,
Old white head laid to rest
On dirty pillow,
And eternity of silence.
Who marks his passing?
The cryptic Christ looks dolefully down,
Yellowed, frozen in wood,
The Virgin's tears dried to salt;
Even God has run off with the money.
The light that sneaks across the wall
Like a moving finger
Never finds him.[53]
Companioned only by time and memory,
Wound in unholy shroud of sheet,

---

[53] The light of God (or Spirit) passes him over. He is not 'chosen' as in Matthew 20:16.

Banished to the fire from pious eyes,
That in no cathedral shall rest,[54]
Thus passes his glory from the world
At the dying of the day.

Far away,
The clock tower chimes the vespers hour,
The nightingale sings the nocturne
And starlings wheel above the pier.

Notes

The title of the poem is taken from Matthew 20:16 *"So the last shall be first, and the first last: for many be called, but few chosen."* The poem is intended to highlight the difference between the sentiment expressed in that verse and the reality that the last often remain the last and die forgotten. Thus, this is very much a poem about age and irrelevance. Further, however, I am suggesting that each person's death is their own

---

[54] A reference to the Turin Shroud which is said to bear a simulacrum of Jesus, and is thus a physical icon of remembrance. Our old man's sheets will instead be consigned to the fire and all memory of him lost.

personal crucifixion, their own personal Passion, and I thought it would be an original and exciting idea to portray the Passion of an elderly person completely unknown and marginalised by society. To that end, I took the apocalyptic imagery of Jesus' crucifixion (the sky darkening, the earth trembling) and applied it to a sunset over a seaside town (my own Eastbourne to be precise). I felt this was an appropriate use of imagery since there is a strong symbolic connection between sunset and death, expressed as the dying of the light. A sunset, while beautiful to behold, is also an apocalyptic event, and in the poem, I sought to emphasise its apocalyptic (even sinister) rather than its aesthetic aspect. The significance of the bird imagery in the concluding verse symbolises the flight of the soul from the body.

The first line, which translates in Latin as *Sic transit gloria mundi*, was originally used in papal coronations between 1409 and 1963, to remind the Pope of the transience of worldly existence. St. Thomas à Kempis used the phrase in *The Imitation of Christ*: "*O quam cito transit gloria mundi*" ("How quickly the glory of the world passes away").

Strangely, while I was composing the poem (which felt more like dictation at times), the Beatles' song

Eleanor Rigby (from their 1966 album *Revolver*) floated into my mind and thus deserves to be cited as an unconscious influence.

The Good Soldier
(Dedicated to Captain Sir Tom Moore)

Let us sing the virtue
Of one, who,
No Achilles now,
Nor Heracles in his prime,
But a soldier good and true,
With silver hair and heart of fire
And honour to his country due,
Runs not into the fray
But sets his course
And wins the day,
No rifle clasped
To enemy engage,
But two old legs
To storm the gates of age.
Blind old Milton
Could only stand and wait,
But thou, with straining sinew
And back straight,
Moved heaven and earth
To his duty do,
Nor too late
To stem the tide of death

That swept our shore.
If, as heroes in our youth,
Our boundaries were fresh and great,
How greater still the challenges
Doth age create?
Go then to thy rest,
Thou favoured son
Who served his country and his queen,
Thy war is won.

Notes

I had been meaning to write a tribute to Captain Sir Tom Moore for his extraordinary feat in raising thirty-three million pounds for the NHS and quite suddenly the words just began to write themselves, and I was left with this beautiful poem. The reference to 'blind old Milton' refers to John Milton's poem *On His Blindness* in which Milton reframes the meaning of his existence after losing his sight: "*They also serve who only stand and wait*."

Lady of Crows

All day long did battle rage,
Anguished screams of men and horse
Enmired in blood,
More death than victory could assuage.
Boom of cannon and rifle crack
Rent the air,
Sent flocks of birds from forests broke and bare,
And place to hide was found nowhere.
Men pressed forward to the fray,
Fought the bloody fight with main and might,
Cut down like flowers by end of day,
Strewn about the field churned and bare
That once was meadow bright and fair,
As rain began to pour,
And tattered flags loomed from out the smoke
That wreathed and whirled about the wreck
As fog doth drift across a moor.

And from that bloody meadow did I flee,
Turned not to see
What form or shape might follow me,

But plunged through ivy-strangled wood
Until I came upon a tree,
Broad and thick and gnarled with age,
Whose blackened bark was wet with rain and moss,
And there sat down and prayed upon my cross,
Prayed upon my cross, did I.
And of a sudden, a light did shine,
Full upon my eyes, and angel's voice,
So clear and sweet, I trow, it was a sign,
And the angel spoke,
And spoke to me,
As I sat beneath that blasted tree,
 "Beware! Beware!
There cometh one who is not fair,
But flies abroad on bat-winged night
For souls to take unto her lair.
She glides through groves and forests hushed
And floats upon the air,
And those who meet her pale gaze
Are sunk into despair."

I drew my coat about myself,
And huddled sat 'neath that old tree,
About whose roots strange fungi grew
In shapes horrible to see,

And all night long the rain did drip
From twisted branch above,
And ran upon my lip
And sleep could find nowhere,
But from some distant haunt
An owl did screech "Beware! Beware!"
Shortly, I began to doze,
But a strange and eerie sight
Did shake me from repose,
For in that darkened grove
Lay not alone,
But another stood close by
That chilled me to the bone.
A woman stood but feet from me,
Wrapped in firmament of night,
From which a pale face gazed out
And looked upon my plight.
And all about her crows did sit,
On branch and leafy floor,
And circled wild about her head,
Ceased not their awful caw.

"Who art thou?" I said to her,
"And from what pit hast come
To disturb a soldier's rest,

With freezing breath
And birds of death?
To thee I'll not succumb.
Art thou Hekate of the Ways
Who comes where three paths meet?
Or that Lady of Crows herself,
Who moves in darkness fleet,
And walks the fields of the dead
Their souls to take,
Who rise up from their flowery graves
And follow in her wake?"

And that dread spectre spoke
And spoke to me,
Not from her mouth
But all around and in my head,
And naught but rain and darkness did I see.
And this she said,
In voice no pity had,
"I am she who rules the dead,
And I the last they see,
And all men who die bloodily
Those men shall come to me.
Drummer boy and captain both,
Slain upon the heath,

Old men murdered in their beds,
Maids in lakes beneath,
For them no grave is dug,
None for them shall weep,
Lost to the world are they,
Who go down to the deep.
And those who are pure
And those who sinned,
Shall follow me upon the wind,
And with me forever sleep
In barren hall
'Mid deathly pall,
In realm that's dark and dim,
And for each one
A bell shall toll,
A bell shall toll for him."

Then, said I,
"But I do live,
What doest thou want with me?
A soldier of fortune, I by trade,
And fortunate be."

"Thou hast cheated death,"
She said,

"But shalt not cheat it twice,
For on this day thou shouldst have died
And upon thy soul a price.
I shall come for you
When the moon is dark,
And the wind is high,
And storm clouds scud across the sky,
And you shall know that I am near,
For man and beast alike shall flee
And the stars shall hide in fear.
When the lights have all gone out,"
She said,
"You shall know that I am near."

Then the men
Who'd met their deaths that day
Rose up from grassy grave,
Stood up from where they lay, they did,
And began to make their way.
Hollow-eyed, faces skewed,
Bodies torn and rent,
And followed her into that fell grove,
Into that fell grove they went.
And all about the crows did flap,
The crows did flap and fly,

And cawed loudly in the murk-filled brume[55],
"Thou shalt die! Thou shalt die!"
And I was left alone
To ponder 'pon my fate
Not knowing when my end would come,
Be it soon or late.

And when the priest
Doth ring the bell
And good folk go to church,
I fear the bell doth toll for me,
It summons me to Hell.
For she hunts upon the hag-haired haze,
In the misty midnight air
With ghostly host in train,
She flies, on her pale mare,
And those who see her passing by
Shall no more be sane,
But fall and kneel down in prayer
And bid her go from whence she came,
And hide their fearful face from her,
Nor dare to speak her name.

---

[55] Brume = mist or fog, from Latin 'Bruma' meaning 'Winter'

Notes

The mythic basis for *Lady of Crows* is the Morrigan, the Celtic goddess of the battlefield, who takes the souls of the unshriven unto herself, and for whom the crow was a totem animal. Morag, Morgan and Morgana (as in Morgana La Fey) are all derivatives of this goddess's name. There is also a Slavonic version of the same goddess by the name of Morena. There are influences of Poe's *The Raven*, Coleridge's *Rime of the Ancient Mariner* and Robert Burns' *Tam O'Shanter*. I deliberately introduced chaotic rhyming in the poem to instil a sense of unease in the reader.

Lovers in Chains

Lovers kiss in orchards,
Lovers smooch on trains,
Lovers press in sunny streets
And doorways when it rains.

Lovers read poems
To while away the hours,
Lovers part with angry words
And make it up with flowers.

Lovers are tortured,
Lovers are slain,
Lovers feel anguish,
Lovers feel pain.

Lovers go to war
To fight to be free,
Lovers die in battle,
Lovers drown at sea.

Lovers are beaten,
Lovers sleep in chains,
Lovers die in death camps,
Lovers die in flames.

Lovers who have loved for life
Are from their lovers torn,
Lovers who say goodnight
May never see the morn.

Lovers die of sorrow,
Lovers go insane,
But lovers keep on loving
Through the storm and rain.

Notes

This is a poem to the enduring power of love that all the tyrants and dictators in the world cannot destroy. Its symmetrical structure, regular rhyming and use of repetition make it belt along, and it is a useful counterpoint to some of the darker poems in this collection.

Manderley

I must drive down to Manderley again,
Manderley by the sea,
For though of ash and timbers charred,
Manderley calls out to me.

I remember Manderley,
Set in the south wind, defiant on its heights,
'Mong fruitful orchards and ancient oaks,
Secret palace of strange delights,
Sketched in chequered light of cloud
Or wreathed in mists,
Approached by wooded lane that turns and twists,
Of shadowed gables and fairy towers
Where, in childhood books,
Ruined princesses weaved paper flowers,
A maze of rooms, puzzle of the mind,
Of endless corridors and mysterious doors
One never knew what lay behind.

Oh Manderley, though now but
Shattered glass and scorchéd stone,
In my youth, while yet alone,

You were the summer of my heart,
A house of creaking elegance
And ancestral charm, of extravagant art
And secret soul,
Across whose rolling lawns
A gentleman might stroll
On evenings soft and warm,
Of cathedral windows and panelled halls,
Of stately bedrooms and masked balls,
Where people laughed and people danced,
People watched and people glanced,
Or stole outside to admire the view,
And while its sleepers dreamt,
Manderley, high upon its cliff, dreamt too.

Joy it was to stand at garden's edge
And watch the rollers break
Down in the bay,
To dream of kingdoms far away,
Listen to the susurrating sea
Soughing 'mong whitened shards of shell,
The soft synth of ocean swell,
Or gaze up and see
Swallows spryly strim the dawn,
Wing the mallow-tinted clouds of morn,

And now I know with certainty,
For all the love and death and pain
From its blackened plot of earth
Manderley shall rise again.

Notes

Manderley is named after the ancestral home of the
de Winters in Daphne du Maurier's novel *Rebecca*. In
this poem, Maxim de Winter looks back at his youth
in Manderley, prior to his disastrous marriage to his
first wife, the beautiful and manipulative Rebecca,
after whom Daphne du Maurier's novel is named. In
the novel, the new Mrs de Winter comes to live with de
Winter at Manderley only to find the house dominated
by the lingering memory of his first wife, Rebecca,
sustained by Rebecca's devoted housekeeper Mrs
Danvers. After Mrs Danvers' attempts to side-line de
Winter's new wife fail, and discovering that de Winter
shot his first wife after she confessed to being pregnant
from an affair with another man, the housekeeper
burns the house to the ground.

The attentive reader will notice that the first line
of the poem is adapted from the first line of *Rebecca*

which reads, "Last night I dreamt I went to Manderley again", but also draws inspiration from the first line of John Masefield's *Sea Fever*: "I must down to the seas again, to the lonely sea and the sky..."

Rebecca is a Gothic novel that relies on psychological tension rather than supernatural intervention. Rebecca's 'presence' is sustained by Mrs Danvers' preserving of her wing of the house in exactly the way it was when Rebecca was alive, even down to her monogrammed stationery, and undermining the new wife at every turn. That said, Manderley is not merely a plot locale but is a character in its own right, possessing its own oppressive atmosphere. It is ambiguous as to how much of Manderley's atmosphere is generated by Mrs Danvers' preservation of Rebecca's memory and how much by the house itself. It is possible to argue (as a subtext) that Rebecca is so completely identified with the house that she becomes 'part' of Manderley after her death (her personality merging with it) and that the psychic link between Rebecca and the house is catalysed by Mrs Danvers. However, this is a personal interpretation.

So, the gothic architecture of Manderley augments the psychological tension of the novel, but what gives Gothic houses 'atmosphere'? When we use the word 'Gothic' in referring to houses, we are talking about the Gothic Revival of the late eighteenth to the mid-nineteenth century, largely coincident with the Romantic era in literature, which was partly a reaction against dehumanising industrialisation, and partly a reaction against excessive formalism which emphasised style over emotion. Gothic houses, with their high-pitched roofs, windows with pointed arches and cross-gables, their sprawling 'wings' and turret rooms, lend themselves to the imagination. The Gothic country house supplanted the previous Neoclassical style based on neat geometrical lines and curves derived from Greek temples. The key element that makes Gothic architecture 'atmospheric' is its 'heaviness' combined with its propensity for shadowy recesses. Again, while Neoclassical appeals to the rational mind, Gothic (in its lack of symmetry and shadowiness) appeals to the unconscious emotions, conveying a sense of unease.

In the United States, the energies released by the reunification of the country after the Civil War saw a boom in industrialisation (the so-called Gilded Age) which ushered in the age of the American tycoons who advertised their wealth and status by building huge sprawling Gothic mansions totally at variance with the antebellum colonial style (the Winchester house being a case in point). It was from such mansions that the American Gothic tradition emerged, which formed the inspiration for Shirley Jackson's *The Haunting of Hill House*, and for Stephen King's *Rose Red,* but arguably also informed H.P. Lovecraft's Cthulhu mythos whose 'non-Euclidian geometry' was derived from the Gothic architectural form, hence his references to "shadow-gabled Arkham".

The description of Manderley in the poem is taken from the novel *Rebecca* but especially from the film sets of Alfred Hitchcock's 1940 screen adaptation.

Mirror, Mirror

Mirror, mirror, be my eyes,
My faithful friend who never lies,
Seek out what I need to know,
And in thy glassy surface show.

Show me pictures for to see,
Send me spirits to speak with me,
Answer faithfully, answer true,
Reveal what I ask of you.

Mirror, mirror, black as night,
Thy darksome eye reflects no light,
Draw me down and into thee,
And show me what I need to see.

Last night I dreamt a girl so fair,
Of snow-white skin and raven hair,
Of blood-red lips and bluest eyes,
One so beauteous I should despise.

Mirror, mirror, is it she,
I once thought dead to be?
For I cannot bear that one so fair,
Should ever breathe the self-same air.

Is she daring? Is she bold?
Does she threaten what I hold?
Or is she just a silly child,
Doomed to die in forest wild.

And if it proves that she doth live,
I shall her a poisoned apple give,
Then shall my beauty be without compare,
And kingdoms shall I capture, and kings ensnare.

Mirror, mirror, be my guide,
Cast thine eye far and wide,
In thickest forest, on rushing tide,
For from me she shall not hide.

Tell me truly, tell me all,
For if she lives then I shall fall,
Mirror, mirror, on the wall,
Who *is* the fairest of them all?

Notes

Mirror, Mirror was inspired by the Wicked Queen in *Snow White*, named Ravenna. For antecedents, we can cite Morgana La Fey, the sorceress of the Arthurian cycle, and even further back to the Greek goddess Eris, Goddess of Discord (see below).

Snow White was collected and originally published by the Brothers Grimm as *Sneewittchen* in 1812, and finally revised in 1854. Two rival origins of the story have been proposed. In the first, *Snow White* was based on Margaretha von Waldeck, daughter of Philip IV, Count of Waldeck-Wildungen *(1493–1574)* and his first wife, Margaret Cirksena (1500–1537). The first wife dying young, Margaretha's new stepmother, Katharina of Hatzfeld, sent Margaretha away to Wildungen in Brussels, where she fell in love with a prince who would become the future Philip II of Spain. The parents were against the romance since they were Lutherans, as was Philip's father Charles V, Holy Roman Emperor. Margaretha mysteriously died at age 26 and was believed to have been poisoned.[56]

---

[56] Sander, Eckhard (1994). Schneewittchen: Marchen oder Wahrheit?: ein lokaler Bezug zum Kellerwald.

A more likely source, however, is Maria Sophia Margarethe Catharina, Baroness von und zu Erthal, born in 1725 to Philipp Christoph von und zu Erthal, the local representative of the Prince Elector of Mainz. Maria Sophia's mother died in 1738 and her father was remarried in 1743 to Claudia Elisabeth von Reichenstein, who put her own children before her new husband's. Interestingly, Claudia Elisabeth owned a magic mirror which can still be viewed today in the Spessart Museum, in the Lohr Castle where the stepmother lived.[57] For the purposes of this poem, I have assumed the use of an obsidian glass mirror, also known as a 'black mirror'.

Both stories are associated with mining interests that may have given rise to the story of the seven dwarves. Margaretha's father owned copper mines that employed child labour, and in Maria Sophia's story, there was a mining town called Bieber just west of Lohr, set upon seven mountains, that also employed children whose growth may have become stunted as a result of working in narrow tunnels.

---

[57] Bartels, Karlheinz (2012). *Schneewittchen – Zur Fabulologie des Spessarts*. Geschichts- und Museumsverein Lohr a. Main, Lohr a. Main; second edition.

The poem is set after the Wicked Queen's failed attempt to send the huntsman to kill Snow White, after which Snow White blossoms into a beautiful girl, the fairest of them all, confirmed one day by the Wicked Queen's mirror which can only speak the truth.

The symbolism of *Snow White and Sleeping Beauty*

The Thorn

In one version of the story, Snow White's mother, the Queen, pricks her finger on a needle and her blood drips onto the fresh snow covering the black windowsill. In another version, she pricks her finger on a rose in the garden and the blood falls on the snow. She says to herself, "How I wish that I had a daughter who had skin as white as snow, lips as red as blood and hair as black as ebony." She becomes pregnant with a daughter but dies during childbirth, after which the Wicked Queen seduces the King, murders him, and seizes the kingdom.

So far, so good, but let's look beneath the surface of things as poets are meant to. Both the needle and the thorn are sharp objects: symbolically, they are the same thing. In order to understand what has happened, we need to turn to Norse and Saxon runic tradition, and a particular rune known as the *Thurs (Þurs)* rune, also known as *Thurisaz* in Proto-German, which, in post-Viking Scandinavia, came to be known as the letter *Thorn*.

Thurisaz or *Thurs*.

Thorn derived from Thurs rune

Thurs (Þurs) means 'thorn' (hence the letter *Thorn* which succeeded it), but since many runes have double meanings, the rune doesn't only refer to a physical thorn because *Thurs* also refers to the giants of Norse mythology (Thursar or *Þursar*), and the giants (like the Greek Titans) represent the primordial chaotic forces that preceded (and lie behind) the ordered universe. They are literally 'the forces of the Other Side', and in Jungian terms, the forces of the Unconscious, which is itself a gateway to the Other Side. Hence when Princess Aurora in *Sleeping Beauty* pricks herself on the spindle (for which read *thorn*) she falls asleep, i.e., enters the unconscious dreaming state. Maleficent, who has cursed Aurora, is another prototype of the Wicked Queen or faerie, the counterpart of Ravenna in Snow White, and it is no coincidence that the sleeping Aurora is surrounded by a briar rose that grows up around her – another reference to the thorn. Snow White's mother pricks herself and dies in childbirth (returns to the Other Side), but read between the lines: she sheds blood, so there is a blood sacrifice to the Powers of the Other Side – that is how her wish for a daughter of Snow White's description is granted. But since the thorn has entered her finger, the powers of the Other Side have also flowed into her and are inherited by her daughter. This is where things get interesting! I have said in the *Foreword* to this collection that the Unconscious/Other Side is double-edged: it contains both terror and beauty, (terror as dark magic and sorcery, beauty as otherworldly beauty and inspiration) so it is not far-fetched to suggest that the Wicked Queen represents the Terror aspect of the Unconscious while Snow White represents the Beauty aspect. How does Snow White surpass the Wicked Queen in beauty? Because the same power flows in her. How does Snow White survive the Wicked Queen's schemes (the huntsman, the overtight bodice, the poison apple)? Because she is under the protection of those same powers. Remember, and this is critical to understanding, the thorn is a symbol both of aggression and of *protection*, and just as the Wicked Queen represents the sinister sorcerous aspect of the thorn, so that same power exercises a protective aspect over Snow White.

The *Thurs* rune is composed of two other runes: the *Is* rune and the *Ken* rune. The *Is* rune derives its name from *ice* and the *Ken* rune from *torch*. So together, the runes denote the interaction of opposing forces (ice and fire) that brought about existence in Norse myth. For our purposes, however, ice represents something that is 'locked in', and that 'something' can be described as 'primal knowledge'. The *Ken* rune represents the association between two ideas: light and knowledge/understanding, hence the Scots expression 'Ye ken what I mean?' ('ken' being a Norse loan word into Scots). Every time we depict someone having an idea by drawing a lightbulb above their head, we are replicating the same idea of association between light and knowledge: hence we speak of the 'illumination of the mind', conveyed by the Greek word *gnosis*. So, the conjoining of *Is* and *Ken* is symbolising the mobilisation or activation of the primigenial gnosis deep within us: in other words, knowledge of the nature of our own Being. Note that the *Thurs* rune points right, so it is indicating a transference of knowledge from the left (the Unconscious/the Nightside) to the right (the Conscious/Dayside).

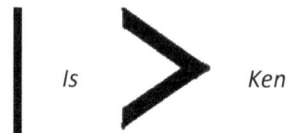

Is   *Ken*

The Apple

The poison apple represents the dayside and nightside of Consciousness, but also the dayside and 'other side' of Existence, by virtue of the fact that it has a face turned toward the sun and a face turned away from it: it is red on one side and green on the other. It is the red side (the poison side) that the Wicked Queen gives Snow White to eat from. Furthermore, cut an apple across and the pips are arranged in the shape of a pentagram, and a pentagram may be depicted upright for protection and inverse for malice.

The reason for the association of the apple with evil is a linguistic one, as well as the symbolic one mentioned above (that it has a face turned toward the 'other side' of existence). The linguistic connection is down to the Latin 'malum' which means both 'evil' and 'apple', derived from the Greek for 'melon'. The apple belongs to genus Malus, part of the family Rosaceae which includes the rose. It is because of this word association that the fruit of the Tree of the Knowledge of Good and Evil in *Genesis* was depicted as an apple. It is also because the word 'apple' in old English originally stood in for any type of fruit other than berries. Interestingly, from the fourth century after the Christianisation of the Roman Empire, the word 'pomum' replaced 'malum' as the word for apple, hence the French 'pomme'.

Mythically, the apple is the fruit of beauty and discord (representing its two faces). In the *Iliad*, Paris gives one of the golden apples of the Hesperides to the goddess Aphrodite, with the promise to give it to Helen of Troy, and thus the Trojan war is set to begin. The full story, however, goes like this:

The apple in the *Iliad* comes from the Garden of the Hesperides. The Hesperides are daughters of the Goddess of Night, Nyx. The apples confer eternal youth, health, beauty and immortality. In addition to the Hesperides, the apples are also guarded by Ladon, a hundred-headed dragon that never sleeps (think of the golden fleece guarded by the hydra – it's the same idea). Eris, Goddess of Discord, furious at not being invited to the marriage of Thetis and Peleus, takes one of the apples and throws it among the guests. The apple is inscribed with the words 'To the fairest' and causes commotion among the guests. This is where the Judgement of Paris comes in because Paris ends the quarrel by awarding the apple to Aphrodite as 'the fairest of them all' (does this ring any bells?). The careful reader may discern a pattern emerging: in *Sleeping Beauty*, Maleficent, furious at not being invited to Aurora's christening, curses her to prick her finger and enter a catatonic state, so Maleficent is clearly a cipher of Eris (who appears in the Arthurian romances as Morgana La Fey). In *Snow White*, the place of Paris is taken by the mirror itself who awards the title 'fairest of them all'. So, *Snow White* and *Sleeping Beauty* have common antecedents in the Homeric epics.

In Norse mythology, the place of the Hesperides is taken by the goddess Idunn (or Iduna), keeper of the apples of immortality eaten by the gods. In the Arthurian romance, Arthur, mortally wounded by Mordred (his 'dark twin'), is taken across a lake by three priestesses (possibly representing the Three Norns or spinners of fate) to the Isle of Avalon, which was also known as 'the Isle of Apples' and is essentially the land of immortality: the Garden of the Hesperides translocated to dark-age Europe.

The Kiss

The kiss by the handsome prince is also a common feature both of *Snow White* and *Sleeping Beauty*. It is the kiss that breaks the curse. In a Jungian sense, it is the release from the thrall of the Unconscious and the achievement of the fully integrated Self in which the Unconscious and Conscious minds now exist and cooperate in perfect balance. Christianity gave a twist to the idea by identifying the prince as the principle of the Spirit (male) awakening the Soul (female) to spiritual knowledge, but the essential principle is the same.

So where does the redemptive prince come from? My money is on Orpheus in the Greek myths. Orpheus, son of Apollo and possessor of a lyre that can charm the beasts, marries Eurydice who, soon after their wedding, is bitten by a viper and dies. Orpheus descends into the Underworld to retrieve her and charms Hades himself into releasing her. Hades agrees to let her return to the realm of the living but on the condition that Orpheus must not look back... which is precisely what happens, and Eurydice is lost forever, after which Orpheus, desiring death, is torn apart by wild beasts. So, in the Orpheus myth, the story doesn't end well. Notwithstanding, the myth of descending to the underworld to bring back a loved one was an established trope: Demeter descends to the Underworld to bring back Persephone (albeit for only six months of the year). Before her, Inanna/Ishtar descends into the Underworld to bring back her lover, Tammuz, from the clutches of her sister, Ereshkigal, in the Sumerian myth. A similar story exists in Norse myth: Loki having slain Baldur, the god of light, with a branch of mistletoe, Odin sends Hermod on his horse, Sleipnir, to Helheim to bargain for Baldur's release. Hel grants his wish on one condition: that all the gods must agree to allow Baldur back among the Aesir, and all did, except for one giantess called Tokk who said, "Let Hel hold what she has!" But Tokk was none other than Loki in disguise, and so Baldur remained in Helheim.

The Wicked Queen

The archetype of the Wicked Queen or Faerie (also common to *Sleeping Beauty* and *Snow White*) has already been covered in the above discussion but to summarise: her archetype goes back to Eris, Goddess of Discord who appears as Morgana La Fey in the Arthurian cycle, Ravenna in *Snow White* and Maleficent in *Sleeping Beauty*. Symbolically, however, she represents the adversarial powers of the Other Side which sow confusion in the ordered universe, and symbolically the power of the Unconscious which threatens to overwhelm the waking mind.

The Missing Socks

I've lost a sock,
A pair to be precise,
I don't know where they've gone
But to find them would be nice.

They aren't in the washer,
They aren't in the bin,
They're not mixed up with underpants,
Who knows what I put them in?

There they are!
I must have gone insane!
Who would have thought a pair of socks
Would cause me so much pain!

Underneath the duvet!
Who would think to look there?
After I turned the house out
And was beginning to despair.

It's like this since I lost my wife,
Things keep going astray.
I need to find another wife
To organise my day.

I really am at a loss,
Not knowing what to do.
I wasn't made to live alone.
Damn it! Now I've lost a shoe!

Notes

Although framed in humorous verse, there is an underlying theme of sadness to this poem: a man growing old alone after his wife has died and gradually falling apart. I really do think that, on the whole, men are more fragile and vulnerable than women, particularly as they grow older, and women seem to adapt better to solitary life. Possibly this is because women have wider circles of friendship and support networks, while men retreat into the shed. Funnily enough, I really did lose a pair of socks, and that was the inspiration for the poem!

Ode on a Summer Night

Night is a woman, soft and round,
Whose tresses hang low over sea and sound,
And the glittering stars that garland her hair
Light home the weary seafarer.

Night is a fruit, pungent and sweet,
Sagging from orchards ripened in heat,
Damson and plum with dusky hue,
Black cherries dripping with honeydew.

Night is a garden fragrant and warm,
Scented with jasmine where honeybees swarm,
Soft winds blow among mallow and rose,
Foxgloves and lupins nod and doze.

Night is a lover, sensual and smooth,
Whose song stills my thoughts and fingers soothe,
Our skins seek pleasure in the humid night air,
And our lips speak the love that only we share.

Night is a goddess, accepting and wise,
No act of love doth she despise,
Priestess of love, she tells not the priest
Of all that transpires at the wedding feast.

Night is a mystery, a secret untold,
A masquerade waiting for the dance to unfold,
And the masquerade dancers, fox, crow and owl,
All bow to her, wound in her cowl.

When Somnus[58] closes the lids of day,
Then we, night's children, come out to play,
To revel and dance in woodland green,
And court our Dark Lady, night's honoured Queen.

Notes

This poem is a homage to Night, conceived of as feminine in contrast to the harsh light of day. The light separately delineates reality while, in night, all things are melded; to the day belongs logic and reason, to the night belongs intuition and magic. The poem intends

---

[58] The Roman god of sleep; his Greek counterpart is Hypnos.

to convey the heaviness, languor and sensuality of a warm summer night through a succession of images and experiences.

Ophelia Lies Floating

Oh, my love! Oh, my sweet!
What have you gone and done?
Outside, the dawn is breaking
But you shall never see the sun.
Below, the city teems with life,
But your flat is deathly still,
I searched for you and called your name,
Could not shake that awful chill,
And when I found you, caught my breath,
And still cannot believe
That what I see is really you,
And my eyes do not deceive.

My beautiful Ophelia lies floating in her bath,
Her hair streams out like ocean kelp,
Skin cold and drained of blood,
Too late to ask for help.
Serene and quiet, your eyes lie closed
As though lost in thought,
But the angry wound upon your wrist
Tells the violence you have wrought.
Oh, my lovely Ophelia,

Why did you end your life today?
You didn't even write a note
But simply slipped away,

And now I face the world alone,
A world that doesn't care,
A world that's empty without you,
A life I cannot share.
In terror, I tried to pull you back
From your dark descent,
So many words I spoke to you
And all of them I meant.
I tried to stop the bleeding,
I tried not to despair,
I tried to bring back your soul,
But my hands met empty air.

Too late, I watched my love sink down
Into the murky depth,
And I would follow where you've gone
Till I run out of breath,
And brave the ocean pressure,

Brave the cold and pain,
Brave the endless night of Death,
To have you back again.[59]

How I miss your secret smile,
Your laugh so bright and gay,
The fleeting expressions on your face
Like the fleeting of the day.

Books and poems, kisses and looks,
Clubbing after dark,
Shopping for blouses and picture houses,
Laughter in the park.
My delicate Ophelia,
Willowy and slight,
Blue eyes sad and wet with tears
Or sparkling and bright.
I never knew your inner thoughts,
The self I could not see,
The changing seasons of your mood
Were a mystery to me.

---

[59] There is a classical allusion here to the story of Orpheus and Eurydice, whereby Orpheus descends to the underworld to bring Eurydice back from the world of the dead.

But now I think I should have asked,
Tried to understand your mind,
Even though you shut me out,
My God, I was so blind!
But now you're lost to the world
And you're lost to me,
And I cannot understand the reason
Though I struggle ev'ry day to see.
And the last memory I have of you
Isn't the Ophelia of my days,
But a naked girl lying in her bath
With an empty gaze.

Notes

The inspiration for this poem, and the reason for its title, is that of Ophelia in Shakespeare's *Hamlet*. Ophelia is Hamlet's potential wife, who, although in love with Hamlet, becomes deranged over Hamlet's erratic behaviour and deteriorating sanity, not least when Hamlet stabs her father Polonius behind the arras. She commits suicide by drowning and is found floating in a brook. The idea occurred to me to update the scene to the present day by presenting Ophelia as a vulnerable teenage girl. Several paintings have been made of the scene, the most well-known being *Ophelia* by John Everett Millais, but John William Waterhouse and Alexandre Cabanel also depicted the scene.

Suicide is often regarded as a taboo subject in poetry, but I feel that something that is too dreadful to be talked about is a perfect candidate for talking about. From the outset, I made the decision that I would not exploit death for its shock value, but neither would I romanticise it (as in, for instance, the famous painting of the poet Chatterton lying dead in his garret room with one arm romantically draped over the side of the bed). Rather, I chose to focus on the feelings of the young man who discovers his girlfriend lying dead in the bath: first the shock, then the recrimination. "Couldn't I have done something to stop it?" is a classic response but one has to realise that everyone has a private side to their personality that is turned away from the sun, which is their Mystery (and what we might call their Unknowable Self) and, however long one has known a person, one simply does not have access to that private side of them... and sometimes they can do something so unexpected and unpredictable, it will shock you, and you never saw it coming.

Pompeii

The sand runs through,
The shadow of the dial lies long upon the hour,
And time is measured in the beat of a dying heart
Whose sound fades out
Upon the birdless air,
And everywhere,
The black pall obscures the blood-eyed sun,
The blind sun,
Closed by the Titan hand of winter.
The mask of reason slips upon the well of chaos,
And faith to splinter.
Those who have no eyes cannot see
The jester's leering face,
And above the din,
The scream of human race,
One who listens might hear the soft folding of wings.
Great men lie in chunks of greatness,
From out whose coiffed and curléd heads
Cold eyes admire our shoes coldly,
Where once, boldly,
Cast scorn upon the dregs,
And between their broken breasts

And shattered legs
The hot wind sings.
If granite can crack,
If bronze can burn,
What hope for us?
The Beast writes the Book of Man
In words of blood;
Its pages float among the pyres of cities,
Carried on the flood,
And the sedge of all our dreams,
All we hoped to be,
Swells upon the burning tide,
The bitter tide,
That bears them out to sea.

I would sing of lemonade and laughter
And love in the long grass,
Of trysts on sunny slopes
'Mid purple vine and orange grove,
Or in azure bay, 'pon golden sand,
With wave-washed feet we'd rove,
And you – hair like autumn spelt
Stirred by Tyrrhenian winds,
Sloe eyes creased in silent mirth;
We who loved, though were poor,

Love and lie among asphodels,
On some Hadean shore.

Wrapped in sleep's sweet succulence,
We heard the Kraken roar,
Saw the swelling doom tide,
Infernal engine wreathed in fume and flame,
Thanatos' awful face[60]
From whom men run but cannot hide,
Like unto some Minoan bull,
Careening and careering in its maddened rage,
Monstrous dark, no god assuage,
And all that once was fair,
Dead and bare
On Vesuvius' smoking plain;
Lissom limbs locked in agony of ash,
Parodies of gods convulsed in stone,
Knotted in the terror of our own divinity,
Where once was flesh and bone.

Oh wind, what jealous child art thou?
A thief of time and memory
That haunts the houses of the dead,

---

[60] Thanatos is the Greek god of death

And cares not what it takes,
Of fondest thoughts left unsaid;
Take now the dust of she I loved
Who in life didst move the very clouds with song,
And lulled the shepherd in his fold
'Neath ancient trees
With plaintive pipe and hum of bees,
And charmed the parchéd earth with softest feet,
So light her step, so fair,
In death, she floats upon the eventide
To follow the sparrows on the southern air.
Come then, many fingered wind,
And with burning breath
Lift up the ashes of my lover's hair,
That once did glister in the dewy day,
And cast them to the night,
Cast all away,
A kiss blown to the stars
From old Pompeii.

Notes

The obvious literary reference to *Pompeii* would be
Edward Bulwer Lytton's *Last Days of Pompeii* but the

stylistic influence comes from W.B. Yeats' *The Second Coming* with its overtly apocalyptic opening, especially in Yeats' reference to 'the blood-dimmed tide'.

> Turning and turning in the widening gyre
> The falcon cannot hear the falconer;
> Things fall apart; the centre cannot hold;
> Mere anarchy is loosed upon the world,
> The blood-dimmed tide is loosed, and everywhere
> The ceremony of innocence is drowned;
> The best lack all conviction, while the worst
> Are full of passionate intensity.

In the poem, I wanted to draw attention to the irony of the people of Pompeii becoming statues, frozen in ash, very similar to the gods they had worshipped. The story is told from the point of view of two lovers who are caught unawares by the apocalypse.

Raging Heart, or The Ballad of Rory John

Now I'm a trapper born and bred
And my name is Rory John,
I've trapped the forests far and wide,
Few places I ain't gone.

Still, I grew tired of the wand'ring life,
Became a settled man,
And took for me a nice young wife,
Name of Betty Ann.

I kept some pigs and chickens,
And hunted thereabouts,
Led some expeditions
And bought from Indian scouts.

I set to build a cabin
And cleared myself a plot,
But soon there came along a man
Who wanted what I'd got.

John Smith was the kind of man
Who takes most what he can,
And John Smith it was
Who took my Betty Ann.

For I came home one day,
From our cabin no lights shone,
And I called the name of Betty Ann
And discovered she was gone.

And I vowed then and there
For want my soul to save,
I'd track down that coward Smith
And put him in his grave.

I knew I'd catch him soon or late,
For I'd learned the tracker's art,
And though he had a start on me
Hope still burned in my raging heart.

I worked the railroad dime a day,
Did what I could to get along,
And all it was that kept me going
Was vengeance' wicked song.

I wrangled horses for a while,
I rode the prairie storm,
Laid my head down where I could
But no fire could keep me warm.

For when I wed my Betty Ann
I swore nothing would us part,
Ain't no mountain, ain't no stone,
Could dam my raging heart.

The storm and me, we're brothers, see,
Full of sound and fire,
Its fearful thunder shakes the earth
And crackles like a wire.

The storm don't care who it hurts,
The strongest man will tear apart,
But no storm ever was as wild
As the storm in my raging heart.

I crossed the Sierra's pink-hued peaks
Through snow drifts high and deep,
Where the bay of wolves in the forest pass
Gives a man no sleep.

I rode the trails for a while
On my mustang sleek and brown,
Until I chanced upon his name
In some neglected town.

Soon I found out where he lived,
By a river he would pan,
And every day brought me closer to the man
Who took my Betty Ann.

One day John Smith broke cover,
I guess he felt secure,
Rode out upon his dappled mare,
Betty Ann rode at the rear.

My raging heart could wait no more,
I sprang before his horse
And challenged him to get down and fight,
Or I'd feel no remorse.

Well, he just sat and didn't move,
His face was white in disbelief,
So I looked him in the eye and shot him down,
And killed the coward Smith.

I called my Betty Ann to come
But a tear rolled down her cheek,
Then she turned her horse and rode away,
Away back down the creek.

And I never saw my Betty Ann
From that day she did depart,
For that single tear upon her cheek
Put out my raging heart.

Notes

Raging Heart is a ballad of the American West, a lawless frontier where men settled their own disputes, and I aimed to capture the grittiness of the landscape and people in the poem. A ballad is a story simply told in verse (no room for flowery description) and was designed for singing. Its protagonists find themselves pitched against forces greater than themselves (government, industry, the law) and it often ends in tragedy or betrayal. Uniquely, it was a popular poetic medium, printed on broadsheets, learned and passed along, becoming part of the nation's cultural inheritance. My first introduction to the ballad was in my early years in school when, as a young child, I was introduced to the *Ballad of Jesse James*, one of the most famous ballads of the American West, in which James is depicted as a popular hero, a Robin Hood figure, who stole from the rich and gave to the poor. The ballad is, therefore, inextricably linked with the social history of the working class.

The protagonist in this ballad, Rory John, isn't so much a hero as an anti-hero, and *Raging Heart* is a tale of vengeance gone wrong. It is the story of a man who sets out to avenge himself against the man who took his wife, only to find his wife has fallen in love with her abductor... or did they plan it all from the start? I have deviated somewhat from the formula by exploring Rory John's inner state of mind, essential to understanding his actions. The reference to 'the coward Smith' recalls 'the coward Robert Ford' in *Jesse James* and is intended as a tribute.

Central to the story is the impact of landscape on character: a harsh unforgiving landscape produces hard-bitten men, as though the actors are chiselled out of the very landscapes they inhabit. Think of the spaghetti westerns or the novels of Cormac McCarthy, which are set in desolate (almost apocalyptic)

266

landscapes and run-down western towns in the middle of nowhere.

It is crucial to realise just how influential the Frontier was to the American mind. The Frontier never went away but became internalised in the American psyche in the ideas of rugged individualism and infinite possibility. America became defined by the Frontier long after the Frontier ceased to exist.

Shot Down in Flames

I saw you in a lighted window
As evening fell on glowing shops,
And traffic swished along rainy streets
Honking 'mid buses and taxi stops.
I stared at you for quite some time,
A goddess chic in skirt and tights
With boots of shiny leather,
And hair with gold highlights.
So pert and pretty were you
Your beauty God acclaims,
But you looked askance at me
And shot me down in flames.

I would have walked the earth for you,
The whole earth wide and round,
To kiss your goddess' sandaled foot
And rejoice in the love I'd found.
A single endearing glance
To set my heart ablaze,
And rest my head upon your lap,
The goddess of my days.
But you wanted nothing I could give,

And scorn your face proclaims,
You could barely look at me
And shot me down in flames.

I'd buy for you a country house
With gardens and a lake,
With deer and hound and horse,
All for you to take.
And you would be the toast
Of everywhere we went
Of every race and country fair
And every grand event.
But you preferred a younger man
Like those common dames,
Said I was too old for you
And shot me down in flames.

I'd make for you a gilded cage
For my pretty bird to sing,
And on your pretty finger
I'd slip a diamond ring.
And all I asked of you
Was one ounce of your love,
A drop of water from your spring,
To hold you like a dove.

I spoke my love to you
But you only called me names,
You turned your ire upon me
And shot me down in flames.

Lover boy took offence,
Beat you black and blue,
And you crawled out into the street
Wearing but one shoe.
Now you are an ageing wreck
And stress lines etch your face,
Gone now is the pretty girl
Who moved me with her grace.
So run on back to lover boy,
I'm tired of all your games,
I could give you what no woman has
But you shot me down in flames.

Go and live with lover boy
If he means so much to you,
I had the power to change your life
And this is what you do.
Enjoy your life with lover boy,
You got what you deserved.
You made your bed so lie in it,

Justice has been served.
Now I know ingratitude,
I've seen how a woman shames,
Nor e'er again allow a woman
To shoot me down in flames.

Notes

So here we have *Shot Down in Flames*: something that
begins as a love poem and ends as a howl of rage. This
is social realist poetry, in the same vein as *The Pretty
Magpie* and *Ophelia Lies Floating*, *The Death Show, Dear
Leader*, and *Strong Love*, and it explores the themes
of dark possessive love and male rejection. At first
sight, it is a poem about an ardent lover spurned by an
ungrateful woman. But is it? The narrative is only told
from the man's point of view. Why does she reject him
so vehemently? Is he a wealthy controlling man who
just wants a trophy wife, the kind of man who thinks
he can have any woman he wants? Or worse, is he a
dangerous fantasist who is stalking her? Can he deliver
on what he has promised? He offers her wealth and
security but can he truly love? And how does he know
her boyfriend abuses her if he isn't outside her house

271

watching her? Did her boyfriend beat her *because* of his attentions? Observe how his reactions change after she has rejected him, turning from Prince Charming to Judge Dredd in an instant, and men can be like this: charming one moment, spiteful and vindictive the next if they don't get what they want... and make no mistake, by the end of the poem he has become a total misogynist. When she is beaten by her boyfriend, there is no concern whatsoever for her wellbeing; it's 'justice' for having rejected him. This is a man who thinks he is God's gift to women, and a woman's love can be bought. So here we have a woman who is torn between a control freak on the one hand and a jealous abusive boyfriend on the other... not an enviable position to be in. Think about the title: exactly *who* is being shot down in flames?

The Story of Gunnar and Hallgerður:
An Icelandic Tale Retold

The Skald Speaks[61]

Harken now,

Sons of warriors of warriors' blood,

Bloodied born of woman's womb

And bloodied die by heft of axe,

Kiss of Skuld[62]

Who cuts the thread of life,

And I will tell of what becomes those

Who scorn the codes that bind,

---

[61] A poet who narrates the lives and deeds of prominent men.

[62] The third of the three Norns, who weave the web of fate (*Wyrd*) of each person. The three Norns are Urðr, governing the past (from whose name *wyrd* is derived); Verðandi, representing what is currently coming into being; and Skuld, representing what shall come (and ultimately the time and manner of death). Readers may notice a similarity with the Three Fates or *Moirai* of Greek myth: Clotho, who commenced the weaving of fate from birth, Lachesis, who decided the length of a person's life, and Atropos, who cut the thread of life and decided the manner of death. The correspondences are similar but not exact, however, but I have made an approximate identification between Atropos and Skuld. Of interest is that the Three Fates/Norns found their way into Shakespeare's *Macbeth* as the Three Witches or Weird Sisters. It is Macbeth's attempts to control and manipulate his destiny that brings about his downfall.

273

Of honour broken and betrayed,
Of judgement unseated in its course,
Of madness of men and poison of woman,
Vipers lacking honour to their kin,
And their law.

A Wedding and a Storm

So, it begins with Hámandar of Hliðarendi,[63]
Who, with his own hands,
Bravely fought and won wealth in foreign wars,
But falling foul of his lord
Sought exile in Ísland,[64]
Far removed from cupidity of kings,
And a fine hall of stone built,
Framed in wood and roofed in turf,
With fields to farm, and cattle fat,
His legacy to his kin and all that followed,
That may ne'er be sold nor squandered
By impecunious son;[65]

---

[63] True to the saga form, the story begins a generation before the main action. The establishment of lineage was a feature both of the Greek epics and Norse sagas.

[64] Norse spelling of Iceland.

[65] Under Icelandic law, the family inheritance could not be sold. 'Impecunious' means 'without financial means'.

And as his fortune magnified,
So acquired power and renown,
For all looked up to Hámandar
And much respected was he
For his fairness and wise counsel.
In time, old Hámandar passed from the world
And ascended rejoicing
To Vallhöll's[66] hallowed halls,
There to join his kin before him,
Heroes all, constant, straight and true,
In death as in life,
For friendship forged in battle is like no other.
But he had raised a son, Gunnar,[67]
Of whom he was proud and expected much,

---

[66] Also transcribed as Vallhalla, the Norse 'heaven' where heroes go after death. The equivalent of the Greek Elysian Fields. The halls of Vallhöll were probably inspired by Vikings' experience of Constantinople.

[67] The name of Gunnar's mother is not recorded in the original, as the storyteller would not have regarded it as important. In Viking society (as in Sparta and many other warrior societies), it was the father who acculturated the son into manhood, and a mother's influence was perceived to be weakening. Hence the term 'mother's boy' which we still use today. Arguably, the toxic masculinity and absence of empathy that typified Viking culture owed to an absence of maternal influence, engendering an institutionalised psychopathy. Put another way, Viking society existed at the boundary between culture and mental illness.

For the honour of family rests upon such sons,

And continuance of the line.

Gunnar grew from boy to man

With the wind in his hair

And the fleck of rain upon his cheek,

A son of the earth,

Hewn from rugged mountain and barren moor,

Of roaring falls, fulsome in flood,

Dark forbidding cliffs

Sweeping steeply up from swelling sea

Beneath a fell sky.

It was giants who had raised those mountains

In the elder time,

Before the Aesir[68] brought order to the nine worlds[69],

Before the first cow had swung its horns,

Yet still the land tried a man

And wore him down;

A land of wind and ice and mist

And relentless rain,

---

[68] Originally, the trinity of creator gods Odin, Vili and Vé, who succeeded the Giants, but the pantheon also included Thor and Tyr. The Greek parallel would be the Olympian gods who overthrew the Titans. There was a second pantheon called the Vanir who were fertility gods like Freyr and Frejya.

[69] The nine words of existence organised around the World Tree, *Yggdrasil*.

Of sleet and hail,
Scorn of Heaven, bane of Man,
And only the food in his belly,
The mead in his throat,
And the fire in his blood
Stood fast against the storm.
And yet he prospered,
Stolid as an auroch[70], he,
That mats the mossy moor with heavy hoof,
And he would do well,
Until there came a day
As summer drew its final breath,
When he stood before the Alþing[71] at Þingvellir
On a brilliant morning,
Where kin and neighbour gathered before the
    great stone,
And harkened to the Lawspeaker,
Great affairs discussed,

---

[70] A prehistoric form of wild cattle that evolved during the last Ice Age, featured in cave paintings. They continued into the Viking era. The last was killed in the seventeenth century.

[71] Parliament. The *alþing* is the great parliament while the *þing* is a lesser assembly. Derived from Old Norse 'alþingi'. Originally pronounced 'all-thing' and 'thingi' but today pronounced 'all-ting' and 'ting' because the 'th' sound disappeared from Scandinavian languages in the Middle Ages.

Disputes settled and neighbours reconciled or not,

For men are quick to take sleight

And swords quick to sing,

And he spied among the crowd

A girl so beautiful

Her hair shone with the sun,

Hair fine as silk as though of pure light it were
    made,

And it flashed brightly as she tossed it

In the cool morning air,

Flashed with gold

As the sun strikes the still waters of a lake.

Her clothes also spoke of wealth and good taste;

What a fine wife she would make,

And how jealous the men

Whose wives had been coarsened by hard work.

Her name was Hallgerður, daughter of Höskuldur,

Descendent of Danish princes,

And she had that haughty bearing

That oft goes with great beauty,

Ill-suited to a small town like Hliðarendi.

So with her Gunnar dallied

And made known his interest,

And inquired of his friend Njall,

Whose farm neighboured his own,

As to her provenance.
Njall, however, surprised him
With ill-omened advice.
"Wed her not," said he,
"For she will be thy ruin.
Two husbands hath she wed
And two sent unto the grave".
But of wise counsel Gunnar would not heed,
His mind set upon his prize,
For obsessed he was of Hallgerður,
Bright and beauteous as morning's song,
And though some said she had bewitched him,
All men know
Lust requires no supernatural assistance,
For in truth,
His great bull's head led him to the prettiest cow,
And not even her uncle Hrútr
Could dissuade him,
And *he* should know…
Her first husband Þorvaldur
Had been bled dry by her extravagance.
"Beauty is a treasure not earned," he had said,
"And some there are who wield it falsely,
As a bright flame lures a moth to its doom".
Still, Gunnar, sore for solace and waxing in want,

Resolved readily her hand to have,

And shelter of his house,

But to his offer had she laughed, with laughter
    loud and long

"Marry me if you dare,"[72] said she, "For no man
    hath tamed me,

But toiled in the trying".

And so he dared.

Bright was the wedding,

And cheerful,

And the weather good,

And all feasted on ox, ale and mead,

And danced with the joyousness

That was rare now in these hard times.

Ere eve, as the feast wound to its end,

The sky did smart and smoke in surprise of storm,

Cancerous clouds swelling and swirling in poisonous
    pool,

Sickly skein, in grievance growling,

Bleak and blackly bloated;[73]

So, guests departed in haste

---

[72] Beth Rogers' rendering has "There aren't many who would want to take the risk." See Notes.

[73] The storm presages the breakdown in Gunnar and Hall-gerður's relationship, reflecting their inner mental states.

And folk homeward wove their way

By lantern's lambent light.

That night, rain rang teeming upon the obdurate
earth,

Hard as the hammer of Heimdall[74],

Nailing fast the groaning ground that pleaded in
pain,

As lightning leapt from out the roiling rump of
wrath.

Hallgerður was cold unto Gunnar

And proud,

And spite rolled easily from her tongue,

As a fish slips through the hand of the fisher,

The bitch of wounds, she,

Whose mordant mouth lashed scorn on all

In Floki's land[75].

---

[74] Heimdall (Heimdallr in Old Norse) was the watchman of the
gods and guardian of the Bifrost bridge which was the only
crossing between Midgard (the realm of humans) and Asgard
(the realm of the gods). Indeed, the Bifrost bridge connected all
of the nine realms. The bridge only opens if Heimdall permits
it. At the commencement of Ragnarok (the end of everything),
he would sound the Gjallarhorn which could be heard through
all the realms. It was predicted that Heimdall and Loki (the
Trickster god) would slay each other.

[75] Although Iceland had been discovered first by Naddodd from
the Faroe islands around 830, and then by the Swedish Sailor,

Ever she would have the best
Whether it could be afforded or not,
And whatever Gunnar's neighbours had
She also must possess.
Sorely had she offended Bergþora,
Njall's wife of many summers,
Esteeming her a fish wife,
Which honour screamed for blood
And crimson ran the iron dark earth that day,
One þrall[76] ne'er to see the morrow,
But it was Njall who had made the peace,
For his friendship with Gunnar triumphed
Over the enmity of the women,
And he knew well the politics of the henhouse,
For the moods of women turn upon a spindle,
And ever it was that women have dragged their
    men into wars
That men's better natures would have passed.[77]

Gardar Svavarsson, the first person to found a settlement was Hrafna Floki Vilgerðason in the 870s.

[76] Þrall = thrall. A slave or indentured worker. One held in bondage.

[77] Although this may raise the eyebrows of contemporary feminists, I have a maxim that current ideology should not be imposed on historical realities. The stereotype of the 'subversive woman' (also known as 'the sinister feminine') was a product

Still, the law judged Gunnar harshly,
And heavy the recompense demanded of him.
Gunnar did not easily forgive his wife
And forsook their bed for many a night.
The climate was a harsh one
And winters unforgiving,
And to make an enemy of a neighbour
Was to be fated.
As Thor sullen in his hall,
As the bear before the gates of winter,
So Gunnar, brooding in his furs,
Kept his silence and his counsel.

A Theft and a Fire

As autumn ebbed, strange sights were seen
About the farm, portending ill.
One evening, the sun burned red with such
    fierceness
As though the fires of Muspelheim[78]

---

of the same patriarchal power structures that gave rise to it.
Put simply, if women are deprived of overt power the natural
consequence is for women to exercise power covertly.

[78] The realm of primal fire, counterpart to Nifelheim, the realm
of ice. Together, they represent the energies of expansion and
contraction in the universe. It is the tension between them that
creates the steam from which existence comes into being.

Had unto Midgard[79] come,

And shone so ruddily upon Gunnar's farm

That Bergþora swore the house dripped blood,

And even Njall,

A straight man, he, not prone to imagining,

Muttered of omens dire.

A fortnight hence, a strange old crone,

Cowled in black and hunched with age

Whom no one knew,

Was seen upon the moor.

White and bleached was her face,

Wan and pale

As the pale faces of the dead,

And woven into her straggled hair,

The bones of children

That rattled and clinked in the wind

As she went her way a-wandering,

And much as men ran after her,

No one might close distance nor catch her.

So folk muttered darkly that of Midgard she was
     not,

But of Helheim spawned, and Hel her queen,

---

[79] Earth, the world of humans, animals and plants.

The realm of cold and unrequited potential[80]
Where men go who have led soft lives
And died peacefully in their beds,
Of children ne'er to sing the urgent song of youth,
Nor follow their fathers into war,
For the scream of life is heard most loudly
In the midst of death.
Winter came early and with vengeance laid on,
As like a host of warriors shivering in their ships,
And hay barely gathered in before sleet
Rained down upon the fields
And gales gustily the farmhouse shook.
Now was the time for gathering in,
Butter churned and cheese strained through cloth,
Animals brought down from pasture
To warm the house and feed on hay,
The weaker slain, their meat preserved,
Salted, cured and hung,

---

[80] The Norse and Greek view of the underworld was fundamentally different from the Christian. While the Christian idea of Hell (ironically derived from the name of the Norse goddess Hel) was predicated on sin, the Greek and Norse underworlds were places for those who had not realised their potential, excelled themselves in valour or had not acquired lasting fame. For the warrior societies of the ancient world, to be remembered for one's deeds was the difference between going to the underworld and going to the Elysian fields/Valhalla.

For food was scarce
And supplies might not last
The season of darkness,
More so Hallgerður's,
For whom sea mist ne'er did melt so fast
As her victuals[81].
Starvation lay upon a knife-edge,
And all wives tended to their stores.
Yet, good neighbour that he was,
Hay and cheese Gunnar had disbursed to
Families who might starve,
Which Hallgerður thought unmanly,
For the fellowship of men was alien to her.
And so it was that he resolved
One day to join an expedition
To gather in fish for salting
And seal for meat and blubber.
And thus, with weather closing in,
Men pitched their boats
Upon the siren-haunted sea[82]
And caught what they could.

---

[81] Victuals = food and drink.

[82] Sirens appear in the Greek sagas, for example in the *Odyssey*, but had their equivalents in the Celtic and Norse worlds. The Scottish version is known as the *Kelpie*. The closest Norse

Hallgerður, realising the straits they were in,
Stores emptying,
Portending shortage and direst need,
And wary of her husband's rage
Should he return to find the storehouses bare,
Ordered a servant to steal butter and cheese
From a neighbouring farm
And conceal the crime with fire,
But his honour sprang up before him
And vehemently declared no thief he.
For all, the spiteful wife averred to whip him
And cast him abroad to fend like a beast.
And so it came to pass that a night hence,
Horses were readied for the raid,
Panniers slung,
Faces blacked, hoods drawn up
And hooves muffled.
By stealth they would pass,
Dark to the moon and silent to the dog,
And ere long,
An orange glow lit bright the fleece of night,
Fulgent as the fires that burn atop the hills

---

equivalent is *Rán*, destroyer of ships and goddess of death for all
who perish at sea, and consort of Aegir, god of the stormy sea.

In days of doom,
And shouts of men carting water from river and well
To staunch the blaze,
All the while,
Hallgerður at her window waiting
Her robbers to return.
That family starved for want of the victuals
Hallgerður had taken,
She who always had enjoyed fine clothes
And warmth of food and fire,
Ne'er fallen to famine,
Nor walked barefoot in snow.
All in the parts thereabout knew
Who had instigated the fire,
Hallgerður's vaunted consumption no secret,
And Gunnar suspected too when he returned,
Tired and cold, to the farm
To find cheese and butter in abundance,
Cupboards brimming and spilling over.
Njall knew it also but foreswore accusation
That might have caused a feud,
But still Gunnar rode by him for a distance,
Testing him for aught he knew.
Now the truth had unfolded,
And with certainty in his heart,

Gunnar returned to his home
And struck his wife full hard upon the cheek,
For which she flashed such look of malice
He would not do it twice.
"If you had been a man," she had said,
"'Twould not have been me had to do the deed".
But the die was cast,
She had dishonoured his house by her violence,
Her mood molten and importune,
Like a wild mare no man might tame,
And Gunnar ere long arraigned before the Alþing,
The penalty of outlawry pronounced,
That he be exiled,
Afforded no shelter,
And any man who found him might kill him...
And there were men greedy enough to take his farm.
Njall had stood for his friend that dolorous day
Before the Lawspeaker,
Before the great stone,
But sterner voices did opinion sway,
Men of meanest motive and calloused heart,
And Gunnar hounded like the stag,
Shot with arrows,
And brought to ground.
He could not plead that it was Hallgerður

Who had done the deed,
And it was all hers,
For a man who cannot control his wife
And is led by her
Earns the contempt of his peers.
Better an outlaw feared
Than a fool mocked.

A Curse and a Vengeance

Leaving his farm, Gunnar,
Farmer and warrior, skilled in war,
Pledged himself in service to a foreign lord,
And many a battle fought under his banner,
But ere long, developing a sickness for home,
Asked leave of his lord to return,
Which was gratefully granted,
For he had fought valorously at his lord's side
And was come among the company of heroes,
Men of renown,
Who feast and drink in the mead hall
On nights of rain.
And so Gunnar,
Of many wounds and many scars,

Sailed the seal road[83] home,
And returning to his farm under cover of darkness,
Beheld his wife Hallgerður
In the company of a man he knew naught of,
For Hallgerður, alone now,
Had sought protection of her family,
And her father, coveting the farm,
Had sent men to secure it,
Lest neighbours, like ravening wolves,
Descended to take it.
Enraged was Gunnar,
Intemperate and beside himself,
Swollen and sore, with jealousy consumed,
So combustible it might at any moment erupt
As a geyser's steamy spume sprays up
From out the hoary hide of earth,
For a hot temper makes wax of reason.
Hallgerður had brought him low,
His very name disgraced,
And now had taken another man
Into his own house.
In his delusion, angrily he beat upon the door,
And when it was opened,

---

[83] The ocean. In *Beowulf* line 10 we find 'the whale road'.

Flew forth at the man and with war axe raised
Felled him in his fear,
His skull cleaved in twain,
Spilling his brains upon the floor.
Hallgerður, for once, being moved to pity,
Stood trembling, aghast,
For in Gunnar's madness,
Her brother had he slain,
In the flower of his youth cut him down,
As a pig before the slaughterer,
And the blood price would be high.
For all, with bovine numbness, Gunnar stared
Upon his work,
As one whose soul hath fled yet body walks,
Nor moved to clear it up,
The world his enemy now.
Ordering Hallgerður to her bed,
He sat awhile before the fire,
Enjoying the mastery of his own home
Which he vowed to defend unto his death.
But Hallgerður, festering in wrath,
And feigning sleep,

Carved the runes[84] of death upon the post,
By prick of thumb gave them life,
And lowly called on one so terrible,
Men should rather die than speak her name,
Angrboða,[85] midnight hag, Jöttun-born,
She-fiend of darkest murk and deepest fear,
Of writhing tentacles, of raking claws
And slithering hair,

---

[84] The Norse runes originated from the North Italic Etruscan alphabet, which was taken by traders up through central to northern Europe and adapted by the peoples of northern Germany and Scandinavia around 250-150 B.C. The runes were a proto-alphabet rather than a true alphabet. In a true alphabet, the letters are named after the sounds they represent but in a proto-alphabet the letters have names which signify ideas or things they represent... things that were important to the people of the time. The Norse world was a pre-literate culture, so the runes were never used for practical writing, but rather inscribed for symbolic, religious and magical purposes. The original Scandinavian runes consisted of 24 characters arranged in three rows called aetts. The entire rune sequence was known as the Elder Futhark, named after the first six letters. See Pennick, Nigel. (2002) *Complete Illustrated Guide to Runes*. Element Books. pp 68-69.

[85] A jöttun (or giantess from Jötunheimr) and wife of Loki, the god of chaos and misrule, who gives him the underworld goddess Hel, Fenris wolf and the serpent Jörmungandir. She is the mother of monsters who will bring about Ragnarok, the end of existence. Her name means 'the one who brings grief' or 'harm bidder'. Privately, I believe that Grendel's mother in *Beowulf* may have been based on her.

Mother of monsters, turning in her lair,
Spawner of serpent and of wolf, Loki's brood,
Trickster god who didst Fenris, snapping,
Rip from blackest womb,
And laid upon her plague-bruised breast,
To suck the milk of death from poison teat
And drink deep the foaming wine of frenzy.
Hallgerður, of remorse unshriven, did this,
Reached down into that lightless place,
Daughter of her mother's arte,
Taught in shrouded whisper by secret flame,
As strange shadows moved across the wall,
And thus did pass the hour,
Her curse gone down
And retribution near.
And death *did* come
And came by night.
Five warriors stalked the sodden moor
'Neath corpse light of waning moon,
And to the lonely farmhouse made,
With gifts of horror,
Given all too soon.
Five murderers they,
Men killers, night strikers,
Battle-maddened,

Sons of Oðinn, raven-born,[86]
War axes tight-grasped in whitened fist
And swords keen to bite,
Serpent blades, forged of damascene arte,[87]
Scabbarded for the journey,
Until unsheathed in anger
As a man stands before a woman
In the glory of his nakedness,
And coming upon the place
Laid waste.
Loud the pounding upon the door,
Hard the rain of blows
And breathing press of men,
Till broken, splintered through and through,

---

[86] Refers to Odin's ravens Huginn ('Thought') and Muninn ('Memory' or 'Mind'), representing Odin's ability to project his consciousness. Ravens are also birds of death, denoting Odin in his death aspect.

[87] 'Damascene' refers to pattern welding, whereby the main shaft of the sword was composed of interwoven strips of iron, fused by heat then hammered and cooled, the cutting edges being forged separately to the main blade. When cool, this left a serpentine pattern in the resulting steel. The technique originated in the Islamic world and increased the resilience of the blade to shattering. Iron that contains more than 0.35% carbon becomes steel and Viking blacksmiths worked with iron of min 0.8%). The leading manufacturer of high-quality swords from the 9th to 11th centuries was Ulfberht, a Frankish armourer based in the Rhineland.

Framed in the void by moon's sallow sheen,
Five avengers armoured,
Giants of men, with axes raised,
In coats of mail they,
Helmeted in iron and gold,
Tunics dyed with blood
Of fifty wars
And cloaks heavy with rain;
Berserkers[88] broiling in want of war,
Ruffians, red-faced,
Drunk on mead and herbs of wrath[89],
And venom in their veins.
Into the house of doom they poured
And laid about with axe and sword,
Ne'er chair nor table left unturned,
The rushing tide of death washed all around.
Yet Gunnar, knowing his fate was nigh,
And yearning yet for hero's death,
Launched himself with battle cry
Into the fray.
As a bear baited, torn by tooth,

---

[88] Ferocious warriors who leapt into battle and fought without body armour. Renowned for their frenzied fighting.

[89] Probably henbane.

In agony of wound,
Of lifeless limb and flailing feet,
Slipping and sliding in baneful blood,
Gunnar, for his wife, cried out,
To Hallgerður, for help,
But she, the skulking cat,
Had fled already in the night,
Slipping quietly out as he had dozed
Content before his fire,
Her brother's brains yet lying about the floor,
And at the last, denied redoubt,
Gunnar with mighty cry
Gave up the joyous bright glory of his life
In one red wash of woe,
To be sprayed across the hearth
At which he had warmed his feet
In winters past.

A Song of Mourning[90]

Thus passed Gunnar to the land of his fathers,
By a woman brought low,

---

[90] During their courtship, Hallgerður is described as 'Bright and beauteous as morning's song'. Now, in the closing of the tragedy, we have a Song of Mourning, the reversal in fortune of the protagonists.

As Baldur to Hel's dour realm
By mistletoe sent
And life and joy forever gone
From Valhöll's vaults,
His light put out.[91]
For Gunnar all folk keened,
A man of promise he,
Scion of a noble line,
Who wrought the land by his own hand,
And bent it to the plough,
And in his youth and vigour
Earned golden words,
A man to share ale with and call friend,
Betrayed by such vain and shrewish nature
As would pluck the eyes of reason
From heads of men.
Pitiless the wanton works by women wrought,

---

[91] Baldur, the fairest and brightest of the gods, has a premonition of his own death, and to this end, his mother Frigg obtains promises from all the nine worlds that nothing will hurt him, but Loki, transformed into a servant girl, obtains from Frigg the knowledge that only the mistletoe plant can harm him. Loki then gets Baldur's blind brother, Hod, to aim a branch of mistletoe at Baldur's heart, which strikes him through. The passage is comparing the death of Gunnar with that of Baldur and saying that Gunnar too died as an act of treachery and mourns the loss of his 'light'.

Undoers of dynasties, poisoners of cups,

The dagger that lurketh behind the curtain of sleep.

How tangled had been Gunnar's *wyrd,*[92]

That his life had come to this,

To suffer such reversal

And such death,

For what lies within a man's own hand

And what to Fate

Is a mystery to all.

Months passed, and folk still recounted

The story of Gunnar and Hallgerður,

But in time it would be overshadowed

By mean and bloody strife,

Great families vying for land,

And settling of scores,

Quiet men silenced by din of war,

Farms torched and farmers slain before their wives,

Rich harvest for the burners of the dead,

And all the while the King of Norway

Cast envious eyes upon Ísland.[93]

---

[92] The web of fate or destiny of each person, woven by the three Norns. Over time, our word *weird* has come to mean something strange and otherworldly.

[93] King Haakon IV. In 1262-4, Iceland was absorbed into the kingdom of Norway.

And of Hallgerður, life passed quietly,
Nor did her beauty fade
But her hair ever gold as ripened wheat
And cheeks pale with the milk of wrath
That glowed with the whiteness of snow,
And so remained until one day,
Before the Alþing at Þingvellir,
Hallgerður her bright tresses tossed
In the cool morning air,
And the glorious glint of light was noticed
By a passing merchant from Norway,
But of *his* fate, none shall bear witness
But the wind and the grave

Notes

There are two main traditions of literature in Iceland.
The first is poetry, which is differentiated into the
Poetic Eddas[94] (tales about the creation of the world,
the giants, the Norse gods and their rivalries, and the
end of the world – Ragnarok), and Skaldic poetry,

---

[94] There is a Prose Edda, written by Snorri Sturluson in the
13th century.

written to celebrate the deeds and generosity of kings and lords (with a touch of embellishment perhaps). Eddic poetry always used simple metrical forms and the author was always anonymous, whereas skaldic poetry could use quite complex non-rhyming metre, ranging from the relatively simple *fornyrðislag* to the 'courtly metre' known as *dróttkvætt*, and the *skald* was always a named poet. Norse poetry was composed to be recited and was transmitted orally, only being written down in the early Middle Ages. In skaldic poetry in particular, meter is interwoven with cadence (the up and down modulation of voice), alliteration (successive words that begin with the same letter), *heiti* (the poetic substitution of one word for another, e.g. 'steed' for 'horse'), kenning (the joining of two words to form a figure of speech e.g. a king is a 'ring-giver', a sword is 'bane of shield', 'wound-fire' or 'shield biter')[95] and caesura (a break in the middle of a line which lends driving momentum to the poem). The *Hávarmál* and the *Völuspá* are two of the best known Eddas, but it is not hard to imagine *Beowulf* beginning as a skaldic

---

[95] The raven banner of Harald Hardrada was known as 'Land Waster'.

poem prior to being written down as an epic poem in Anglo-Saxon times.

The second tradition is the Sagas. A saga (from the Old Norse verb *segja* meaning 'to tell')[96] is a narrative prose form, centred on a single protagonist or group of people, and offering tales of heroism and strife, of honour, justice and revenge. Of these, there are three main forms: the sagas of kings (*Konungasögur*), the sagas of Icelanders (*Íslendinga sögur*), also known as the family sagas, and the legendary sagas (*Fornaldarsögur*). Examples of kings' sagas are the *Heimskringla* and *Jómsvíkinga* sagas. The family sagas include Nijall's saga, Egil's saga, the saga of Eric the Red, and the saga of the People of Laxárdalr (*Laxdaela* saga). An example of a legendary saga would be the Saga of the Völsungs (*Völsunga Saga*).

The sagas are, in general, stories about real people, but, being derived from oral accounts, can include elements of the legendary, as in the Saga of the Völsungs. There are often intrusions of the supernatural also such as ghosts and curses, but here there is a

---

[96] There is also a Norse goddess called Sága, goddess of events in time. The noun 'saga' is spelled *sögur*.

difference between the Norse sagas and the epic poems of the broader Germanic world.

The Middle High German *Nibelungenlied* and the Anglo-Saxon *Beowulf* are epic poems, although, as said above, *Beowulf* may have originated as skaldic poetry. The epic poem was the ancient equivalent of cinema, offering a seamless blend of fact and fantasy, often centred around a quest which the hero must fulfil to achieve his destiny and become fully himself. Whereas in the Norse sagas, there is no interaction between the gods and men, in the epic poem, the hero struggles to fulfil his destiny in spite of the capriciousness of the gods and other supernatural agencies. Whereas the Norse sagas are generally biographical, the epic poems concern themselves with the legendary. The tradition of the epic poem stretches centuries back in time to the Greek epics such as *The Iliad*, *The Odyssey,* the *Argonautica* and Virgil's *Aeneid*; indeed, we might trace it all the way back to the *Epic of Gilgamesh* from ancient Sumeria. The quest of Jason for the Golden Fleece, Odysseus' struggle to make his way home to his wife: the epic quest began at the very intersection with prehistory before flowering once more in the Germanic Dark Age legends of Siegfreid and Beowulf.

Sagas endured because people wanted their names and deeds to be immortalised, but we must remember that most of the Icelandic sagas were written down in the thirteenth century, several hundred years after the events, often from oral accounts. Many were written by one man: Snorri Sturluson, often referred to as 'the Homer of the North'. He was writing during a time of civil war between landed families (see below) and there was an urgency to record the ancestral histories before they disappeared. Sturluson himself was assassinated during this conflict by members of a rival family.

The 'family sagas' detail the struggles, successes and feuds of particular families, and these are unique to Iceland (which never adopted the feudal system of the rest of Europe where no one would have written a saga about ordinary folk), and it is to this group of sagas that *The Story of Gunnar and Hallgerður* belongs. Presumably, family sagas would have been recited at family or clan gatherings.

The Story of Gunnar and Hallgerður is contained within the larger *Njall's Saga*, set around the year 1000, which is also the time when Iceland was Christianised, although the traditional Viking mindset and culture continued to hold sway for many decades,[97] and I have emphasised the pagan aspects of Norse myth and religion at the expense of Christianity. Originally founded in 874 A.D. as a 'proto-democracy' or commonwealth governed by the legislative body, the *Alþing*, and by the Grey Goose Laws or *Grágás*, by the thirteenth century, Iceland had begun to dissolve into civil war as powerful land magnates fought for dominance, a period known as the Sturlunga era (1220-1264) which ended with the absorption of Iceland into the Norwegian kingdom under Haakon IV in 1262-4. Although the saga would have been written down in the thirteenth century, the story is based on oral accounts dating back to the eleventh century.

I first came upon the story in *Medieval Warfare* magazine Vol. 9, Issue 6, in a modern prose rendering by Beth Rogers PhD of the University of Iceland. The saga is in the vein of a teaching story about honour and what happens when a man marries a woman who is not good for him. Thus, it serves a similar purpose to the Greek *Odyssey* and *Argonautica* in teaching young men about the different kinds of women they are likely to

---

[97] The runes were not banned by the Church in Iceland until 1639.

encounter in life and the different ways in which men and women wield power. But I saw it also in the larger sense as an exploration of the 'sinister feminine': the dangerous, destructive woman, the *femme fatale*, the *beldam* (from the French *belle dame sans merci*[98]), and this poetic adaptation is intended as an exploration of one aspect of the feminine psyche and not as an anti-feminist diatribe. The 'sinister feminine' featured in the Old Testament in the story of Samson and Delilah, in Greek tragedy in such plays as Euripides' *Medea* and Aeschylus' *Clytemnestra*, in the sixth century Merovingian queen Fredegund, and it was also explored in Elizabethan theatre: in the scheming Lady Macbeth (not forgetting the deceptive Weird Sisters) in Shakespeare's *Macbeth*, in the seductive Queen Gertrude in *Hamlet* who may be more complicit in murder than we suspect, and in Webster's *White Devil* and *Duchess of Malfi*; not least in the treacherous Milady de Winter in Alexandre Dumas' *The Three Musketeers* (1844). In fairness, as mentioned earlier in a footnote, it was the patriarchal power structure in the first place that gave rise to the stereotype of the 'subversive woman'.

---

[98] 'A beautiful woman without mercy', and the title of Keats' famous supernatural poem.

The story also offers an insight into the structure of Scandinavian society, composed of tight-knit communities where honour to clan and obligation to neighbour were paramount, and the actions of one's wife reflected on the honour of the husband. This was a society in which a perceived sleight could trigger a generational feud. Although ostensibly a story about love gone wrong, *The Story of Gunnar and Hallgerður* is also (in its original context) about the squandering of inheritance through bad choices in marriage: Vikings were not a romantic people (they didn't have the luxury of being so) and their principal concerns centred on honour, family and inheritance. Naturally, being a clan-based society, anyone outside the network of family and ties of loyalty was fair game to be exploited or killed. There was no abstract concept of 'humanity', human rights, 'social good' or common morality, and whereas, in our own time, war is an exceptional event, it is fair to describe Norse society as a 'culture of war', so much so that by the eighth century, the runic alphabet had itself lost all those runes which related to non-violent human interaction, the 24-letter

Elder Futhark being replaced by the 16-letter Younger Futhark.[99]

Aware that an academic translation is not the same as a living, breathing story, I have attempted a free retelling of the tale in my own words, simplifying the story and reconstructing it in the poetic form, thus removing it from its original prose context. In short, I have re-imagined it, and the resulting poem thus departs in many respects from the original, nor is it intended as a literal retelling.

The problem facing me was how to use the epic voice to recite a story of an Icelandic farming community that is not by nature epic. The solution was to *make* it epic by imagining it read before a company of warriors in the mead hall, calling on 'the five warriors' who come to exact revenge on Gunnar, and introducing a supernatural theme (the early omens and Hallgerður's curse) not present in the original; the description of Angboða is inspired by H.P. Lovecraft. I have introduced Gunnar's mistaken killing of Hallgerður's brother in anger as a motive for the revenge attack upon the farm and filled in the

---

[99] Pennick, Nigel. (2002) *Complete Illustrated Guide to Runes.* Element Books. Pp68-69.

gaps about what Hallgerður was doing during Gunnar's exile. As to what happened to the farm, presumably it devolved to Hallgerður, (as Icelandic law – and Norse law in general – allowed a woman to hold property under her own title[100]) but she would have been in a precarious position so would have looked to her family for support and security, hence her brother's presence at the farm. Throughout, my objective has been to create a sense of immersion in the landscape, the characters and their motivations, to get into their minds and evoke a sense of 'being there'. The only phrase I have borrowed verbatim from Beth Rogers' version is the expression 'bitch of wounds', used to describe Hallgerður, and a wonderfully evocative phrase it is.

Pronunciation guide

In this poem, I have used some letters unique to Scandinavian languages, so it is important to know how these are pronounced.

---

[100] This would change under the influence of Christianity.

þ (lower case) and Þ (upper case). Known as the letter *Thorn* in Icelandic and Old English, it was derived from the Old Norse *Thurs* (*Þurs*) rune (Proto-German *Thurisaz*), which symbolised not only a thorn, but also the primeval race of giants known as *Thursar* (*Þursar*) or *Jöttun*, which represented the forces of chaos constantly trying to undermine the ordered universe. For practical purposes, it represents the 'th' sound as in 'thick' or 'thin'. For example, the Icelandic parliament (which is still called the Alþing) would have been pronounced 'Althing'. Likewise, the Anglo-Saxon 'aþeling', meaning a prince, would have been pronounced 'atheling'. The god 'Þorr' would have been pronounced 'Thorr' (with an elongated 'r'). Pronounce 'thick' while placing your fingers on your Adam's apple where the larynx is located and your Adam's apple doesn't vibrate. For this reason, we say that the letter *Thorn* is 'unvoiced'.

Thurs rune   *Letter Thorn*

ð (lower case) and Ð (upper case). Known as *Eth*, this was pronounced like the 'th' in 'with' or 'they', i.e., more like a 'v' sound. So Hallgerður would have been pronounced 'Hallgerthur', and Angrboða pronounced 'Angrbotha'. Pronounce 'with' while placing your fingers on your Adam's apple, and your Adam's apple vibrates. For this reason, we say that the letter *Eth* is 'voiced'. *Eth* never occurred at the beginning of a word.

Although the 'th' spelling still persists in modern Scandinavian, the 'th' *sound* itself disappeared from Scandinavian languages in the Middle Ages, (1300s for Danish and 1400s for Swedish and Norwegian), being replaced by 't', except in Icelandic. So 'Althing' would be pronounced 'alting' and 'Thorr' would be pronounced 'Torr'. While Scandinavian languages abandoned the 'th' sound, English retained it. *Eth* was replaced by 'Dh' and then by 'd'. So Oðin becomes Odin, but his name wasn't originally pronounced with a 'd'. Concurrently, the letters *Thorn* and *Eth* similarly disappeared from Scandinavian alphabets, except again in Icelandic where they still persist. This was because Iceland was colonised relatively late in the ninth century so its language is closest to Old Norse.

Much of this dropping of Old Norse letters had to do with the Christianisation of Scandinavia (the runes

311

and the letters derived from them being considered pagan) and the preference for the Gothic script in northern Europe (particularly the German Empire) from around 1150 to the 17th century. The letter *Thorn* was replaced by a letter that resembled a Y, which is how we get expressions like 'Ye olde curiositie shoppe' in English, although the 'ye' was still pronounced as 'the'.

 *The letter Thorn was substituted by a letter resembling a 'Y' so that Þe became 'ye'*

This is not to be confused with the second-person plural personal pronoun 'Ye' which meant 'you', where the 'y' sound comes from the letter *Yogh*, derived from the Carolingian letter G. *Yogh* has nothing to do with yoghurt!

The death knell for *Thorn* and *Eth* occurred with the invention of the Gutenberg printing press around 1440, which standardised printing using the medieval Gothic script known as 'Blackletter', and which did not contain these letters.

33 *Letter Yogh*

æ (lower case) and Æ (upper case). Known as the letter *Ash* (*Askr* in Old Norse), the digraph (or ligature) 'ae' was originally pronounced 'a' as in 'Alfred'. Thus 'Aesir', the creator gods of Norse mythology, would be pronounced 'Asir'. This is confusing because the same 'ae' digraph occurs in Latin, pronounced variously as 'eye' and 'ee'. Hence, we pronounce 'praeternatural' (from the Latin *praeter naturam*) as 'preeternatural'.

W (lower case) and w (upper case). In both Old Norse and Anglo Saxon, the letter 'w' is pronounced softly as a 'w' and not as a hard 'v' as it is in modern German. Old English used the letter *Wynn*, borrowed from the *Wunjo* rune, meaning 'joy', to represent the 'w' sound, which dropped out of English around 1300 due to the import of the 'uu' combination from the French. By the eighth century, the *Wunjo* rune itself had already dropped out of the Elder Futhark and was missing from the Younger Futhark, which is why we don't find it in Old Norse literature.

Wunjo rune from Elder Futhark

Þ þ

Letter Wynn

The Yew Tree
(After Edgar Allan Poe)

Last night a fly crawled in my head
And I began to hear
The voices of the dead,
Who whispered to me all night long,
Not stopping e'en at break of day,
But always and eternal plied
Their sibilant song,
Saying to me, "There are such sights to see
But you shall only see them
If you become as we".
Wherefore, went me to the ancient yew
That shivered in the morning dew
And hanged myself from sturdy rope
That I might see the Other Side
And know that it were true.
Then took me knife and cut me down
While breath remained and lest I swoon,
And when I opened up my eyes
Full wonder met my view;
A whole world peopled with the dead
Who walked through windows and through walls,
Through nightmare gardens and gothic halls,

Until at length I left this earth
And flew upon the roaring wind,
Past spinning worlds and flaring sun,
Past and future all as one,
And at length lay worn upon the turf
In churchyard far from human home,
Through which the fog did writhe and turn
In ways that chilled me to the bone,
And there among the mildewed stones,
Cold and damp with sick decay,
An old crone stood,
Wrapped in black and eyes of grey,
Who said to me, "Come away
To yonder wood
And there shalt see
What no man should".
Wherefore I went with her to that foul wood
Of dripping branch and rotting leaf,
So dark it was beyond belief,
And there in grove of gnarléd oak,
Garbed in raven-feathered cloak,
Spat full into my mouth her stinking spume,
So wretched, upon it I did choke,
And bade me walk with bleeding feet
The new dug grave

Of each poor robbed and nameless corpse
Who called up from beneath the ground,
 "Return to us the life we crave!"
Then I didst stumble, turn and run
From that dread wood where shone no sun,
As their spirits rose from leafy mound
And blindly hovered 'mong the trees
That henceforth I would shun,
But to my home ran for very life
To my children and my wife,
As dawn began to break upon the east,
And straightway burned the ancient yew
That shivered in the morning dew,
For no more would I endure
This disturbéd state of mind
That simple folk judge unkind,
And laying myself upon my bed,
That cursed fly crawled out my head,
And now I see what all men see
Until the day this life shall leave
And the spirits of the dead
Shall come for me.

Notes

The Yew Tree is a disconcerting nightmare trip through alternate reality in continuous verse and using irregular rhyming to create a sense of breathlessness and panic. It begins with a form of supernatural assault: a spirit inhabiting the body of a fly enters our protagonist's head and opens the doors of otherworldly perception... really a form of initiation. Our protagonist cannot cope with what he sees and refuses the gift by symbolically burning the yew tree, after which the spirit leaves him. Henceforth, he is like 'other men'. So, the poem explores the subtle boundary between spiritual experience and mental illness, between inspiration and madness. It questions the comfortable idea of a 'unitary Self', and it posits the opening of spiritual perception as both a blessing and a curse.

The Yew Tree draws on the association between the fly and the raven as messengers of the dead, since flying creatures were associated with the 'Powers of the Air' (for example, Beelzebub or Baalzebuth as 'Lord of the Flies'), and the night hag often seen by victims of sleep paralysis. Possession through the ear of the sleeping person is a tradition going all the way back to the Sumerian exorcism tablets, and was said to cause buzzing in the ear and, in extreme cases, the hearing of spirit voices. The poem also contains references to necromantic rites that involve walking with cut feet over the graves of the dead to establish communion with spirits, and to strangulation as a means of inducing altered perception, with mythological reference to Odin who hanged himself from the World Tree to obtain the runes (although, in this case, Odin is suspended face down toward the underworld – think of the Hanged Man of the Tarot). The yew is, of course, the tree of death since it traditionally grows in or near graveyards and is extremely poisonous, but also, being evergreen, is a symbol of life after death. The action of spitting in the mouth is derived from ancient shamanic methods whereby the 'magical virtue' of the shaman was transmitted to the initiate or one to be healed.

An inspiration for *The Yew Tree* was Poe's *The Raven*, with its similar helter-skelter pace and urgency, although I have eschewed Poe's use of a double rhyme in each line. However, readers may also find inspiration in the hellish paintings of Hieronymus Bosch and Goya (for example *Vuelo de Brujas*), and in *Night on a Bare Mountain* by Mussorgsky which was so beautifully animated in Walt Disney's *Fantasia*.

Poems
of
2022

A Solitary Man

I'm a solitary man.
The comforts of love have I known,
Kindness given and kindness shown,
With wise men and philosophers I have talked,
And with Jesus walked
The dusty mile,
Done good where I pass,
Earned applause from some
And others none,
But it don't bother me what I can't control,
I look after my own and do what I can,
I'm a solitary man.

The wild road have I trod,
Seen cruelty by Man no man should see,
Kicked my heels in southern ports,
In sultry bars knocked back shorts,
Walked the lights on Broadway,
In Vegas played my chips,
But the city's too dirty for long to stay,
So I took my burden and walked away,
The problems of the world ain't my own,

I take my pleasure where I can,
I'm a solitary man.

The boards of life I've played[101],
Visited amusements,
And sights, I've seen them all,
Taken my turn on the merry-go-round[102]
And found no peace withal,
The consolements of women
Picked up for a night,
Left me feeling empty
And afforded no delight;
And at length I said 'let it be',
And left it all behind,
All the empty horses and all the straw men,
The ambitious and the blind,
The politician with the dazzling smile,
His glittering wife
And the whole darn world of human strife;
Now I hold my life in my hand

---

[101] In other words, the 'game of life', as in a gaming board.

[102] The fairground imagery symbolises the distractions of the world.

And somewhere there's a plan,
I'm a solitary man.

And always I return to the solitary life,
Watch the settling of the dust of time,
The stars wheel and suns burn
And frost coats my leathers in icy rime,
A pack, a knife and a ten-dollar bill
And the call of birdsong on evenings still,
A water bottle, a campfire and sleeping on hay,
Jumping the carriage
'Twixt night and day;
In the fight with death, life will always lose
But while I live, this life I'll choose.
I'm a solitary man.

Notes

A Solitary Man is the story of an American who feels
overwhelmed by modern city life with all its ambition,
competition and decadence, and embarks on a journey
through the back roads of the states to find simplicity.
No longer does he carry the world on his shoulders; he
looks after himself. I chose to portray him as a middle

aged, rugged type of man dressed in leathers, very much after the fashion of the archetypal frontiersman of American legend.

The Franciscans have a saying, 'Remove the meaningless to reveal the meaningful', and the ideal of spiritual simplicity (in contrast to spiritual poverty) is the cornerstone of all spiritual traditions. By rejecting the false and the worldly, our protagonist has taken his first step on the path.

The poem ultimately takes inspiration from Roger Miller's classic song *King of the Road*.

The Antlered Man

Wipe not thy mouths, my treasured ones,
Till thou hast drunk the god's blood
That twists the innards of the mind,
And in its fever,
Moves the soul to wilder clime.
Time will be when blood and guts of faun
Shall hang in strings from mouths
Glutted with wine,
Ivy ground by whitest teeth arouse,
And women call the Great God Pan
To loose the chains that bind;
When green juice o'er red lips shall flow,
And pale hips lewdly dance
With arching back and blooded breasts
Before the antlered man;
Time will when moon-washed feet
With manic might
Shall pound the pine-strewn floor among the tall
    trees
To swoon of pipes,
And ye shall whirl and scream in the mad night.
Our lord Dionysus is a nail

Driven in the head of reason,
Whose cup doth make the senses rock,
The bonds of form destroy,
And the unsung song of basest Nature
Shall wind and ring through forest thick,
Dangerous desires unlock,
That seek thee darker love and stranger joy.
Soon, my treasured ones,
The mind will bend
And you shall run amok
In heedless passion,
Blood lust without end;
Maenads maddened by the gods touch,
Lank haired, wild and wan,
Thrash through thicket, tear through tree
Rampage, rip and rend.
Make haste, my treasured ones,
And take the winding track
That leads up from the sea,
To where the antlered man doth wait;
In the place where no birds sing,
In the glade where the hell moon shines,
He 'waits thee patiently;
Where death is life and life is death,
And all Existence holds its breath,

And his brides run wild and free,
Dance to the sound of beating drums
And fly the air in ecstasy.[103]

Notes

In Titian's *Bacchus and Ariadne* (1520-23), Bacchus (the
Roman name for Dionysus, or, more strictly, Dionysos)
leaps from his chariot to greet Ariadne, abandoned
on the shores of Naxos by her lover Theseus. It is a
beautiful Renaissance painting, lush in colour and
detail, and somewhat romantically inclined as far
as the left side of the painting goes, but look closely
and there is a darker side to the painting, for among
the crowd of revellers following Bacchus on the right
(shadowed) side is a child dragging the decapitated
head of a calf behind it while another reveller holds
aloft the severed hind limb of a faun. A third figure
struggles as his body is wound and constricted by
serpents in the manner of Laocoon in Homer's *Iliad*
who attempted to warn the Trojans of the Greeks'

---

[103] A reference to drug-induced out of the body experiences, the
foundational myth of the flying witch.

deceit but was struck by Athena with sea serpents for his trouble. In Sophocles' version, he was said to be a priest of Apollo who had married against his vows.

The rites of Dionysus, which in Roman and Hellenic times assumed the role of a mystical religion (characterised by Orphism) had a very different origin in the Greek dark ages as an ecstatic cult, in which Dionysus assumed the 'spirit of the vine' who intoxicated his celebrants. The cult is thought to have originated in Thrace where Dionysus was called Sabazius but may have migrated from North Africa centuries before. The classical story of the birth of Dionysus by Zeus from Semele, the infant Dionysus' death at the hands of the Titans who tear the child apart and eat it, the destruction of the Titans by fire, and the birth of Man from their ashes, is a later attempt to absorb Dionysus into the Olympian hierarchy. Yet the Olympian myth points to a powerful truth that Man is human but with a divine spark, and it was this spiritual understanding that provided the foundation for the Hellenistic mystery cult, Orphism, and the later Roman variants, which eschewed the ecstatic dancing and violence of the earlier cult. For an understanding of what the earlier cult was like, we can consult Euripides' play *The Bacchae* which describes the god Dionysus taking revenge on King Pentheus of Thebes, of the house of Cadmus, for banning his rites. The source of Dionysus' anger was that the original King Cadmus had disputed his daughter Semele's conception at the hand of Zeus, instead ascribing Dionysus' birth to human origin, thus denying Dionysus' birthright. Dionysus cleverly exploits King Pentheus' weakness: Pentheus wants to see the Bacchae dance and so he hides in a tree where his hiding place is betrayed and, in her frenzy, his own mother Agave tears off his head.

The primitive rites of Dionysus took place in a clearing marked out for ritual use. The Bacchae (Latin) or Maenads (Greek) donned faun or leopard skins, wore crowns of leaves and berries, and carried a thyrsus which was a staff of giant fennel wrapped with ivy leaves and topped by a pinecone (in other words a phallic symbol). They would drink wine probably mixed with entheogens (possibly ivy or henbane) and dance ecstatically to the beat of drums and pipes. Visualise the kind of dances involved in Haitian vodou, and they would have been very similar, particularly in the trance-inducing backward neck flick. Deep in ecstatic trance they would twine snakes in their hair and run wild through the forest, tearing apart whatever animal they found, even descending on farms and tearing apart cattle and goats. They became such a threat to settled society that their rites were banned in several Greek city states. At the heart of the rites was the idea of the primal spirit of life transcending the outward bonds of form: the Spirit is so expansive that, in its ecstasy, it literally tears matter apart.

The poem explores the boundaries between order and spontaneity and what defines 'innocence'. The innocence of our natural state is very different from what we define as innocence in a socialised environment, i.e. someone who is bright, open and curious, and who isn't calculating and duplicitous. But what are the consequences of returning to our natural instinctual innocence? Is loss of the state of natural innocence the price we pay for civilisation? We say that a baby is innocent, but a baby is a monster of selfishness, and without socialisation would grow up to be completely feral and unaware of anyone else's needs except its own.

Can the women followers of Dionysus be considered proto-feminists rebelling against the strictures of early Greek patriarchal society, or do they simply speak to us of the depths of feminine wildness? Certainly, one of the cult's devotees was Olympias, mother of Alexander the Great, and there was a strong woman! But I think the rites of Dionysus also illumine the dark vein of wild sexuality that throbs deep in the nature of every woman. The cult affords us an uncomfortable look at what lies beneath the veneer of socialisation: the Unconscious or Deep Self is a seething cauldron of animalistic instincts and emotions that lies just below the surface. Finally, the poem raises questions about the assumptions of Judeo-Christian religion: is the violence of nature reconcilable with Divine love?

I have left the identity of the antlered man vague. Is he a cult leader wearing the headdress of a stag or is he an inhuman spirit or entity, a 'god' in the most primitive animistic sense? And is there a parallel between the god Dionysus surrounded by his women followers and the Black Man of the Sabbat in the medieval witch cult? A fascinating conjecture indeed! This, then, is a poem that speaks of something dark and disturbing in the primitive psyche enacted in the ecstatic cults of the ancient world, not the 'sanitised paganism' reinvented for modern times.

The Ashes of My Heart

O my dear Joanna,
The truest love I ever knew,
Though I swore together we'd grow old
And I'd be true to you,
You I'll never see again
And my letter bids adieu.

Today they take me from my cell
And hang me from a rope,
Though I strived to be a good man
And did my best to cope,
Now these words I write to you
Mark the end of all my hope.

My conscience would not let me rest,
I couldn't handle what I saw,
Every day atrocities,
Each new day a war;
My gentle nature took offence,
My heart bled like a sore.

Corruption like a crimson stain
Spread throughout the land,
And above it, towering over all,
To a military band,
The grimly smiling general
With a crop clasped in his hand,

Who with flippant wave
Rolls out his corps,
Soldiers raping women,
Men shot by the score,
And armed police with batons
Riding horses o'er the poor.

And so I went to fight
For I could stand no more.
I loaded my revolver,
On my back a rifle bore,
And sailed a boat to foreign lands
On a stranger shore.

I went to fight oppression,
I went to fight the state.
Enmity became my art,
My heart consumed by hate,

And I didn't realise what I'd lost
Until it was too late.

In my zeal I was blind,
Of vengeance did I sup,
The fire of rage consumed me
The anger burned me up,
But all the anger gave me
Was poison in my cup.

I executed prisoners
With sacks pulled on their heads,
I bombed the homes of peasants
And burned them in their beds,
And with each new act of war
Still more the next one dreads.

The horrors I committed,
I was not to blame,
I was forced to do them
All in freedom's name,
And all the things I'd fought against,
I did just the same.

The shelled-out towns I wandered
Among the bodies and debris,
I won the cause of freedom
But no people left to free;
Ask not why the baby cries alone,
It cries because of me.

I forsook the love we had
For that higher state of mind,
Possessed by vain idealism
That forgets how to be kind,
And for the sake of conscience
I left you all behind.

I fought a war not mine to fight,
In delusion took a stand,
Now I am a stranger to myself
And a stranger to my land,
Exiled in the ruins of misery,
Of cities sunk into the sand.

Nor can I return, Joanna,
But forever be apart,
My duty was to you, my love,
Too late again to start,
And all I have left to give you
Are the ashes of my heart.

Notes

Ashes tells the story of a man, who out of ideological conviction and a natural sense of justice, goes abroad to fight as a mercenary in a foreign war. He could be one of the many British men who went to fight against the fascists in the Spanish Civil War or one of the idealistic young Muslim men who left Britain to fight for the Islamic Caliphate. It really doesn't matter. Ideological and tribal wars always result in mutually assured destruction, in which the very basis of civil society is brought to ruin, warlords take over, and no one learns the lessons of history. In the end, one militia group is as bad as another, and 'freedom' becomes a hollow word, justifying all manner of civilian atrocities. The question the poem asks is a timely and eternal one: how a civilised and principled person can become a monster when he becomes part of a theatre of war. I think one reason is that when we identify with an abstract ideal like socialism, justice, equality, freedom or religion, we override our higher emotions like kindness and empathy which govern our moral compass, and so the end justifies the means. Of course, war itself releases dangerous atavistic impulses and a kind of 'group bloodlust' or 'red mist' takes over, in which we no longer recognise ourselves. *Ashes* is a companion piece to *The Pipes of Scarrowness*, which is similarly about naïve, idealistic young men signing up for a cause they do not fully understand.

Bartholomew Fair
(Traditional)

Sing me a song of red, red roses,
Rosy and wanton[104] as the dawn of the day,
Sing me six bridesmaids bearing their posies
In blue silken dresses that swirl as they sway.
Sing of a young man who'll give those red roses
And plight his love on the point of his knee,
Sing I shall marry my love who proposes,
And a fleet ship to carry me over the sea.
Sing oh that young man shall not forsake me,
Say he shall have the courage to dare,
For I would have many children by thee,
Promise thou'll marry me at Bartholomew Fair.

I'll sing thee a line of fine dandy dancers,
Gaily decked out in yellow and green,
I'll sing thee a carriage drawn by white prancers[105],

---

[104] While 'wanton' has the connotation of 'promiscuous', I am using it in the context of desire. The dawn is the 'swelling' or pregnancy of the day, and thus mirrors the theme of fertility and marriage, symbolised by the rose. This is not merely a poem about love but about love and desire.

[105] Horses.

A crimson carriage fit for a queen.
I'll sing thee a troupe of fast[106] musicians
To play us out with fiddle and pipe,
And I'll serve thee a table with fairest provisions,
Of goose and of game and plumbs that are ripe.
I'll sing thee a bed of swan feather mattress,
The fairest bed thou ever hast seen,
And thou shalt have my children, my darling,
Nor aught our love shall come between.
I am that young man who dareth to love thee,
And at the point of my knee, this I do swear,
In the high month of August, together we'll be,
For we shall be married at Bartholomew Fair.

Notes

Bartholomew Fair is a poem set in the late medieval period when the annual Bartholomew Fair, held at West Smithfield in the parish of St Bartholomew the Great, was held on 24th August from 1133 to 1855 when it was suppressed for vice: too much licentiousness for Victorian prudery to bear! Originally, it was a cloth

---

[106] That is, playing dances at a fast tempo.

fair and lasted three days, extended to two full weeks in the 1600s, but shortened to four days in 1691. When the Julian calendar was replaced by the Gregorian calendar in 1752, the fair thereafter recommenced on 3rd September. The fair would be opened by the Lord Mayor of London, who would stop off for a glass of 'sack' (fortified white wine) at Newgate Gaol from the Governor. The Guild of Cloth Merchants would then process to the fair to test their measures for cloth. The Elizabethan playwright and contemporary of Shakespeare, Ben Jonson, wrote a play of the same name, and in Daniel Defoe's *Moll Flanders*, Moll meets a well-dressed gentleman at the fair.

The young lovers who plan to marry at the fair are fantasising about a wedding they can't possibly afford, but the marriage laws were quite relaxed in medieval times: parental consent wasn't required, and one didn't have to marry in church, or even seek out a priest, hence our young couple arrange to marry at the fair. It was enough to say 'I take thee as my wife/husband'. Parish registers weren't created until 1538 and there wasn't a national Register of Births, Marriages and Deaths until 1st July 1837, so *proving* one was married was problematic, relying on witnesses. If one opted for a church service, from 1215 the 'banns' (announcements) would be read out in church on three days, a day apart, before the marriage to ensure there was no legal impediment and the service would take place in the church porch[107], not at the altar. There would also be the legalities of dowries. The betrothal ring originated from the price of the bride's dowry paid in gold, but it wasn't always a ring; it was called a 'wed', hence the term 'wedding'.

I suspect that the poem, as communicated to me, was originally a song that had become lost to tradition. I didn't realise it at the time, but the prevalence of colours in the poem relate to the different coloured cloths that the cloth merchants would trade at the fair.

---

[107] See Chaucer's *Wife of Bath's Tale*, in the *Canterbury Tales*.

Benediction

I have felt the benediction
Of sun breaking through rain,
Its beams dissolving the darkness
And bleak sheets of pain,
Banishing the scowling coverlids of cloud
And malevolence of thunder
Peeling and loud,
To curtain the hills in fulgent drapes
That pattern the fields
In scintillant shapes,
Lighting grass and meadow in lustrous greens,
And picking out the broom
That sports its yellow sprays
In the evanescence of blue skies
And cloudless days,
While, clustered in the copse
That nestles on the Downs,
The slanting sun endows
The mossy bark of oaks
In richly tinted browns,
And the dreamy wafting
Of somnolent breeze

Turns to diamonds the drops that cling
To spindly branches of stooped old trees.
I have felt the kiss of warmth
Upon my face,
Breathed the sweetness of grass,
And my soul sings out
To the sun's embrace,
For even as rain soaks
And winter numbs,
No matter how dark the day,
Redemption always comes.

Notes

"If, with patience, you can endure the adversity of rain, you can accept your transfiguration by light, for as the light of the sun caresses Nature, so the light of the Spirit caresses the soul."

This was a message communicated to me in the early hours of one morning. The previous day, I had endured a postal round in torrential rain. Suddenly the rain petered out, the clouds parted and the sun poured through, endowing everything in golden light. The grass sparkled like tiny sequins and the water coursing along the side of the road spangled in dazzling flashes. I was so transfixed that I stopped, and in that moment when all thought was suspended, its image seared itself into my consciousness. Light has always been a living metaphor for Spirit since time immemorial, but I can honestly say that when one meditates on a scene like that in a state of no-mind, one can feel something within coming into life.

I have evolved certain meditations involving Nature, based on the principle that meditating on the beauty of Nature awakens the light of the soul. One such meditation is to study one's surroundings and the objects in them in minute detail: how the sun plays on the rugged contours of brickwork, making the deep ruddy colours of the brick seemingly glow; observing how the sun lights up an old stone wall, picking out the olives and greens of the lichens spreading out in patches; observing how the sun glances off a bottle in the gutter; how a web glistens in morning dew or a water drop spangles like a diamond suspended on a branch; how the light makes transparencies of leaves, endowing them in a luminous green, and many others... and all this is done in a state of no-mind with all thought suspended.

Another meditation is to take oneself to a wild place and sit beneath a tree, experiencing the alternations of rain and sun, and accepting both with equal equanimity. It is a powerful lesson which teaches us that, eventually, the light pours through.

Burned by the Sun

I have dreamed of Beauty
And would before her stand,
But now in Beauty's presence
Am unmanned,
And defenceless 'gainst this Beauty
That burns me like the sun,
These palsied limbs rebuke my will
And cannot run,
Nor love's lament shall rise from voice
Of one new-nibbed whose song is yet unsung[108]
For Beauty in her plenitude
Stops my eye and tongue
And compels me look
And ne'er turn away,
This wretch in Beauty's house
Is bound to stay[109].

---

[108] A young man with little life experience who struggles to articulate his feelings. 'New-nibbed' refers to the practice of cutting a nib for a new ink quill and is a metaphor for a naïf. One 'whose song is yet unsung' refers to someone who has just started out on life's journey.

[109] In the sense of 'captivated'.

But if I touch Beauty
And make her mine,
Then no more
Shall Beauty shine,
But dull become,
Of earth endowed,
Mere mortal maid
Where once was goddess proud.
Dare I walk in Beauty's fire
Or, fearful, pine away and die,
Hand stretched out to empty air,
In winter wind my bones to lie?

Notes

There is human beauty and then there is a certain type of beauty that transcends the human. It shines with an otherworldly light and inspires both love and terror at the same time. I call it preternatural beauty, and it can be intimidating, but the only way to relate to it is by humanising it. Once the 'goddess' becomes relatable as a mere human personality, however, that preternatural beauty diminishes, or maybe one simply becomes blind to it. Our protagonist has a choice: pine away for an unattainable beauty or possess it and reduce it to the human level. The poem has its roots in the European courtly love tradition of medieval literature whereby the knight saw in the beauty of a woman a glimmer of the radiance of Divinity, and through chaste love, that is, the non-consummation of desire, found purity of soul.

There is, of course, an alternative interpretation: that the vision our protagonist is seeing is not a real physical woman at all but either a projection of his own Unconscious mind or a supernatural entity: a Lilith-like figure. Various things suggest this: he dreams 'of Beauty' and suddenly she appears in front of him; he dies with his hand stretched out to 'empty air'. Whatever interpretation the reader chooses to adopt, here we have a man whose entire being is paralysed by a vision of unattainable beauty, whether it is of a real woman, a supernatural entity or a projection of his own mania.

The Constant Watch

Like a watch is my heart,
Beating out each second
With the perfect precision of a Breguet[110],
Neither the gaining nor losing of time,
A dutiful servant performing its duties
Without so much as the crease of an eye
Or curl of a lip;
Made neither in Paris nor Lausanne,
Wrought neither of dials nor wheels,
It is the best keeper of time
This side of Heaven,
And who am I to argue with God?
Yet was this heart not made for joy?
Should it not skip a beat
As I draw my fingers about
The yielding softness of a rounded breast,
A nipple taut to an ardent tongue,
The smooth cantilever[111] of a hip caressed,

---

[110] A make of French watch.

[111] A cantilever is a projecting beam that extends out, fixed only at one end and supported by a strut, e.g., a balcony or a cantilever bridge which is formed of two cantilevers joined in

351

Or jump in my chest at the enigmatic smile of a
    mistress
With laughing eyes that beckon the master to bed?
Should it not rejoice as the sun
Lights the lustrous strands of a girl's hair
That billow about her freckled face
In the morning air,
With deft fingers, rippling her blouse
That it brushes like the teasing of a tender hand
'Gainst sensual skin made for love?
When dawn,
Like a rouged *prima donna*[112],
Makes her grand entrance,
Sweeping across the stage
To sing the aria[113] of morn
And blackbirds trill the coloratura[114],
When all Existence unites in the climactic chorus
Ere the curtain drops and bouquets thrown upon
    the boards,

---

the midline. The hip joint is also a cantilever. The term is used
in this poem in its aesthetic sense.

[112] The lead female operatic singer.

[113] A solo operatic song.

[114] A melody or aria with improvised flourishes such as trills and
broad sweeps of the scales.

I remain strangely unmoved,
A passive spectator to the pageant of time,
For whom life is witnessed
Like a military parade, cabined by
The compulsive symmetry of reason,
That abhors the insolence
Of the unscripted delight.
Yet time was, I would gaze in wonder
At the soft glow of Christmas lights
On a snow-decked fir,
The shimmering boom of thunder
'Mong mountain pines,
The dappled iridescence of a cathedral window,
Or sunlight as it glinted between branches of a tree
As I sped along the lanes
Laughing in the wind of my own momentum,
Content to be.
They return to me now...
A flotsam of echoes, strewn on a sea
Of torn and broken memory,
A wide-eyed child,
Entranced by the furry warmth of a sunbeam
On a bowl of peaches,
The showering of rust-hewed leaves
In autumn gusts,

The lengthening of shadows on late winter days,
Striping the meadow in golden haze[115],
And yet the moment when I succumbed
To the anaesthesia of life
Eludes me,
As though I am become in substance
Like a dead log,
That once belonged to living tree,
Bedecked by lichen,
Strewn by the wind upon some forest floor,
That shall never know the joy of igniting, or see
The beauty of a spangled web pendant with dew,
Breathe the sweetness of petrichor[116] after rain,
Nor yearn the coolness of wet grass on
    trammelled feet.
How rare these moments, and how few,
In one declined[117] so far
From the compass of his own nature
That another's joy stirs not his own

---

[115] "There's a bright golden haze on the meadow", from the song *Oh, What a Beautiful Mornin'*, *Oklahoma*, Rogers & Hammerstein, 1955.

[116] The scent of earth and grass following a fall of rain.

[117] The angle of declination is the difference between magnetic north and true north. In other words, his 'compass' (his nature) no longer points true.

But his very heart hath flown,
Where once did nest
In yellowed journals scratched in ink
Of glee and tears,
Garnered now in dust of years,
Of love liveried[118] in lorn[119] and loss,
And stars that shall never cross[120].
Content is that man at the final hour who says
"I have lived!"[121]
Yet what prospect a man of straw
But to be scattered by the hurricane of death,
Leaving no sonnet to light the lights of lovers,
Nor stanza to stir the sleep-knit soul;
Who could have blazed but begged,

---

[118] Livery is a uniform or colour scheme worn by servants or applied to coaches. The American use implies an equestrian outfitter, as in 'livery stable'.

[119] Lorn is usually employed as an adjective in such words as 'lovelorn' and 'forlorn' meaning 'absence of' or 'lonely'. I am here using it as a noun meaning 'loneliness'.

[120] "From forth the fatal loins of these two foes,
A pair of star-cross'd lovers take their life (5–6)"
Shakespeare, William, *Romeo and Juliet*, 1597.

[121] There is a saying that goes, "To be emptied at death, one must be filled in life." To die fulfilled is to look Death in the eye as an equal and not as a victim.

Cavern'd in the drear dudgeon of the cloistered
    mind,
Girt alone in dreams
Of forgotten cities, rivers of Mars,
Kings of orient and wandering stars,
And without realisation,
Become already a shadow of himself,
Even as his heart ticks down
To the day it dies,
And his watch, unmoving,
No longer points the hour,
But silent lies.

Notes

The Constant Watch is probably one of my most
confessional poems and describes the state of
withdrawal from sense and feeling as one ages, which
happens almost imperceptibly until one day one wakes
up and realises one doesn't feel with the same intensity
as one once did; as the poem puts it, one is never more
to know the joy of 'igniting'. The poem describes how
the intensity of sense experience builds the peak
experiences that sustain us through life, but also how

the ascendancy of the rational mind interposes a veil between thought and feeling such that one never feels as intensely as one did when young. The poem also explores my inability both to experience and express physical and emotional intimacy, resulting in the sensation of being 'imprisoned' in my own mind, like a kind of 'locked in' syndrome.

Dark Knight (of the Soul)

In Gotham City it's always night,
Sirens like fireflies flash blue and bright,
Black and white cop cars squeal round bends,
The folk live on credit but nobody lends,
Lurid neon reflects off the streets,
And the shuttered shop windows are full of
    deadbeats,
Rusting iron bridge and graffitied train,
Murky sidewalks painted in rain,
A vandalised picture whose colours have run,
With brutalist buildings that block out the sun,
Its hopes and its laughter washed down the drain
And all that's left are the drugs and the pain;
Bruce Wayne, sleek and swell,
Winging through Gotham like a bat out of Hell,
But under the cape and the hard black shell,
Bruce Wayne ain't doing too well,
Haunted by daddy gunned down by a clown
In a lawless town that's dead and brown,
A bit of a bastard all agreed
But still your dad, I'll concede,
And now you see his face in every rotten punk,

Every robber with a gun and every drunk,
And all that's left is vengeance to expiate the pain,
But still the flashbacks come again and again.
You hang on your butler like a wounded bird
And you can't love a woman, so I've heard,
You'd crumple inside without a fight,
You're all about vengeance, but where's the light?
You've bitten more than Man can chew,
When you look into the abyss, the abyss looks
    back at you[122].
When the fight is over, will you see the morn?
For the Dark Knight, will there be a dawn?
Are you predator or are you prey?
Either way, your world's gonna end one day.
I understand you've done your best,
But Gotham's a city of freaks
And you're a freak like all the rest.

---

[122] "Battle not with monsters, lest ye become a monster, and if you gaze into the abyss, the abyss gazes also into you." Friedrich Nietzsche, *Beyond Good and Evil.*

Notes

What would the Joker say to Batman if he were lucid enough? I have always loved the Batman comics and films for their sheer dark romantic quality, and they deserve to be considered a part of mainstream literature. The inspiration for Batman borrows from nineteenth century gothic romanticism and transposes it into a setting that is both future and retro. At the same time, the motif of the flawed hero is firmly wired into Shakespearian tragedy. The Joker also has a history steeped in the myth of the Trickster or malevolent god, with affinities to the Norse Loki and Roman Saturn.

I chose to compose this poem as a series of straight-forward rhyming couplets, thus lending a driving momentum to the verse. Thus, it is radically different from my more rhetorical discursive poems. In particular, I wanted to capture not only the conflicted personality of Bruce Wayne but also the flavour and feel of the future-retro Gotham City.[123]

---

[123] Gotham was actually a nickname for New York from the early nineteenth century, first used by Washington Irving in 1807.

The Dodger
(Adapted from First World War music hall song)

The Two Policemen

Now we've found you, now we've caught you,

You scruffy little man,

We're itching to arrest you

And throw you in our van.

We'll put you in a uniform

And to the Front you'll go,

To be shot up in the mud of Mons

And mown down in a row.

Then you'll be a hero, son,

Dead in bits, it's true,

But this country don't like cowards,

So I'd sign up if I were you.

The Dodger

I'm a writer, not a fighter,

A British institution, I might add,

I've written thirteen novels

And to lose me would be sad.

Queen Victoria read one
While sitting on the loo,
She hadn't laughed so much since Albert died
And didn't know what to do.

I'm not a man of action,
I'm a man of letters, don't you know,
If you tried to march me twenty miles,
I'd be a little slow.

I'm an intellectual
Thinking's what I do,
When it comes to practicalities,
I haven't got a clue.

The Two Policemen

He's a writer, not a fighter,
A better class of chap,
Our country needs his kind of brain
Even if he can't read a map.

He's no sense of direction,
His eyesight's rather dim,
Never mind the Jerry,
Our problem's surviving him.

The Dodger

I can't tell a bullet
From the arse end of a shell,
And when someone takes a shot at me,
I start to feel unwell.

I think I'd look ridiculous
With a basin on my head,
And those pineapples you call grenades[124],
I'd peel them instead.

Put a rifle in my hand,
Don't know the barrel from the stock,
But get me writing propaganda
And I'm solid as a rock.

---

[124] A reference to the Mills bombs invented by William Mills in Birmingham in 1915, based on the Belgian Roland grenade. It gradually replaced the old stick grenades.

I'll make heroes of your soldiers
And reduce your foes to tears,
I'll win the moral war for you,
Of that you'll have no fears.

I can't shoot to save my life,
My weapon is my pen,
I've killed more men with a bottle of ink
Than you can say 'Amen'.

Please don't send me to the Front,
It's a waste of a degree,
Now I've stacked his cellar,
The Dean will vouch for me.

The Two Policemen

He's a writer, not a fighter,
Can't you blinking see?
He's no urchin off the street,
He's from university.

Such exceptional intelligence,
We simply can't waste that,

This man will win the war for us,
If not, I'll eat my hat!

The Dodger

Thank goodness that's all over,
And if you'll leave obligingly,
I'll just pop over to the caff
For a scone and cup of tea.

I must confess, for a moment there,
My knees went wobbly,
But now you all know who I am,
It's peace and harmony.

And if old Georgie needs my help,
He can come and call on me,
I'm a writer, not a fighter,
Why, it's plain for all to see!

Motley Crowd

He's a famous author,
A symbol of our age,
Everybody reads him,
His books are all the rage.

'Twould be a crime to waste him
In some stupid war,
He's a writer, not a fighter,
And that's for blooming sure!

Notes

Don't you just love it when the little man gets one over on authority? *The Dodger* is not intended as a poem but as a satirical song, emulating the bawdy routines of the late Victorian and Edwardian music hall and the Vaudeville era in the United States; there are also elements of Gilbert and Sullivan operetta (which evolved out of music hall), while the stage play *Oh, What a Lovely War*!, filmed in 1963, also served as an inspiration.

In the First World War, conscription began in 1916. The song centres on a draft dodger who is arrested by two military policemen and must talk his way out of being sent to the front-line, which, by the end of the song, he apparently succeeds in doing, convincing them that he's a genius. Beneath the superficial music hall jollity, however, there is the more sinister theme of an entire generation of young men being sent to the front-line as cannon fodder to fight a war not of their own making, propelled by nationalist sentiment among the British public, and the two policemen make it quite clear that he's not expected to live. As Siegfried Sassoon wrote in his 1918 poem *Suicide in the Trenches*, the front-line is "the hell where youth and laughter go". There is no doubt that the First World War (and all wars following it) involved a massive loss of intellectual and artistic ability. The moral question the poem presents is this: should an individual be expected to give their life to a war created by politicians? The Dodger's argument is clear: "If you want me to use my talents writing propaganda, I'll write propaganda, but I'm not going to waste my life for your stupid war." Our dodger is literally pleading for his life.

For a poignant treatment of the First World War, see *1913*, towards the end of this section.

The Dream of Odysseus

A Storm and a Calm

Come, Odysseus, lay down thy head,

For the brightest sun hath shone[125],

The topless towers of Ilium[126] lie burned

And the heroes are all gone,

Ajax and Achilles, Patroclus too,

And old Agamemnon[127],

---

[125] Odysseus has won out over all others. He is the star of the siege of Troy.

[126] A tribute to one of the most famous lines in literature:

> Was this the face that launch'd a thousand ships,
> And burnt the topless towers of Ilium?
> Sweet Helen, make me immortal with a kiss.

Christopher Marlowe, *Doctor Faustus*.

These lines occur in the scene when Faustus instructs Mephistopheles to summon the spirit of Helen of Troy that he may gaze upon her beauty. The name Ilium (Latinised form of Greek Ilion or Ilios) is a variant of the Greek Troia, hence the title of Homer's *The Iliad*.

[127] Agamemnon, King of Mycenae, on his return from Troy, was murdered by his wife Clytemnestra, who had been having an affair with the younger Aegisthus while he was away at war. In revenge, she is slain by her son Orestes, with help from his sister Elektra. The story forms the basis of Aeschylus's *Oresteia* trilogy.

His fate sealed by his wife abed,
Shall haunt the halls of the Mycenaean[128] dead.
Rest Odysseus,
The wind no longer beats its wings
Agin[129] thy sails,
And the storm that blew is blown,
And for thy grievous crime[130]
The dragon's teeth are sown[131],

---

[128] Mycenaean civilisation was the dominant culture of the Greek Peloponnese from around 1750 to 1050 B.C. and was centred on the citadel of Mycenae on the Argolid plain, famous for its cyclopean architecture. An Achaean people, they were invaded by the Dorians from the north around 1050 B.C.

[129] Dialect form of 'against'.

[130] Odysseus' crime was to blind the Cyclops Polyphemus, even after Polyphemus had warned him that he was a son of Poseidon, the god of the sea. In retribution, Poseidon sent a storm that set Odysseus' ship off-course.

[131] The phrase, 'to sow the dragon's teeth', means to initiate an action meant to prevent trouble but which actually brings it about. The story originates with Cadmus (who famously brought the Phoenician alphabet to Thebes) and who killed the sacred dragon that guarded the spring of Ares. The goddess Athena told him to sow the dragon's teeth, from which sprang a group of ferocious warriors called the *spartoi ('sown men')*. Realising he was in danger, he threw a precious jewel into the midst of the warriors, who turned on each other in an attempt to seize the stone for themselves. The five survivors joined with Cadmus to found the city of Thebes. In the story of Jason and the Argonauts (from Apollonius Rhodius' *Argonautica*), Jason, on his mission to retrieve the Golden Fleece, obtained the remaining dragon's

And what storm it was Poseidon sent
To best thine arrogance!
Typhonian lightning that leapt and leered
From leprous sky,
Coiled and cracked in cordite air
As thunder thrashed in mortal throe
And all things fair
It mocked, in laughter long and low,
And at the heart of it my song
That sang above the storm,
Rang amid the rigging
And murmured in the mast,
And filled men's hearts with thoughts of home
And women warm.
No more the blind bulls of the sea,
In tempest toiling, hurl their heavy heads,
About thy bow,
Dash indifferently its timbers taut,
In works of wrack and waste,

---

teeth with the aid of the duplicitous King Aeëtes of Colchis who
offered the Golden Fleece to Jason if Jason would sow them
into the ground. Jason did this and successfully overcame the
warriors with the aid of King Aeëtes' daughter, the sorceress
(and priestess of Hekate) Medea, who gave him the means to
resist fire and steel. Interestingly, the phrase also occurs in
Hindi.

Nor Poseidon's fists relentless pound thee now
With bitter brine,
Mighty god of the sea of unquiet wrath,
Fury foaming in his beard,
For whom the ocean is as wine.
Becalmed is the ship of the Greeks,
Motionless as a mosquito on the sea's skin,
That glimmers like glass in the breathless air,
Nor augury the gods hath sent
But rigs limp as a man spent,
And men the bleak horizon stare,
Drunk in drought, man and boy,
Who watch by night the stars shower
As the spears of the Achaeans[132] rained
On the plain of Troy.

---

[132] Homer used the word Achaean to describe Dark Age Greeks
(c.1750 to 1050 B.C.) in general. They inhabited the area of
the Peloponnese (the southernmost point of Greece including
Laconia – Sparta – and Arcadia). Homer uses Achaeans, Argives
and Danaans interchangeably. The Myceneans were an Achaean
people but were attacked and displaced by the Dorian invasions
from northern Greece from around 1100 B.C.

The Coming of the Siren[133]

Sleek Odysseus, cunning and sly

Skulking in his ship, waits the morning star,

And wind to roar,

No more to oar

The unforgiving sea, but enjoy

His wife on Ithaca's friendly shore;

Handy with a knife, *that* one,

Endowed by the gods with a snake in his eye[134],

Who ne'er charged screaming to the fray

But ever sought the secret way,

His enemies to destroy.

And now Odysseus too succumbs to sleep,

Curled on the boards amid his men,

Cocooned in his web of fate[135],

Spectral and white,

---

[133] A mythological entity, part woman from the waist up and bird from the hips down, who lured sailors to their deaths with her song (see Notes).

[134] There was actually a Viking named Sigurd Snake-in-the-Eye who was reputed to be a son of Ragnar Loðbrok, but in this usage it means someone cunning and deceptive.

[135] I thought it an original idea that the siren would be able to 'see' Odysseus' fate that had been spun for him by the Moirae or spinners of fate, of which there were three: Clotho, who spun the thread of life; Lachesis, who measure the thread of life (i.e. its length); and Atropos, who cut the thread of life.

That billows and blows in the ancient moonlight.
Odysseus frets and Odysseus cries
And fills the night air with his sighs,
And I alone walk the ship
That reared and bucked on Trojan tides
In serpent hiss of spray, the war begun;
By storm undone, late the lissom waters lap and loll
As into night the day elides.
Harken, Odysseus, and welcome me,
For I come to thee from out the sea,
Fragrant with spikenard and oils of delight,
And flowers that bloom in the Indian night,
Legs nimble as the crane,
That stealthy stalks the singing sand,
Flanks that glisten like the dew
That beads the verdant leaf and
Drips from fronds in forests of rain.
With henna'd hair and ochred eye
I kneel and beside thee lie,
To croon the care-worn crib[136],
With sweetest music melt thy pain,
And brush thee with tresses
Lank and damp,

---

[136] To sing softly as though to a baby.

Naked in the flame of the terracotta lamp.

Beautiful am I,

That the gods did cower at their work

And high Olympus quake,

Dark avatar of Night's wrath

Enwrapped in fairest flesh,

Come Odysseus, awake,

Lay down thy quest and bend,

All care set aside

And with me abide

For I shall love thee in the soft sea swell,

And love thee to the end,

In sandy idyll far removed to rest,

To eat of lotuses[137] in the Arcadian noon

And make love with me beneath the moon,

In languor deep caress my hips,

---

[137] The phrase 'lotus eater' denotes a pleasure seeker and it derives from another episode in *The Odyssey* when Odysseus' ship is blown off-course to an island whose inhabitants eat of the lotus. Odysseus' men partake of the plant and are overcome with a blissful forgetfulness, having to be dragged back to the ship and chained to their rowing benches. The Greek word *lôtos* can refer to a number of plants, but the blue lotus of the Nile would probably be the most likely choice as it is an entheogen with narcotic properties, although there is a possibility that it refers to the opium poppy whose seed pod resembled that of the true lotus.

Eat of olives from my breast
And fill my mouth to overflowing
With wine from thy lips,
And faraway I'll take thee
To seek pleasure in my den,
To the isle where the women dwell
Who nest 'mong skulls of men
And perch upon the sun-bleached crags
To sing and comb their hair,
Gnaw on bones in mariners' rags
And drive men to despair.
But lo! The red limned lips of dawn
Part and swell
To plant their kiss of warmth upon the world,
And with thee can no longer dwell,
My time is spun,
And like the melting mist away I wend
To sing my salt song without end
And let thee be and fare thee well,
To waken in the grey dun morn,
Bloodied by talons and tunic torn,
Alone, uncertain and unmoored,
In thine own unhallowed hell.

Notes

After completing *Burned by the Sun*, I had a lot of left-over material which I had thought of using in a poem about Samson and Delilah. Somewhat whimsically, I had intended to call it *Why, Why, Why Delilah?* after Tom Jones' song; I'm glad I didn't write that! I was also entertaining the idea of writing a poem about the sea, and so the two concepts converged in this poem. The poem itself employs a hybrid of loose rhyme interposed with rhyming couplets, driven by an alliterative beat.

The Odyssey, attributed to Homer around the ninth century BC, and thus around four hundred years after the original events of the Trojan War, is the sequel to *The Iliad* which describes in prose poetry the beginnings and main action of that war. On his way back from the Trojan War to his wife Penelope in Ithaca, Odysseus and his men land on the island of the Cyclopes, a race of one-eyed giants. Imprisoned by the Cyclops Polyphemus, Odysseus escapes by rendering Polyphemus drunk and blinding him, in spite of Polyphemus' protestations that he is a son of Poseidon, the god of the sea. So enraged is Poseidon by this action that he sends a storm which blows

Odysseus' ship off course. It is during his wandering of the Black Sea and Aegean that Odysseus encounters the sirens who drive men mad with their singing and lure them onto the rocks to devour them. Wanting to hear their song, Odysseus instructs his men to tie him to the mask and ignore any instructions to free him, while telling them to plug their ears. I decided to re-imagine the encounter by having the siren board Odysseus' ship in the guise of a beautiful woman and entice him to abandon all thoughts of returning to his wife and instead steer his ship towards the isle of the sirens; presumably, Odysseus' reward is to enjoy the pleasures of the flesh and be eaten last! The sirens also appear in Apollonius Rhodius' *Argonautica* in Book IV (on which the story of Jason and the Argonauts is based), which relates that when the Argonauts sailed their way, Orpheus sang so divinely that only one of the Argonauts heard the Sirens' song.

The sirens were a chimera[138], that is, a composite of different animals including the human. From the

---

[138] A chimera was a means by which the peoples of the ancient world understood the concept of 'otherness', that is, something not of this world. It is instructive to compare the descriptions of demons in ancient Sumerian and Babylonian tablets with those given in 15th to 17th century *grimoires,* or books of magic, and they both describe demons with chimeric characteristics.

waist up, they were beautiful naked women, while from the waist down they were birds. They were variously said to be the daughters of the sea god Phorcys or of the river god Achelous by one of the Muses. However, their origin lies not in Greece but in Mesopotamia and the Levant. One antecedent is the Sumerian Lamashtu demon with a hairy body, a lioness' head with donkey's teeth and ears, long fingers and fingernails, and the feet of a bird with sharp talons. From the Lamashtu, several demonic representations occurred such as the Lamia (a woman with horse legs) and the Akkadian Lilu demon, of which the Hebraised Lilith is an exemplar, also depicted as a woman with bird feet. For the link with the sea, however, we should look to the Phoenician goddess Atargatis whose statues depicted her with the body of a fish. Atargatis is the foundation of the mythical mermaid. So, the siren is a composite of the Lilu demon and the mermaid. On a cultural level, the siren is an archetype of the predatory feminine: the highly sexualised, dangerous, destructive woman who ruins men by 'drinking them dry'. I don't think this is merely a matter of patriarchal cultural prejudice; there *are* women like that. "Once she got her claws into him, he was never the same."

I have re-imagined the siren for this poem, granting her the ability to materialise out of smoke and assume the form of a beautiful human woman. In her real form, however, she is a lethal seductive killing machine.

Why, we may ask, does the siren seek out Odysseus? My own belief is that it is because they both share the same nature: predatory, cunning and deceptive. Throughout *The Odyssey*, Odysseus gets the women he deserves such as Circe and Calypso, all of whom attempt to divert him from the constancy of his path home to his wife. It is as though Odysseus must be 'deconstructed' by these encounters in order to be a fit man to return to the faithful Penelope; in modern parlance, he needs his rough edges smoothed off and to grow up. In its proper Greek setting, however, The Odyssey was also a teaching story read to young men about the different types of women they were likely to encounter in life: the ones to marry and the ones to avoid.

Four Hundred a Year and a Cow
(Scenes from Hogarth No. 1,
eighteenth century)

If thinkest thou my boldness hath offended thee,
How bold, then, would you have me be?
For faint heart doth not win fair maid
But should at home hath stayed,
To prune my pear tree
And hunt with hounds...
Zounds! I'd sooner hunt thee!

Dost consider me a rake,
That I frequent the racecourse and the inn,
My porter to sip and play at dice
With old Bill Pride and Matthew Price?
Is it a sin
To walk with ladies in the park
And sport the fashion of the day?
Why, an entire wardrobe for you I will pay.

The slops of piss pots I can take,
The stinging rebuke of a lady's hand,
That too, I'll be damned!
Though I love my claret and my beef

And, come midnight,
Leave the table for underneath,
And pipe I'll puff and brandy sup,
I look like a gentleman when I'm standing up.

A house, a farm,
And four hundred a year[139],
Not bad for a squire's wife,
Upon my life!
And if you stay at home and stitch,
Who'll scratch my itch?
Or if, when rolling home,
I fall into a ditch,
Who'll put me to bed
And lay a compress on my head?

---

[139] 'Four hundred a year' refers to the income of the young squire's estate in guineas. The guinea was minted as a gold coin in 1660, but because of fluctuations in the price of gold, the value could go up and down. By 1680, the value of the guinea was worth 22 shillings. By 1717, the value was set at 21 shillings (£1, 1s in old currency or £1.05p in decimal). In 1816, the new 'sovereign' pound coin was introduced, but all pound coins minted before 1816 retained the value of 21 shillings, hence referred to as guineas. The term 'guinea' arose because the gold for the coin came from the African gold coast. As a rough guide, £400 in 1765 would be equivalent to £67,180 today (£1 = 167.95).

I need you to reform me,
Fill me with charity and love,
And though I fall asleep in church,
I'll be as gentle as a dove.
O my Lucy true,
When will you begin to see
There's nothing to be lost
By marrying me?
As sensible ladies can attest,
All men are the same...
I'm just (marginally) better than the rest.

Notes

Set in the eighteenth century, the young squire is in the marriage market and ardently pursuing a young lady of means who is not spectacularly interested in him... but he refuses to be rebuffed! The problem is, he is loath to give up some of his more dubious pursuits in the quest for love. Will he win his maid? Whilst composing the poem, I was reminded of the scene in William Makepeace Thackeray's *Vanity Fair* in which the old baronet Sir Pitt Crawley goes on bended knee to propose to the young social climbing Becky Sharp.

The poem is inspired by the paintings of William Hogarth (1697-1764) who made his name as a humourist, portraying the underbelly of Georgian life, peeking beneath the curtain of social respectability to the reality of life beneath. He depicted scenes from Georgian society in series such as *A Rake's Progress*, *Gin Lane* and *Marriage* à *la Mode*, which contrasted and paralleled high society and life in the gutter. Hogarth ingeniously planted visual 'tells' in his paintings, clues whose symbolic meanings unravelled the story of what was happening. This poem takes inspiration from *Marriage* à *la Mode*, which satirises Georgian conventions of marriage and money.

J'accuse

How brazen this girl
Whose mocking eyes,
Shine like a cat's in a lantern beam,
Or glint like diamonds
In mirrored hall 'neath chandeliers tall,
And demure looks are not what they seem
But mischief simmers in every curve of lip,
Of pouting mouth
And insouciant sway of hip,
Cheeks dimpled with fizz of laughter
As the sun breaks through heaven's rafter,
And raven fronds draped desultorily
About white marble neck,
Defiantly tossed,
So unman me that I am lost
And, misty eyed, would embrace the noose,
If you but led me to it,
As though the very Devil let thee loose
To seduce my wit.

But I am master in this court,
And will ne'er be bought
With cheap entrancements,
And thou, whose wanton wiles
Hath brought thee to this port,
Will answer more with tears than smiles;
For I, with jurisprudence,
Shall lay bare this hoax
And truth will coax
From honeyed words
Intent to disarm my sense.

The old clerk,
A funny bald little man
That, while impotent, does what he can,
Whose shrewish wife bakes buns
For the church fete,
And would ne'er consider an elicit date,
Adjusts his spectacles awkwardly;
His timid mind cannot compass
The enormity of thy crime,
Nor countenance licentiousness
In a woman so sublime
As thee.

Pity the job of the court recorder
For robbery hath he witnessed
And murder too
And scandals of the highest order,
Meticulously catalogued in his cramped hand,
But naught so shocking as this,
That decency cannot stand:
Thou stole my heart
And hath, in a stroke,
Torn my world apart,
My head with confusion filled
And heart with ungovernable joy
As though I were but a toy
For thy whims,
An old warthog
Grubbing among leaves for truffles
That no woman of virtue could ever mark
But brush straight past me in the park.

Did he who made Eve make thee?[140]
That hath no modesty,
But naked and shameless before me stand,

---

[140] A nod to William Blake's *Tyger*: 'Did he who made the lamb make thee?'

Confessing thy guilt
With breasts cupped inviting sup,
As nubile fingers southward stray
To that lush delta
'Mong dunes far away
Where cranes flock to drink;
Poor Nature cannot contain such beauty
But matter sundered and blown apart,
Continents collide and sink
And sea boils and blood to rush;
Desire, slipping its leash,
Points the accusing finger
And trembling hands long to linger
On thighs pert and plush.
And having found thee guilty
Of thy crime,
If it pleases this court,
I sentence thee to bed,
To be bound about by silken cords,
And sweetly scourged,
Our mouths to wed,
Skin blushed with feathered touch,
That lights each nerve and ecstasy rewards,
And perchance to swim in thy salty cove
Where the sea slaps sleepily

And mermaids sing mid cooing of birds
And wouldst give thyself to me
In that place where a woman moans
But are no words.

Notes

A retired judge (probably single or else estranged from his wife who no longer affords him pleasure) fanaticises about trying a young girl in his court for her beauty and voluptuousness, which ends (of course) with his complete abandonment of reason and succumbing to desire. This, then, is the heart of the poem: the more rational we become, the greater the desire to abandon reason and 'let go', returning to our primal state of sexual innocence. There is an element of sadness in the poem too: aware of his own age and lack of handsomeness, he likens himself to *'an old warthog grubbing among leaves for truffles'*, which is, to say, looking for young love.

The Last Goodbye

Sleep, smooth thy withered brow and sorrow spare
As alone I sit beside thy bed and stare,
And wonder on my fate and what become of me
When thou art carried out on the great eternal sea.

How ephemeral is Time, how frail skin,
As paper that in rain doth melt and thin,
And through its crumpled creases we do fall
To break in pieces one and all.

And I to my home must wend alone,
Bereft of the friend that I hath known,
A memory I can neither kiss nor hold
Nor thy warm and beating heart enfold.

Oh Death, how cruel to take the one
And leave the other to travel on,
In our heedless youth we asked not why
For each first kiss there's a last goodbye.

Notes

There is an innate sense of injustice when someone we have loved for many years dies, and it is also natural at that time to contemplate one's own future. How will I manage financially? How will I deal with the paperwork? How can I afford the funeral, the legal fees? It is not selfish at all to think of oneself at such times. So, I have attempted to tell the story from the perspective of the bereaved, and it is a common human experience.

Late Blooming Rose
(After Robert Frost)

When I was young and my life new spun
My years stretched ahead to the rising sun,
And now the sand is nearly run,
Taking back the years is an uphill climb,
And I wonder what became of all that time.
Square of shoulder and lank of limb,
I smoked behind bike sheds and hallways dim,
Lounged on the porch in the southern heat,
Ripped blue jeans and looking cool
Were all that mattered to this holy fool[141].
Wouldn't beg apology from no man,
No Sir!
Folk gave me crap, I told them straight,
Didn't know how to communicate,
The feelings I had, I couldn't get out,
I wasn't ready for that first date,
I'm a rose that bloomed late.
Alone and dreaming out of school,

---

[141] 'Holy fool', in this instance, refers to someone who has the potential for greatness of being but is blind to it.

I gazed at my reflection in a pool[142],
Kicked a ball about the yard,
The while men hammered and sang,
Forged the mighty engines of the world
In din and clang,
And writers wrote in artful word
But their words I neither saw nor heard,
I played the clown for others' mirth,
Mistook attention for respect,
Indifferent to my worth,
Gave my gold out in the street[143],
And laid my life at others' feet,
The dead-end jobs they came and went
Money earned and money spent,
But still I walked the old familiar track
As I grew older day by day,
And never saw the broad and tree-lined way.
Now in the autumn of my age,

---

[142] A reference to the Greek myth of Narcissus who grew old and died gazing at his reflection in a pool. Hence the expression 'narcissistic'.

[143] This line is a pun on the word 'talent'. A talent of gold or silver was a measure of bullion, a talent of gold being roughly 100 pounds in weight. So 'giving one's gold out on the street' is a way of saying 'wasting one's talents'.

I'm a calmer man and wise as sage[144],
Childish things I've put away[145],
The insecurity and the rage,
My voice is mellow as the mellowest smoke
And I stand taller than the tallest oak,
My roots run down into the earth
And I weather the storm 'cause I know my worth.
The path I walk is the path I chose,
I'm a late blooming rose.

Notes

Late Blooming Rose is a poem about youth, insecurity, impulsiveness and missed opportunities. Everyone matures out at different speeds. It's easy to dismiss

---

[144] This will interest you. What is the connection between 'sage' meaning 'wise' and the plant of the same name? Well, it all goes back to ancient Greek and Celtic cultures. Sage is a cleansing and purifying plant and ancient belief had it that the essential oils of the sage could induce clarity of mind. In ancient Greece and Rome, the plant was sacred to Zeus/Jupiter and thus to wisdom and virtue due to its 'elevating' properties, and the same belief held in Celtic cultures.

[145] "When I was a child, I spoke as a child, I understood as a child, I thought as a child: but when I became a man, I put away childish things." (1 Corinthians, 13:11)

a person as a failure when they are simply a late developer, as I was. Damn it, I didn't know what I was good at into my thirties and I am full of regrets for the opportunities I missed! So there is an element of autobiography in this poem, and it is a truth that is hard to admit to myself. But now I have.

The Mummers' Play

How blind I was,
Wrapped in my ambition,
That I noticed not your lingering look,
Eyes wet with longing,
Desire like clear water poured into crystal,
Shot by sun,
Those little gestures of affection
A silent mummery of the heart,
And even when I saw you in my dream
I kenned not the meaning,
A distant figure
Standing out in the water,
Hair billowing about your shawl,
Your skirts lapped by little waves
As you pushed the boat out upon the lake,
I, listing against the wind on farther shore,
Rifled by rain, castled in coat,
And would I have stepped into that little skiff
Pushing down into illimitable depths,
Gained my balance on the creaking wood
Taken my seat on the worn board
Shined smooth by oarsman's heave,

And let the tide carry me back with you,
– If I had but taken that chance –
I would have loved.

Notes

Very simply, this is a story about missed opportunities in love and eternal regret; about not reading the signs. I chose a purely prose style as I wanted to write a very sparse poem which, in its looseness, fluidity and lack of embellishment, reflected a deep melancholy.

The dream sequence is highly Freudian. He is standing on the 'farther shore' symbolising isolation; he is cut off – from the stream of humanity and from his own emotions. He is resisting his own impulse to love, symbolised by the wind, instead pulling his coat closer around him in a defensive posture. Perhaps he is afraid of commitment or of losing his independence, or maybe he is simply afraid to yield to his natural feelings of attraction to this woman, the 'tide' that would have carried him back with her. The boat assumes a living metaphor for opportunity, for reaching out, which, in the end, is not taken; our protagonist has literally 'missed the boat'.

A mummers' play is the acting out of a masked mime. Characteristic of many is the death of a hero figure and their return to life by a doctor. They were popular among the poor in antiquity and are still performed in villages in northern England. The tradition was brought to America by Swedish immigrants in the late seventeenth century, and in the eighteenth century, the mummer's play became popular in Philadelphia. The January 1st Mummers' Parade in Philadelphia became popular from the 1860s. The use of the word in this poem refers to the acting out of love and desire through silent hints and gestures.

My Grave Shall Weep in Snow
(Traditional)

Do not say you love me
If you cannot watch me die
For on that day the flowers shall brown
And leaves shall fall
And no swallows flit the sky.

Don't tell me love's forever
If you cannot let me go
For on that day the wind shall keen
And clouds shall scud
And my grave shall weep in snow.

Notes

Love and Death are partners in an intimate dance to
the music of time. To love someone is to watch them
grow old and die, but there is a sense that the travails
and infirmity of age are what make love real.

Night is a Courtesan

Night dispenses her charms like a courtesan,
Masqued and mascara'd,
Coyly revealing her luminous face
From behind her veil of Mystery,
As she doth hasten,
Softly gliding, pert and proud
Among the milling of the crowd,
In sweep of hooded cloak 'cross cobbled court
On some secret assignation to consort
With the old fat signore
Who pants in anticipation of her coming,
His pulse dangerously high;
A game of concealing and revealing,
Of climax withheld to the last sigh,
Mingled scent of skin and musk,
The unhurried consummation of dusk.

My beautiful courtesan!
Thy face gazes up impassively from the mirror
    world,
Of wet pavements and squares vast,

Of palaces sunken in the past,
A thousand faces in a thousand limpid pools,
A thousand hearts to break,
A thousand ships to launch,
That even fabled Helen ne'er surpassed,
Though her lovers were but angry fools.
O Splendid Night!
Wert thou conceived to torment
This nobody, who alone,
Stationary 'mong rooks[146] and revellers
Who sell and stroll, and wares extol,
Lifts up his head in wistful wonder
Forlornly to behold
A face frozen in youth,
A dimpled cheek, an enigmatic smile,
Persian grey eyes inviting a man
To sell his soul?
A concubine of kings art thou,
Who kissed the rings of emperors;
For one such as thee, no act is too demeaning,
Thou knoweth the art of love but not its meaning.

---

[146] Rook = thief. Corvids (including blackbirds, crows, ravens and magpies) are attracted by bright shiny objects, which they often steal.

The stars sing out thy beauty, O Night,
Whose clear-eyed innocence rebukes the frowns
Of stiffened old clerics and dried up popes,
And I, a mooning Pierrot
Gadfly among gas lamps,
Hero of false hopes,
A troubadour of the street serenading 'mong song
    birds,
Mere jester for thine entertainment,
Crooning a love song that shall never know love
To one whose face is as the whiteness of a dove.
Fain would I make for thee a necklace from my
    weeping?
There be pearls enough for thy slender neck,
For the tears of dewy morn weep less than I
Who art but a mote, a speck,
A round-eyed idiot who gawps and gapes
And vainly stretches out his hands
To grasp Night's drapes.
Am I then so poor, you cast not your smile upon me,
Or exalt by dint of praise?
O pale Madonna,
Heaven's prostitute, I pause
To lay for thee a rose upon the cobbles
And thy scorn is my applause.

But see! All lights go out,
The oil turned down,
The candle snuffed,
Each doll's house caped in quiet,
Bright squares of orange now blackness of tombs,
And only the 'quisitive cat slinks along the rutted
    way,
Beneath the darkened rooms.
Tonight you will visit each man in his bed
And fill his thoughts with forbidden sin...
Even I, this worn-out sot,
Who hath no room to let thee in.
Shall I sleep and not remember
How you touch me in my dreams
Or am I too far fallen to figure in your schemes?
Shall you stoop to kiss
Such one of disassembled mind
Who in the gutter lies,
Drunk and left behind,
After the parade has passed,
Good folk gone to church,
And dandies shout abuse
As along the lane I lurch,
Kicked by children, run down by carts,
Struck by turds and mocked with farts,

And on my back in muck and dirt
With ripped trews[147] and torn shirt?
Still I sing to thee, my beautiful courtesan,
Whorled in jewels and lace[148],
And keep my faith of years,
Strain forth my fingers to touch thy face,
So wan and so sublime,
That floats above this ragged world
Unsoiled by grit and grime.
I ask of thee, O Lady Night,
Is just one kiss a crime?

Now, my love, my life is run,
For good or aught, what's done is done,
And at last I know equality of Man;
Wouldst thou my laboured lungs
With softest night airs fan?
Wilt thou bend thy head
And gentle rays pour down
To caress my cragged brow,
Iron smooth this hard-won frown,
And soothe thy servant who lies in watery pools,

---

[147] Archaic word for 'trousers'.
[148] Stars and clouds.

Whose heart unclenches and body cools?
What blessed fool am I,
When others loveless go abed to lie,
To die with my lover's image in my eye.

Notes

While translating the imagery for this poem into
words, a forgotten quote from Oscar Wilde surfaced
in my mind: *"We are all in the gutter, but some of us are
looking at the stars,"* and so for the lovelorn nobody in
Courtesan. Socially marginalised and bereft of the love
of a woman, he has fallen in love with the moon, and
her face is the last thing he sees as he dies. The poem
began as a hymn to Night, imagined as a courtesan
dressed in black hooded cloak with the face (the moon)
peeking out from within it, but in the course of writing,
it actually morphed into a poem about loneliness and
neglect.

The overall flavour of the poem is Italian, evoking
long languid nights in sleepy towns dotted with
romantic castles and villas, infused with an air of
dilapidated decadence. Finally, *Courtesan* explores the

paradox that the experience of physical love can be both sublime and spiritual, and rude and earthy.

Of Gods and Kings
(A Poem of the English Civil War)

Who can turn the wheel of the stars?

What hand shall ride the horses of the sun?

Oh, who greeneth the wide earth

And maketh the deer to run,

Bringest rain to the parched

And nourish the corn to grow,

That men with weathered skin shall till and sow?

Father art thou to intemperate and unruly kings,

Exalted in ermine, crowned in hollow air

Who brood and plot on pond'rous thrones,

Lay waste the weald and put fire to the fair,

And think them mighty, though have no care,

For they weigh not the common man

Nor admire the rose[149],

But ever and eternal strife hath chose

And say them 'No hallowed city nor humble home
    be spared',

As armies mill and swarm, despoil the pleasant
    land

---

[149] In other words, dedicating their lives to creating a more beautiful world.

And ships of war with cannon blast
Send sailors to the sand,
Yet canst they swell the swooning sea
To fret and froth
Or loose the arrow of tight-stringed storm,
Caress the lamb in softest breeze,
Clothe the verdant vale in sunbeams warm?
Shake, oh kings, and fear the trumpet blast,
The last shall be first and the first shall be last[150],
For the Prince of Peace shall come in power and
    sound[151],
Uproot the tyrant in his tower
And joy ring all around,
And with his hand shall still the oaken fold[152],
Stir the wheat that whispers
In singing seas of gold,
As kings decay in motley rags,
And in their tombs lie cold;
Disdaining night shall rue their ruinéd walls
Where spring flowers nod and sway
And the fluting wind shall haunt the empty halls

---

[150] Matthew 20:16 "So the last shall be first, and the first last: for many be called, but few chosen."

[151] A reference to the Second Coming of Christ.

[152] In other words, bring peace to the land.

Fallen in decay,

And shall he walk with gentle feet the fields of the
  slain

Whose armour moulders in the mud

As swords rust ruddy in the rain,

The broke-backed slave, cleave his chain,

And from the daunted man shall lift the yoke

That the light of the world[153] shine out again

Through the fury and the smoke,

And the wolf shall dwell thereafter with the
  lamb[154],

Become as one the timid and the bold,

And Man shall live for evermore

In Eden as of old [155].

---

[153] Christ refers to himself as "the Light of the World" in John
8:12.

[154] Although often quoted liberally in church, the phrase "And
the lion shall lie down with the lamb" never actually occurs
in the Bible. The true text from Isaiah 11:6-9 reads, "The wolf
shall dwell with the lamb, and the leopard shall lie down with
the young goat, and the calf and the lion and the fattened calf
together; and a little child shall lead them. The infant will
play by the cobra's den, and the toddler will reach into the
viper's nest. They will neither harm nor destroy on all My holy
mountain, for the earth will be full of the knowledge of the Lord
as the sea is full of water."

[155] Although this could be interpreted as a literal reference to
Eden, it could also be interpreted symbolically as a return of

Notes

The English Civil War (1642-51) pitted a Puritan-dominated parliament against Charles I, a Stuart king with Catholic sympathies and autocratic tendencies, married to a French Catholic queen. Leading the Parliamentarian army was Oliver Cromwell who eventually became Lord Protector of the new Protectorate (1653-1659) after the execution of King Charles. The poem is penned by a religious radical of the time and envisages the Second Coming of Christ and an end to the tyranny of kings. Having been on the receiving end of Catholic absolutism, Protestants had interesting things to say about liberty, and it is fair to say that had there been no sixteenth and seventeenth century Reformation then there would not have been an eighteenth-century European Enlightenment with its theories on the rights of man and constitutional government derived from John Locke and Thomas Paine. Not all Protestants held to the same views, however. Cromwell was religiously radical but

society to a state of innocence.

socially conservative[156]. He despised tyranny but he also believed in a God-ordained social hierarchy. Pitched against him were Protestant radicals such as John Lilburne's Levellers and the communistic Diggers who believed in a 'levelling' of society in what amounted to a socialist interpretation of Christianity. That interpretation goes back to the earliest days of Christianity before its organisation into a priesthood when it was essentially a 'charismatic' gathering of equals, and to the line in Matthew 20:16 in which Jesus says *"So the last shall be first, and the first last: for many be called, but few chosen."* That phrase is couched in apocalyptic theology: the end of time approaches and the Kingdom of God will be established in which all social distinctions will be abolished. Unsurprisingly, some thought they should be abolished *now*. Indeed, the Middle Ages were filled with millenarian cults who aimed to do exactly this. One such example were the Dolcinists under Fra Dolcino who were suppressed in 1307 and advocated equal rights for women, the

---

[156] Cromwell's social conservatism was the Protectorate's undoing. He appointed his eldest son Richard Cromwell, as his successor (purely out of convention), even though Richard Cromwell was weak and unsuitable, having no connections with Parliament or the Army. His younger son, Henry, would have been a much better choice as successor.

abolition of marriage and an end to corruption in the church; their rallying cry was *penitenziagite*, an Occitan[157] word derived from the Latin *poenitentiam agite*, meaning 'repent' and directed at the Church. They were not the only ones. The Brethren of the Free Spirit, active between the twelfth and fifteen centuries and influenced by the theology of Joachim of Fiore, advocated salvation through possession by the Holy Spirit which elevated them above moral and social law and rendered the Church obsolete. They used Galatians 5:18[158] as their justification for freeing themselves from both secular and Church law. During the early fifteenth century Hussite[159] wars in Bohemia, the communistic Waldensians of Bohemia (Czech Republic) allied themselves with the Hussites against the Holy Roman Empire and became known as radical Taborites. During the German Peasant Revolt of 1525,

---

[157] Occitan was a Latin-derived language of southern France (Provence, Languedoc and Gascony), Catalonia and Northern Italy from the Dark Ages through to the early modern period. The region of Languedoc in southern France takes its name from 'the language of Oc' or Occitan. Aranese Occitan, a derivative of Gascon, is spoken in Catalonia to this day.

[158] *"Those who are driven or led by the Spirit of God are no longer under the law."*

[159] Followers of Jan Huss, an early Protestant reformer, burned at the stake in 1415.

also, the radical anabaptist[160] Thomas Muntzer took the side of the peasants against Martin Luther who sided with the German princes, and from 1534-35, the anabaptists established a commune in the German city of Munster. One of the radical publications of the German peasants, *The Twelve Articles of the Peasantry*, arguing for the abolition of serfdom, employs a biblical precedent: "It has been customary until now to hold us as bondspeople, which is to be deplored, as Christ redeemed and purchased us all with the precious shedding of his blood, the shepherd as much as the highest noble." The Levellers and Diggers of the English Civil War represent the dying embers of the communistic strain of Christian heresy.

The mainstream view of the Church that the social order was divinely ordained goes right back to St. Paul. St. Paul (himself an apocalyptic) refrained from speaking out against the existing order, even though he was aware of its injustices. For example, he did not speak out against the institution of slavery, his rationale being to preserve the existing relationships in society until the coming Kingdom of God sorted

---

[160] Anabaptists practice adult baptism. Examples are the Amish and Mennonites.

those relationships out. Who was he to pre-empt God's Kingdom? Given that the entire economy of the Roman world was based on slavery, it would also have been difficult for the young faith to have changed that, especially as St. Paul *needed* the Roman empire as the seedbed of his new religion, and the last thing he wanted to do was upset the Roman authorities; he also needed Rome to protect him from the Jewish Christians who wanted him dead. Here is what St. Paul has to say about slavery:

> [5] Slaves, obey your earthly masters with respect and fear, and with sincerity of heart, just as you would obey Christ.

> [6] Obey them not only to win their favour when their eye is on you, but as slaves of Christ, doing the will of God from your heart.

> [7] Serve wholeheartedly, as if you were serving the Lord, not people,

> [8] because you know that the Lord will reward each one for whatever good they do, whether they are slave or free.

⁹ And masters, treat your slaves in the same way. Do not threaten them, since you know that he who is both their Master and yours is in heaven, and there is no favouritism with him.

Ephesians 6:5-9

And this is what St. Paul has to say about authority:

¹ Let every soul be subject unto the higher powers. For there is no power but of God: the powers that be are ordained of God.

² Whosoever therefore resisteth the power, resisteth the ordinance of God: and they that resist shall receive to themselves damnation.

³ For rulers are not a terror to good works, but to the evil. Wilt thou then not be afraid of the power? Do that which is good, and thou shalt have praise of the same:

⁴ For he is the minister of God to thee for good. But if thou do that which is evil, be afraid; for he beareth not the sword in vain: for he is the

414

minister of God, a revenger to execute wrath upon him that doeth evil.

5 Wherefore ye must needs be subject, not only for wrath, but also for conscience sake.

6 For this cause pay ye tribute also: for they are God's ministers, attending continually upon this very thing.

7 Render therefore to all their dues: tribute to whom tribute is due; custom to whom custom; fear to whom fear; honour to whom honour.

Romans 13:1-7

So, as per St. Paul, the social order is ordained by God and Matthew 20:16 only applies at the institution of God's Kingdom at the Apocalypse. His words, however, created a dangerous precedent. Protestant slave owners in the American South could read *Ephesians* and exploit slaves with a clear conscience! It wasn't until the Second Great Awakening of 1795 to 1835 that Protestant reformers began to question the morality of slave-owning even when they had

415

questioned the morality of royal tyranny decades before! The Quakers, of course, had always opposed slavery. Thus, the point at which Christianity became a socially conservative religion instead of a socially reformist one goes all the way back to St. Paul, who divorced the idea of spirituality from social reform, and by the time Constantine recognised Christianity in the Roman empire, the ink was already dry on the paper.

The Old Devil
(Scenes from Hogarth No. 2, contemporary)

Do not be deceived by silver hair, my dear,
The finest brandy is longest aged
And this old cask will set you back
A bob or two,
Nor decry this cragged face,
This quarried brow,
Like some gnarled and ancient bough;
Iron grey hair that tumbles wilfully
'bout stubbled chin,
Face carved of Norman stone
Chiselled by the mason's mark,
Hewn by hammer and by spark,
And lips that have sipped of spicéd rum,
In many old Havana bars
Incensed by the smoke of fine cigars.
In the mornings, I'm never at my best
But mooch around in gown and vest,
As dawn breaks over my mock Tudor pile
And by chequered light of day
The hours I'll while,
Reclining on my chaise like a cooling log,
In the afterglow of a vigorous snog,

Dusted by the ash of years,
Settling upon the clinker of souls betrayed,
Of lovers abused and lovers played,
Yet my heart still hot and burning bright
That crackles at the maid
Who pokes the embers of the night.
A sword am I, cast in the flames of some godly forge,
Honed for sharpness,
Tempered for the kill,
And beneath this silky voice an iron sharp will.
There's life in this old dog,
I don't deny,
And would (if I could) stay out all night,
Following some bitch's scent,
Or winsome girl who needs to pay the rent;
Enthroned kingly on my arse,
Sceptred with bubbly and a glass,
After the clubbers have taken flight,
Holding court among the ladies of the night.
All old devils know,
A woman loves a ruinéd man,
But a heart pierced by so many arrows
Cannot easily be healed,
Or wounds concealed.
(although I allow you to think so).

Ha! What does a boy know of love?

Would you, my dove,

Swap this old lion,

Hide mauled by many males,

For the smooth fur of a cub?

More conquests have I won than fabled Alexander,

Kings deposed and queens wed,

And daughters succoured in my bed;

A god am I 'mong wrecks of men,

(Though I confess to twinges now and then),

For whom the nursing home ranks second to the
    pub

Or scouring the bars of a Soho club,

And enjoying the pleasures of another's wife,

For I'll not die till I've drained dry

The glass of life.

In every woman, rich or poor,

Push your luck and you'll find a whore,

Young ones, old ones,

Married or free,

I'll buy you a drink and then we'll see...

Old Odin, well-travelled god,

Stands upon the Bifrost Bridge[161],

As Hel's ship raises its cargo of the dead,

And in dread,

Sees Fenris' jaws devour the sun,

Yet even Ragnarok moves him not,

Nor I, for whom death is but a can

To be kicked along the road,

And when the Furies who, from grim abode,

Swoop down from chimney and from roof

To take me screaming defiance at the gods,

Don't underestimate my power to change the odds!

Notes

The Old Devil is the second in the series *Scenes from Hogarth* (see *Four Hundred a Year and a Cow*) and takes inspiration from both *Gin Lane* and *A Rake's Progress*. It aspires to capture the bawdiness of Hogarth's eighteenth century and transpose it to a contemporary setting.

---

[161] Also called the Rainbow Bridge. Constructed by the Norse god Heimdall, the Bifrost Bridge connects Asgard, the realm of the gods, to Midgard and all the other worlds on the Norse Tree of Life.

So here we visit the old devil: urbane, smooth-tongued playboy, who sees women as conquests, trades on his age and 'vulnerability', views life like a glass to be drained, and who is definitely not read to pop his clogs! In his seventies, he still wears an open-necked shirt and medallion. I think most of us have met someone like this. Very different to the early poems in this volume which anticipate death, the old devil defiantly resists it. In his favour, he is the ultimate survivor and (awful as he is) a refreshing antidote to the smug, puritanical and morally judgemental nanny state society of today. I find it interesting that, however much public morality condemns them, everyone loves an old devil. The poem will doubtless raise the ire of feminists and moralisers as 'demeaning women', but if all poetry were politically correct, no one would read it. The purpose of poetry is to hold up a mirror to life, not to tell people how to live it.

Although I have cited Hogarth as an influence (as per *A Rake's Progress*), there is an affinity with Mozart's *Don Giovanni*, another serial seducer, who, in the opera, reels off his list of conquests. The end of our poem also makes a nod to Don Giovanni at whose climax the statue of the murdered Constable comes to life and a host of devils take Don Giovanni down into hell.

Pavane for a Dead Princess

God rest thy soul and the beauty that is thine
For time and errant memory
Shall dull it not
Nor dim its shine
But ever and eternal blaze
In heavenly halls
As in life did light the palaces of kings,
Its virtue never hide
Nor change erase.
Let nature take what nature gave
For the beauty of thy soul is not to nature slave
But to God belongs
And in God shall it abide,
And the callous catcalls of village girls
And women less thy worth
Shall not offend thee
In that starry realm that floats above the earth.
How the sun did love thee,
That played upon thy face in dappled light of pools,
Where fish swirled,
And clung to every fold of dress,
Caressed thy hair that shone like silk

That in summer breeze unfurled,
But more dear, thy kindly airs and gentle words,
That silenced fools,
The graceful fingers that plucked the harp,
And songs that flowed like milk
Are not forgot,
Nor to the darkness hurled;
Thy spectral step that trod the pillared court
And caught the courtiers unaware
The music of thy laughter and winsome smile
That lit thy face,
Shine a candle to the world.

Sleep well upon thy bier,
Sweet child of mine,
The wars of kings and emperors were not thine,
Nor famine and rapine bled out thy soul
Or ravages of age their toll,
And though my very grief rebel
Time is now to say goodbye,
Untie the knots that bind thee to this port
And bid thee 'journey well',
Yet not with tired old lips shall thee I kiss,
That angry words hath spoke,
But from gardens bright where thou didst walk

On misty morns to song of thrush
A single flower I pluck
And red rose to red lips brush.

Notes

In *Pavane for a Dead Princess*, the old king mourns
the death of his young daughter. The title of this
poem is taken from an orchestral arrangement of the
same name by French composer Maurice Ravel. A
pavane was a stately processional dance in slow time
performed in courtly functions in the 16th and 17th
centuries by dancers dressed in elaborate clothing. The
name originates from the Italian *padovana*, meaning
'Paduan'. I decided to take Ravel's elegiac music and
translate its imagery into poetic form.

The Pipes of Scarrowness

I went up to Scarrowness
In the wake of '45
To find my wife of twenty years
And see if she did thrive.
For the slaughter had been terrible
And redcoats roamed the land
And rebels taken off in carts
Bound by foot and hand.
Oh, the sun shone off the loch that day
As blue as Highland sky,
The misting mouths of cattle wraithed the air
And gulls did scream and cry,
But burned-out bothies were all I saw,
The town put to the torch,
And my lovely Claire sat weeping,
Weeping in her porch.
Mothers nursed their mewling babes
Decked in ragged dress,
And no piper left to play the pipes
In bonnie Scarrowness.

"Wherefore my little Davy?" she did cry,
"Where my bonnie boy?
For he went off in '45
In the Laird's employ,
Went to fight the English
Though his was not the fight,
Tell me that you found him
Tell me he's a'right."
But of my wee Davy boy
I could find no sign,
Though I searched the dead carts
And the corpses laid in line,
But I knew he lay there still
Upon that bloody moor,
Where the crows did circle overhead
And sang their awful caw,
Shot and cut up in a ditch
Pushed down in the mud,
A hundred bodies over him,
A hundred bodies dripping blood.
And I remembered how it was he left my hand,
Hairs new upon his chin,
His eyes bright with fervour,
In the cheering and the din,
The day the men of Scarrowness marched out

Upon a winter's morn
Behind the horse of Laird McDair
Whose loyalty they had sworn.
"Come, boys, and march with me,
Be brave and of good cheer,
For Carlisle shall fall, and Derby too,
And London by the year."
In cap and kilt they marched out,
Stout legged and faces set,
Faces cragged with hardship,
And eyes that brooked no threat,
Through town they marched indomitable
With claymore, dirk and scythe,
To fight for a prince they'd never seen
In a war they'd not survive.
And so they marched into the mist,
T'was the last were seen alive,
And the pipes of Scarrowness, they played them
    out,
For it was '45.

At Prestonpans the day was theirs
And Edinburgh they did take,
South they surged, no stopping now,
The English will to break,

Till Cumberland pursued them like a dog
With the hate he bore
And on that fateful day they took their stand
On bleak Culloden Moor.
"Advance", said the captain,
"Fight!" said the laird,
"Fight and nae retreat.
Fight for Scotland's freedom.
Fight for bread tae eat."
And fought they then
And fought they brave,
Till no man left alive,
And the pipes of Scarrowness were heard no more
In the wake of '45.

And to this day I curse the Laird
And I curse the Stuart cause,
I curse all ambitious men
And their pointless wars.
For such brave and foolish men as these
Took my son away
And the flower of Scottish youth went down
For a preening popinjay.
And yet this land shall have its hour
When the time is right

And one more fitting shall sound the Cause
To end the English blight.
And the wind that sways the gallows rope
And sings among the graves
Whispers to dead heroes hope
That Scots no more be slaves.
And on that day I'll take my gun,
Glad to be alive,
For once more the pipes of Scarrowness shall play
In the wake of '45.

Notes

In the Glorious Revolution of 1688, James II was removed from the English throne. Parliament had reluctantly tolerated James' Catholicism, safe in the knowledge that his daughter Mary, married to the Protestant William of Orange, would inherit the throne. The birth of a male heir, James Francis Edward Stuart, in July 1688, changed that calculation and threatened the Protestant settlement. Thus, in November, William of Orange was invited to invade England by James' Protestant opponents and James II fled to France. Thereafter, William and Mary reigned as dual monarchs, but it was under Mary's sister Anne that the Act of Union (uniting Scotland and England under a single monarchy) was passed in 1707. In the Act of Succession of 1701, it was also decreed that, upon Anne's death, the succession would pass to the House of Hanover and *only* to a Protestant.

James had made several attempts to reinvade through Scotland in July 1689 (Battle of Killiecrankie) and through Ireland in July 1690 (Battle of the Boyne – remembered today in the Ulster Orange marches). In 1701, James II died in exile and Louis XIV recognised his son as James III of England (VIII of Scotland). He became known as the Old Pretender and launched a Jacobite rebellion (after Latin Jacobus = 'James') in Scotland in 1715-16. James III's son, Charles Edward Stuart, was born in 1720, and became known as the Young Pretender, or, more colloquially, as 'Bonnie Prince Charlie'. In 1740, the War of the Austrian Succession had broken out, which had committed the bulk of the British army to fighting in Flanders. Seizing his opportunity, Charles secretly communicated with the Scottish Jacobites who began raising funds for a rebellion. Charles landed on Eriskay Island in July 1745 and declared himself King at Perth in September. That month, the Jacobites won a string of victories at Edinburgh and Prestonpans, then took Carlisle in November. At Derby, however, they were stopped by British troops. It was here that dissention arose between Charles and his generals. Charles wanted to fight, but his generals refused to move without support from France. The army turned back and won victories at Falkirk and Inverness but were now pursued by the Duke of Cumberland, George II's youngest son Prince William. Attempting to protect his supplies at Inverness, Charles staged a battle at Culloden Moor in April 1746 against military advice. The Jacobites were routed and Bonnie Prince Charlie fled the field, hid for several weeks by Flora MacDonald until he could escape via Skye on a ship to France. In the subsequent Highland Clearances, the British dismantled the Scottish clan system and confiscated the lands of the Jacobite lairds.

It is germane to ask what Charles hoped to achieve. The Jacobite rebellion was more about the Stuart claim to the throne than it was about Scottish independence. While he would have reversed the Act of Succession, he may well have kept the Act of Union, with himself and his heirs on the throne of a United Kingdom. While there was support for the Stuart restoration in England, that help never materialised. Charles had hoped, vainly, that when he marched south, the English Catholics would rise to support him. The Catholics, however, pledged their support to the Crown, wary of losing any tolerance they still enjoyed. If he had plunged on past Derby and tried to take London, he would have been reliant on the 10,000 French troops his brother Henry had at the ready and that would have looked like a French invasion. The British didn't like the French. Charles didn't understand that it is one thing to conquer a nation and another to earn its loyalty.

The death of the Jacobite cause occurred when, in 1748, Charles was expelled from France under the terms of the Treaty of Aix-la-Chapelle that ended the War of the Austrian Succession. The memory of Culloden, however, lived on in the memories of the Scots who emigrated to the American colonies and perpetuated the myth of British tyranny that culminated in the American Revolution 30 years later.

The Pipes of Scarrowness (a fictional Scottish town) attempts to convey a sense of what the 1745 rebellion and its aftermath was like as it was experienced by ordinary Scots, but it is also an indictment of romantic patriotism that sends innocent men to die for a lost cause.

Prologue to Macbeth
(From a Lost Folio by William Shakespeare)

Night, a gale and a spray of rain. A barren moorland by a low cliff that drops to a shingle beach upon which the sea pounds relentlessly. A low bank of fog hovers above the sea, its tendrils creeping across the moor. The Weird Sisters stand at the cliff edge with arms upraised to the night sky.

First Witch	Meet we three in gloom and gale, in murk and mist, in rain and hail...
Second Witch	...That scuffs and scours the squalling sea and bitter blasts the barren vale.
Third Witch	The ebbing tide of night doth set us free to work our will in secrecy.
First Witch	Extremest license hath its sway and darkness curse the blighted day!

Second Witch	To scream at the Sun and to bleed with the Moon.
Third Witch	To laugh at the lightning and to spin with the storm.
First Witch	To glide with the serpent and to run with the wolf.
Second Witch	To drain the cup of life and raise the bloodied basin.
Third Witch	Yea, to ride the frighted mare to morn till it gives up its life ere dawn.[162]
First Witch	Hail to the restless spirits who walk the earth.
Second Witch	Hail to the terrible ones who dwell in Darkness.
Third Witch	Hail to the Powers of Night.
All	All hail!
First Witch	Hail to the witch, who art born of fire, and hail to Our Master.
All	All hail!

---

[162] Exhausted horses discovered in the morning would be said to be 'hag ridden'.

First Witch	Then come sisters and dance and sing and sate thy cunts on young boys' pricks. Take thy pleasure from the bearded goat and before it kneel; drink the white milk and feast on the bloody meal.
Second Witch	To burn is to live and to live is to burn!
Third Witch	Lo, the dew of night flecks our faces and damps our feet and the blood red tide doth turn.
First Witch	Then take thy knife and cut the air and raise the cruel wind of despair!
Second Witch	Hail to the Northerner![163]
Third Witch	Hail to the Hairy One!
All	All hail!
First Witch	Let us go down to the realm of Chaos where the wild wind blows.

---

[163] The Northerner was a moniker of Lilith, or Lamia, the seductive Mesopotamian demoness, from the line in Jeremiah 1:14, "Out of the north an evil shall break forth upon all the inhabitants of the land." He was actually referring to the Babylonians.

Second Witch	Let us stand upon the shore between the living and the dead where the seas crash and the thunder rolls.
Third Witch	Let us keep vigil in the house of the ghost.
First Witch	Let us dance and rejoice among dust and bone.
Second Witch	Let us rip the blood of one new lambed to set a beacon to the damned.
Third Witch	Come, Master, attend our feast!
First Witch	Summon him!
Second Witch	Call him!
Third Witch	Bring forth Night!
First Witch	Lo! Our Lord in splendour!
Second Witch	The God of Blasphemy rears upon his hairy haunch and walks as a man!
Third Witch	See! The abomination that sucks at the teat of Chaos!

First Witch	The angels from their watch-towers[164] down are cast, the Divil's kingdom come at last.
Second Witch	The demon kings of earth ride out and ancient Hekate walks fleet the moor in ghostly shout.
Third Witch	Aye, that pale Hekate of sacred name whose hounds bear not heads but tongues of flame.
First Witch	By cope and cowl, by rood and rod[165], we three shall steal from the hand of God.[166]
Second Witch	What meet hath we, sisters?
Third Witch	What ill portend the one whom fate shall bend?
Second Witch	With whom shall we toy? An earl, a thane, a princely boy... a king mayhap?

---

[164] The watchtowers mark the four cardinal points of a magical circle.

[165] These are all religious symbols which have been inverted for magical use. The cope, for example, is worn by a bishop and the rood is the cross.

[166] In Haitian Vodou, a boko (sorcerer) is said to 'steal from the hand of God'. This reflects the pagan idea that the power of Existence is morally neutral and can be used or religion or magic.

First Witch   One of highest stature who knoweth not his fiendish nature.

Second Witch   His name, sister?

First Witch   Thane[167] of Glamis and Cawdor to be, the noble Macbeth do I see.

Second Witch   Such a one that revels in blood and power, but he shall rue the day come the hour. Men are such pretty baubles that chase the light, and for vainest glory die and fight.

Third Witch   Raise him up and watch him fall. A peasant is no fun at all.

Second Witch   How so shall Fate reduce this castle[168] to quarried stone, and mighty hero who won renown shall end his days alone?

---

[167] A thane (Saxon *thegn*) was a nobleman who owned tracts of land in exchange for service to the King. The eponymous Macbeth, already Thane of Glamis (pronounced *glaams*), defeats the rebellious Thane of Cawdor and is given his title by King Duncan.

[168] Refers to Macbeth himself as a warrior rather than to a physical castle. The castle is also a chess piece and the Three Witches are playing a game with Macbeth.

First Witch	A flaw[169] that exceeds the finest art, yet greed and arrogance shall pierce his heart. Ambition doth lead him by the neck as the dog doth walk the master to the wreck.
Second Witch	Aye, and parades itself in servant's clothes, but hides a knife beneath the smile and revels in his master's woes.
Third Witch	No man may know his whole fate, but in its unravelling he sees too late.
First Witch	How now, Graymalkin, child of storm, attend thy mother in pleasing form. By the restless dead who rule the night, deliver this dagger [170]when the time is right.

---

[169] In Shakespearian tragedy, the hero possesses a flaw in his nature that leads to his downfall.

[170] This is the dagger that appears to Macbeth in Act 2 Scene 1.

Graymalkin	For whom doth the anvil ring, on whom the stain, in whose likeness was forged this dire and curséd blade that damns their name?
First Witch	The once and future Macbeth shall bear the stain, who would be king where now is thane.
Second Witch	Come then, sisters, let us stitch a pretty tapestry of pain, the like Macbeth lose all he gain.
Third Witch	Weave about him his web of fate for dawn approaches and the hour is late.
First Witch	Lay the poppet on its back.
Second Witch	Bind it 'bout with cords of black.
Third Witch	Wind in shroud on Divil's rock[171].
First Witch	And mark it out in blood of cock[172].
Second Witch	Nine knots[173] to lie in wait.

---

[171] A natural altar of rock.

[172] Blood contains the life force and so becomes a sacrifice to the Powers of the Other Side.

[173] The Weird Sisters are practising knot magic. In medieval witchcraft a knot was said to trap or contain power and intent.

Third Witch	Nine knots the hook to bait.
First Witch	Nine knots his wits forsake.
Second Witch	Nine knots a monster make.[174]
Third Witch	Nine knots the dead to walk.[175]
First Witch	Nine knots their slayer stalk.
Second Witch	Nine knots he shall fall.
Third Witch	Nine knots his land, his wife and all.
First Witch	Nine knots is all to do the deed and nine to Hell consign his seed. So the work of Night is done ere Macbeth victorious and battle won.
All	All hail Macbeth!
Exeunt	

The number 9 is a sacred number and is the only number whose multiples when added together reduce back to 9.

[174] Refers to the slaughter of Macduff's family in Act 4 Scene 2.

[175] Refers to the ghost of Banquo in Act 3 Scene 4, whom Macbeth has assassinated to prevent him founding a line of Kings, as per the witches' prophesy.

Notes

The Three Witches, also known as the Weird Sisters (from the Anglo-Saxon and Norse *wyrd* meaning 'fate') are derived variously from the Greek Moirae and the Norse Norns, who were spinners of fate, but unlike their antecedents, the Weird Sisters have a malevolent purpose: they are trickster figures, agents of a goblin universe. By only revealing *part* of Macbeth's destiny (that he shall be king), they entrap him into attempting to *control* his fate: first murdering King Duncan, then by murdering his companion in arms Banquo (who was prophesied to found a line of kings *after* Macbeth), and then killing the noble Macduff's family and basically removing anyone who might pose a threat. The irony is that by attempting to control his fate, Macbeth succeeds only in bringing his original fate about and his line comes to an ignominious end. The lesson of Macbeth is that Evil manipulates human free will to destroy itself.

I had originally decided to give the Three Witches names: Old Mother Kettle for the crone, Goodwyfe Drybone for the mother, and Maid Bobbin for the youngest, but that would have clashed with the actual play where Shakespeare refers to them only as Witch

442

One, Two, Three etc. Naming them would also have humanised them, whereas 'nameless' they come across as somehow more malevolent. Note that Shakespeare's stage directions are exceedingly sparse; he sets the scene at the start and after that it is up to the player to interpret how the scene is played.

Quoth the Raven
(Inspired by Edgar Allan Poe's *The Raven*)

A traveller, I, of deserts wide and waste,
Bereft of water and wont to thirst,
To a wild and lonely well made haste,
With a sorrow I had nursed,
For my lost Lucretia
Lay pale in her grave
And where wandered now her spirit
By night and day I'd crave,
And with my question I walked on
To the wan and crumbling wall
That seemed to draw me to it,
So close that I might fall.
Full wide and deep, and black as ink,
As black as ink that well,
Swathed by stairs that spiralled down,
It seemed to me, to hell[176].
And by that well, a woman stood,
Girt in clothes of night,
Shadowed by a grove of palms

---

[176] Hell as in 'Underworld' as opposed to the Christian place of punishment, i.e., akin to the Jewish Sheol.

444

That hid her from my sight.
"Wherefore my lost Lucretia,
Whom lately I did love,
But now lies buried in the earth,
Her soul flown like a dove?
For I hath come to seek her
And hear her voice once more,
And desire to know when she shall meet me
On the deathly shore."
And the wind did blow upon the sand
And the stars they laughed at me
And the woman's robes did rustle
And her eyes shone horribly.
"Never shalt thou meet," she quoth,
"Nor thy lover see,
And though thou walk a thousand miles
Never shall it be.
There art no words to bring her back,
Across the Cimmerian[177] sea,
For I am the Keeper of the Dead

---

[177] A word meaning dark and gloomy, derived from a reference in Homer to a tribe of people who lived in perpetual mist and gloom. They are also mentioned by Herodotus. Historically they were a Eurasian steppe people who arose around 1000 B.C. and migrated into southern Russia until displaced by the Scythians, whence they migrated into Anatolia and raided the

And in death she bides with me".
And as I gazed on, a raven flew
And lit upon her arm,
And such doom was in that raven's eyes
As did fright me with alarm.
"What ghast and nightmare bird art thou
That to thy mistress cleave,
And what fated augury dost thou dispense
So cruelly to deceive?
Shall no candle light my love
To return unto my door,
But alone remain and ne'er forget
Upon that silent shore?"
And that raven it did speak to me
In odd and eerie caw,
So eldritch was the timbre of its voice,
Quoth the raven, "Nevermore."
Thus, its answer spoken
And despairing of my life,
To the tenebrous[178] pit I trod
That I might join my wife,

Greek kingdoms of Lydia and Phrygia, being defeated by King Alyattes of Lydia (r. 610–560 BC).

[178] Dark, shadowy or obscure, from the Latin *Tenebrae* meaning 'darkness'.

For if my lost Lucretia I could not hold
Then I might go to her,
And seek my death in that fey well,
In the demented darkness, where the restless
    shadows stir.

Notes

"'Quaff, oh quaff this kind nepenthe and forget
    this lost Lenore!' Quoth the raven 'Nevermore.'"

The title of the poem is taken from a repeating refrain in Edgar Allan Poe's *The Raven*: "*Quoth the raven 'Nevermore.'*" The meaning of that line in *The Raven* is that the character of the poem will never be able to forget his beloved Lenore, who has passed from the world, and forever be pained by her loss. It is this knowledge that he must always bear the pain of remembrance that drives the author into insanity. The line is echoed in the words of the well's guardian spirit, "Never shall it be," and by the raven itself. Despairing of summoning his wife Lucretia's spirit to hear her voice, our protagonist descends the well to join her in death.

When reading Poe's original poem, certain questions presented themselves: what is the nature of the raven? Where does it come from, and who sent it? Is it merely a capricious spirit or is it a messenger or emissary of some underworld power? In many respects, Poe's poem gains strength from the fact that we don't know the answers. It is clear in Poe's poem that the raven is not a physical bird but an entity "from Night's Plutonian shore". I decided to take Poe's poem in a new direction and interpret the raven as the 'fetch' or totemic spirit animal of the woman "girt in clothes of night" who guards the boundaries of the living and the dead, and might rightly be called the Goddess of Death.

The poem is set in a desert: it doesn't matter which desert; the point is that the desert is a liminal space where the mundane and spirit world meet (which is why ancient ascetics would go into the desert to meditate). The well, too, is rich in symbolism both in Jungian terms as a gateway to the unconscious and mystically as an entrance to Hades or Sheol, in which instance it is often referred to as the 'well of souls', and it is this symbolism that informs the poem.

The Rosary

The wind bloweth where it lists,
Singing songs of lamentation
'Mid falling leaves and mists,
That wreath the hollowed hills
Drably draped in rain
And twine the blackened thorn
That twists in pain.

Shall I recant the heresies of love
Scrolled in shadowed caverns of my heart[179]
Or touch to flame the frail pages
Of fond remembered art?[180]
For though love's kiss hath cooled
And flesh hath fled to earth,
The memory of her burns my lips
And kindles in the hearth.

---

[179] A memory of forbidden love preserved in secret. It is an oblique reference to the Dead Sea Scrolls, heretical texts from the early Christian era that were discovered in a cave at Nag Hammadi in 1945.

[180] The memory of his wife's beauty.

Howl then, bloodless inquisitor, relentless wind,
And plague me with thy prayers,
Thou shalt not pry the secrets of my soul
And I shall shed no tears,
For though thou stir my conscience
And sit in judgement on my life,
Faith is nothing without love,
Nor the joy that was my wife.

Notes

A Catholic priest has defied the Church's law of celibacy and secretly taken a wife (as many priests did in the Middle Ages). His beloved wife has since died, leaving him unable to openly expiate his grief. The first verse uses landscape as a metaphor to explore his emotional desolation in which the wind becomes an accusing voice. The first line of the poem is a line taken from the Gospel of John 3:8, while the penultimate line paraphrases St Paul in 1 Corinthians 13.

The rule of celibacy that dates from the time of St Paul is a curious one since the idea of being 'married to the Spirit' implies a gnostic dichotomy between Spirit and Matter which was itself antithetical to the Church's teachings. The Church would have argued, conversely, a non-dualistic view that while Matter cannot be said to be 'evil' nor Spirit 'good', since both are aspects of God, there is nonetheless a polarity of energy that either draws us down toward Nature (as a mere 'creature') or elevates the soul toward the experience of Spirit. One of the problems with religious celibacy, however, is the repression of those higher emotions such as love that make us human, and more pejoratively, the distorting of the sexual drive. Many of those who have practiced celibacy have been deeply unhappy and unfulfilled individuals and somewhat 'cold' of disposition; the extreme manifestation of this is the 'fanatic'. Personally, I do not believe that one must forsake human love in order to live a 'spiritual life'; a balance is always possible.

An amusing story is told about Thomas Cranmer, Archbishop of Canterbury at the time when Henry VIII split from Rome. The newly 'nationalised' church did not immediately become Protestant (until the boy king Edward VI) and Protestants continued to be persecuted. This left Cranmer (who might be described as a religious 'centrist') in a very difficult predicament because he had secretly married a German Protestant woman and brought her back to

England. He therefore devised a ruse to conceal his wife: he had a box designed for her. Every time he had to accompany his wife on an engagement, his wife would get in the box (loaded on the back of a carriage) and would disembark out of sight at the other end of the journey. I think the story perfectly epitomises the conflict between absurd religious laws and our most human impulses. I know which I would trust!

The Shadow 'Neath the Door

He always comes at three,
I know because I listen out
In the darkness of my room,
And look about
In the coldness and the gloom,
And strain to hear
And catch a glimpse of
Who or what is hiding there.
Tense and watchful,
I slowly turn my head,
And peer into the shadows
That hang beyond my bed.
The laconic drone of a panicked fly
Punctuates the quiet,
Scrabbling to find escape,
Trapped with no way out,
And the percussive beat of blinds
Rattling in the breeze
Through the glazing, cracked and crazed,
Increases my unease.
Kids don't sleep well here at night,
Too many things to fear,

And that's not just the ghosts an' all
But the people lurking near.
Gaunt and leaden is this place,
A house not meant to save,
But built for penance and for pain,
Chill and brooding as the grave.
The sunlight dares not enter,
The dusty windows loom and press,
Numb the skin and whither life,
The babe cries in distress.
Only the damned remain here,
Haunt the echoing halls,
And the shades of angry children
Reach out through the walls.
The corridors, they ache with cold,
The floors are bare and grey;
If God ever once was here,
He's not here today.
From the belly of the building,
The maze that's walked by fear,
I hear the sound of steps
And a door bangs shut somewhere.
I hear the squeak of shoes
Upon the waxéd floor,
Then the squeaking stops as he waits outside,

A shadow 'neath the door,
And I shrink back as the handle turns,
A cat's eye strip of light
And when that goes out it means he's in
And my chest goes tight.
A moving mass of blackness
Bends the pale stripes of moon
That beam in through the broken blinds
And I know he'll touch me soon.
I can hear his breathing,
A choked and heavy rasp,
Of lungs congested by desire,
A perverted sort of gasp,
And then his fingers touch me,
Icy on my cheek,
Twining round my strands of hair
Moving down to seek
My breasts that heave in
Laboured breath, too afraid to scream,
And skin that crawls to get away
From this nightmare of a dream,
And then he rolls the covers back
And suddenly I'm cold
And I just wish he'd finish it,
Release his clammy hold.

Night after night it happens
Till I'm hollow like a sack
A rag doll to be prised and played with,
Twisted on the rack.
I study them at breakfast
And wonder who it is:
The red-faced one with drooping jowls,
The jolly one with the grin,
The stern old bastard what flogs himself
And considers love a sin.
They tell me I am wicked,
But I'm just an accidental kid,
The family's dirty secret
They wanted to be rid.
The priest condemned my mum in church,
Had her sent away,
Then they dumped their shame on me
And every day they make me pay.
When I try to tell the nuns,
They say I'm full of lies,
They lock me up in solitary
With the spiders and the flies.
One day, I'll go and cut my wrists,
Create a fucking stink,
And the fuzz'll lock those fucking priests up

In the fucking clink,
But that ain't gonna happen,
They'll just say I'm ill,
Label me psychotic
And drug me with a pill,
And when they've finished raping me,
They'll send me overseas
To a family who'll exploit me
And work me to my knees.
Why did you betray me, God,
How could you not see?
I thought you loved the children,
But you never heard my plea.
I'm not afraid of solitary,
Don't fear the nuns no more,
But what scares me most is three a.m.
And the shadow 'neath the door.

Notes

The Shadow 'Neath the Door conflates two of the most despicable episodes in recent Catholic history: the appalling treatment of unmarried mothers and children in so-called Magdalene homes in Ireland from the eighteenth century to the 1960s, and the serial abuse of children in Catholic children's homes (usually boys' homes) by Catholic priests.

Let's start with the Magdalene Houses, also called asylums. These operated in Ireland from 1767 to 1996 and were designed to house single unmarried mothers who were put to work to 'atone' for their sins, principally in laundries. Originally Protestant, they were later taken over by the Catholic Church. One of the worst features of these were that the children were separated from their mothers (utterly unconscionable in itself) and put to work in another part of the building or sent away to a completely different home. Conditions were reportedly stricter than prisons, the food poor and the heat intolerable. Many mothers' health collapsed. Essentially, Magdalene asylums were concentration camps for single mothers before the term 'concentration camp' was invented[181]. All that was missing was the barbed wire, the search lights and the dogs.

Media attention has recently focussed on one particular Magdalene House in County Waterford, Ireland: Tuam, run by the Bon Secours Sisters, a

---

[181] During the Boer War 1899-1902, by the British.

458

Catholic order of nuns. In 1975, two boys out playing prised open the concrete cover of a septic tank to reveal the skeletons of children. This, however, was just the tip of the iceberg. The septic tank was in fact a mass grave, and the entire surrounding council estate had been built over it. The Tuam historian, Catherine Corless, requested records of children's deaths in the home and was shocked when the registrar returned 800, only one of whom had been given a Christian burial; the rest had been unceremoniously dumped into a septic tank and left to rot. Deaths of children at Tuam and similar Magdalene Houses were four to five times that of the general population, and a 1944 health board report on the Tuam home reports emaciated and pot-bellied children. The reason why the children weren't given formal burials was, first, to hide the appalling death rate of these children, and secondly, because it was believed by the nuns that children born out of wedlock did not qualify for a Christian burial. The local authorities knew about the abuses at Tuam but chose to ignore them, such was the power and authority of the Catholic Church in Ireland at that time.

Once again, the Catholic church is in the news, this time in Canada, when indigenous tribes in

Saskatchewan discovered 54 unmarked graves at the site of two Catholic-run residential schools. That number has now climbed to 1,100. These government-funded Catholic schools were part of a forced assimilation policy in which 150,000 Metis and Inuit children were forcibly removed from their families and taught to be 'European'. Remarkably, as with Tuam and Saskatchewan, no single person or institution has ever been prosecuted; it seems that some institutions are just too powerful to be taken down.

Two things come out of this: the first is that religious austerity doesn't make nuns and priests better people; it simply represses their most human emotions. Secondly, a vow of celibacy least qualifies a person to look after vulnerable young people on the cusp of puberty.

Now for the Catholic Church's role in child sex abuse. Recently, in 2020, the Independent Inquiry into Child Sexual Abuse (IICSA) in England and Wales found damning evidence of child sex abuse in Catholic institutions including serial rape, masturbation, anal and oral sex, and sadistic beatings. Incredibly, the Pope urged the leader of the Catholic Church in England and Wales to remain in his post; in any normal institution he would have been sacked. Meanwhile in Scotland, the Scottish Child Abuse Inquiry described a Catholic boarding school run by monks in the Highlands, Fort Augustus Abbey, as a "haven for paedophiles". The same inquiry found evidence of systematic abuse at homes in Lanark and Rutherglen. Then there is the sexual abuse scandal in the Catholic Archdiocese of Philadelphia, in Pennsylvania, U.S., revealed through a grand jury investigation in 2005. Having been exposed, however, new charges were reported by a new grand jury in 2011. This time, for once, the law came down hard on the perpetrators who oversaw the abuse.

In the 1950's, also, large numbers of British orphans were placed in the hands of the Congregation of Christian Brothers who shipped them overseas to homes in Australia, the United States and Canada, where hundreds of boys were abused, the extent of which is only just coming to light. This abuse continued into the 1980's.

Although child sex abuse isn't exclusively Catholic, it occurs with less frequency in Anglican homes, and I think the reason is the rule of celibacy that represses a person's natural sexual instincts which ordinarily would be expressed through a loving relationship. The other reason why it is more common in Catholic homes is the secretive power relationship of the

461

Catholic hierarchy which 'looks after its own' and is more intent on avoiding publicity than on removing perpetrators of abuse. This is the pattern: when a priest is ordained, there is an unspoken agreement that in exchange for loyalty to the Church, the Church will cover up the sins of the priests. What the Church needs is a police force acting independently of the ecclesiastical hierarchy to bring cases of child abuse to civil prosecution, but that will never happen. For too long, the Catholic Church has been a law unto itself, and it is time it was made subject to the law like everyone else.

In fairness, abuse also occurs with regularity in non-church local authority children's' homes, as evidenced in Rochdale, Rotherham and Telford, between 2000 and 2012 where Asian gangs predated on young white British girls. The source of this abuse wasn't a religious one: the fault lies in the dark side of Asian patriarchal culture which demeans and represses women, and (some) young Asian men who view white girls as sexual objects. In this instance, the failure of the local authority and the police to investigate was hampered by political correctness: a fear of 'racial profiling' and 'upsetting' the Asian community, and a blanket refusal to believe the children who were making the complaints. The lesson of Rotherham and Rochdale is that politics got in the way of policing.

The Storm that Blows the Rose
(After Christina Rossetti)

The storm that blows the rose
Bends not my heart,
For my heart bends but to thee,
And the sun that melts the storm
Is like the love you give to me.

The clouds that race the sky
Chase not my love,
For my love doth cleave to thee,
And the sun that fills my home with light
Is like the smile you give to me.

The wind that shakes the trees
Sitrs not my soul,
For my soul stirs but for thee,
And the summer airs that stroke the leaves
Are as the words you speak to me.

The waves that toss the ship
Tip not my course,
For my course is set to thee,

Thou art my port and guiding star
Whose arms do shelter me.

The rain that rends the rye
Rends not my heart,
For my heart cannot be rent,
Like a diamond is my heart
And in thy hand it rests content.

Ne'er storm nor wind nor rain
My love shall wash away,
But every morn I wake with thee,
Sweet lover of my life,
Sunshine warms my day.

Notes

I have always enjoyed the poems of Christina Rossetti, who made her name with *Goblin Market* (pub. 1862). Do you remember *In the Bleak Midwinter* that you probably sang as a Christmas carol? That was by penned as a poem by Christina Rossetti in 1872, set to music by Gustav Holst in 1906, with a choral version by Harold Darke in 1909. My absolute favourite Rossetti poem, however, is *A Birthday*, a young woman's ecstatic celebration of falling in love, and *The Storm that Blows the Rose* is intended as a tribute.

Since Christina Rossetti's work is now in the public domain, here is *A Birthday*.

My heart is like a singing bird
Whose nest is in a water'd shoot;
My heart is like an apple-tree
Whose boughs are bent with thick-set fruit;
My heart is like a rainbow shell
That paddles in a halcyon sea;
My heart is gladder than all these,
Because my love is come to me.

Raise me a daïs of silk and down;
Hang it with vair and purple dyes;
Carve it in doves and pomegranates,
And peacocks with a hundred eyes;
Work it in gold and silver grapes,
In leaves and silver fleurs-de-lys;
Because the birthday of my life
Is come, my love is come to me.

Strong Love

So I come on too strong…
Nature makes no apology for itself,
Nor of itself is wrong,
For love's artifice is but a cloth spread
Upon the stain of passion,
Which I would not ration
But yield all restraint,
For love's initiate knows
Flesh to flesh doth cleave,
And aching desire relieve,
In bucking backs and cries of joy.
Why so coy
When I know you like it rough?
The keen plane of my hand excites
And although we have our fights,
'No' doesn't really mean 'enough'.
Such a pretty dove,
Whose panicked eyes and stricken heart implore,
And would yet beg for more,
A ripe cherry to be plucked,
And I'll take my bite before
Time and madness canker love.

Am I a dog to be tickled behind the ears?

I am a wolf with a wolf's appetite

And the wolf knows no tears,

Nor expiation of its sins,

For as the wounded can attest

Its nature always wins.

My lust is a demon that walks on ceilings

And would possess you

And have you speak in tongues,

Wherefore confess your feelings

To this devil who would slide inside you,

And with you naked lie

Till desire breaks o'er the battlements of sleep,

And passion become a storm swell

That breaks the wall of reason

And all away doth sweep.

I would harry you like the Northman,

And sell you in the slave marts of Baghdad

To pout accusingly at fat old Arabs with
     slobbering lips,

And would you pay the *Danegeld*[182] to be rid of me,

I would raid again across the sea

---

[182] Literally 'Dane gold', the gold used to pay off the Vikings to stop them raiding in Dark Age Europe.

With many ships.
Do I so overwhelm you
That you cast me out into the rain?
Is all the pain you give not really yours,
For which I carry the can,
And my life a series of unpacked cases,
And endless tours,
Each hotel an apology
For being a man?

Notes

As with *Shot Down in Flames*, which deals with obsessive love and sexual jealousy, *Strong Love* is an exploration of the darker aspects of the male psyche: the mind of a sexual psychopath. At its core is the difference between a woman's enjoyment of sex as a celebration of both emotional and physical intimacy, idealised as romantic love, and the man's more naturalistic inclinations. The sexual psychopath uses a woman to fulfil his fantasies (enslavement in this poem), but, having no capacity for empathy, he is incapable of love. The poem is told from the man's perspective. It is clear that the woman's desire for a softer form of lovemaking challenges his masculine identity and his 'right' to express his 'masculine nature'. But is there not room for compromise? A sensitive, considerate man will always find out how a woman *likes* to be made love to; he doesn't just plunge in like a Viking! While it is true that women often have fantasies about being 'mastered' by a strong man, they remain fantasies, and the reality is very different. Truly, a relationship is only as good as the quality of mind both partners bring to it. This man's relationships don't last very long before he is kicked out and moves on to another woman... and these are probably tempestuous relationships while they last, with bouts of intense physical sex alternating with screaming matches and plate-throwing, terminating with the man's expulsion from the house. Notice how, toward the end of the poem, he tries to blame the woman's rejection of him onto her own feelings of inadequacy – a classic trick of the manipulator. In short, the poem depicts a sexual psychopath who uses women for his own pleasure and to assert his male dominance.

The Wilding Shore
(Inspired by M.R. James)

I walk the wilding shore 'twixt the ocean and the
    land,
Amnesic waves cool my feet,
Wash clean the memory of sand,
Exposing to my eyes the silent and the dread,
Crowns of Anglian kings
Lost to lore, bones of warriors undead,
While strands of kelp like tattered rags
Dry upon the rock,
And drape the rotting piles of piers
Where ancient ships would dock;
And scattered here and there,
Shells lie waiting to be found,
That speak in voices of the dead,
The voices of the drowned,
And I hear them call my name
As I pick my panicked way,
To flee the figure that follows, black against the
    sun,
Coat flapping in the wind on a windless day.
I stumble 'long the lonely shore,
'Bove rusted haft of Saxon sword

And razor line of broken jaw,
Knowing not what is in my mind
Nor real anymore,
And dare not turn about and gaze upon the face
Of the one that doth pursue me,
The fiend that giveth chase.

Notes

M.R. James (1862-1936) was a distinguished medievalist and antiquarian who occupied such elevated roles as Provost of Eton and Provost of Kings College, Cambridge. During his researches, he came across the darker aspects of church history: tales of hauntings, cursed relics and clerics meddling in books of magic. Thus, his stories were not drawn purely from imagination but were grounded in *what he had found*. The son of a clergyman, James was raised in Suffolk at the family rectory in Great Livermere, Suffolk, and the wild, desolate Suffolk coast featured in several of his stories, especially *A Warning to the Curious*. Centred on a Suffolk town called Seaburgh (based on Aldeburgh, home of James' maternal grandmother) the story concerns itself with an archaeologist, Paxton, who stumbles upon one of the three holy crowns of East Anglia. These were the crowns of the Kings of the Eastern Angles, the last of whom, Edmund, had been martyred by the Vikings in 869. The crowns were said to have been buried to keep England safe from invasion; one had already been dug up and one lost beneath the encroaching sea, but the third lies under the earth until Paxton finds it and digs it up. Unknown to Paxton, however, the crown had been guarded by a family called Ager down the generations. When the last guardian, William Ager dies young at age 28, his spirit remains earthbound to guard the crown. As soon as he has retrieved the crown, Paxton feels a presence following him. He replaces the crown, hoping the presence will stop tormenting him, but the guardian spirit does not forgive so easily...

The Wilding Shore concerns itself with liminal spaces, neither here nor there. The shoreline is a liminal space: between sea and land, sleeping and dreaming, Conscious and Unconscious. Deserts are also liminal spaces: holy men would retreat to meditate in them, Jesus was tempted by Satan in one. Similarly, empty houses are liminal spaces because they exist at the boundary of human communities and a space that has been vacated by people and is, well, empty.

One might say, that when humans leave a place, the powers of the Other Side move in; or is it just that, in a liminal space, we become more psychically attuned to that space? Our psychic antennae literally enlarge and expand, and I concede that some people are more sensitive than others, even when they don't know it... until they see a ghost.

The Wilding Shore is a sister poem to *The Damned*.

1913
(A war poem)

Of course, I remember Heyward,
That lovely old manor set in the valley
By the Thames, willow-washed, winking in sun's
    flare,
Jacobean[183], of high leaded panes and chequered
    corners,
With its stepped gable[184], genteelly castellated,
Proclaiming its privilege 'bove redoubted[185]
    regiments of tile[186],
The while its warm brickwork baked in noon heat,
Glowing in rich reds,

---

[183] Referring to the reign of James I, 1603-1625. From the Latin 'Jacobus', meaning James.

[184] See Notes.

[185] 'Redoubted' = as an adjective, someone who is 'respected, formidable, renowned, worthy of respect', having the same meaning as 'redoubtable'. From 'redoubt' meaning a fortress or defensible place. As a verb, meaning 'grouped in a defensible position'. Both senses are appropriate here: the house is stylish but formidable (adjective), the tiles are grouped in a battle formation (verb).

[186] Note the military symbolism: it's there even in peace time, in the great old houses built by the nobility who descended from the warrior elites.

Foursquare and firm amid its gardens' gaudy
    greens,
Of late and fond-remembered joy
Recalled since then in misty scenes.
A rose trellis scaled the southern side
And petals showered in pinks and reds
As we sauntered down the Long Walk,
Arm in mine,
Immersed in idle talk,
You in your white linen dress,
Straw boater circled by black ribbon,
Hair tied back in a ponytail that bobbed against
Your shell-white neck as you moved like a dream,
Thoughtful grey eyes lost in poesy,
Little wisps of auburn hair
Dancing in a beam,
Swept by scherzos[187] of warm breeze racing through
    grass,
Teasing your skirt,
Exciting the little hairs on your arms
As you brushed pollen from my shirt.
I said something,

---

[187] A vigorous, light, or playful composition, typically comprising
a movement in a symphony or sonata.

And your almond eyes creased in laughter,
Like sloes softly squeezed,
Sparkled bright and gay,
So it was, that perfect day.
We yearned to touch,
And there were times, my darling,
When the urge became too much
And I had to look away.
I watched you float down the steps to the garden,
Caressing the curlicues of stone balustrade,
And demurely linked fingers
Along the avenue of orange trees
Teasing with bitter fruit[188],
Picnicked beneath the great elms,
Firm of root,
Crinoline[189] rustle of leaves like swirling skirts,
The delicate calligraphy of shadowed branches
Inked on paper smooth lawns,
O'er which had dawned many thousand dawns[190].
In a moment of boldness,
I gave you my ring:

---

[188] Note the symbolic importance of 'bitter fruit'.

[189] A hard-wearing dress fabric common in the Victorian era.

[190] The age and permanence of the house contrast with the wholesale destruction of the coming war.

Faces blotched in latticed light,
We drank to England and to love
That last summer before the blight.
It was the end of an age, but we knew it not.
We thought that summer would go on forever,
 didn't we?
Endless garden parties,
Paté and poetry,
Chablis and champagne,
We had no idea
That after that summer,
When came the rain,
The world would never be the same.
There was a regatta that day,
You remember how the lawns sloped down to the
 river,
Full of little punts with brocaded[191] ladies in
 absurd hats
Nursing parasols in the prow,
And the air was full of song;
Life for us was like that — we drifted along
In the stream of our own idleness, untouchable,

---

[191] A rich heavy fabric woven for women with raised patters of gold and silver thread.

And now it's all gone,
The lounge suits and the lace,
The ease and the grace[192],
Usurped by uniforms
Of torn and tattered green,
Like the moss that grows
In dead men's mouths,
Mud and rats,
And enemy unseen,
Of hatred and hunger,
Of war and want,
Of murder by machine,
Where rain hysterically hammers
On helmets made of tin,
Pocked and picked by shrapnel,
A flood of tears above the din,
Drowning the churnéd fields
Where lonely men expire,
Badly hung pictures on barbéd wire,
Milled to meat by melting guns,
Our reward for bravery to England's sons,
Trudging through the muddy maze

---

[192] The story is told from the view of the British upper classes. Life for the working classes would certainly not have been a life of 'ease and grace'!

Past souped-up guts and hairless heads,
The blown-off leg still in its shoe,
Just to gain a paltry mile or two:
"Victory's just a trench away!"
The mental paralysis of war[193],
"Over the top!" "Give the Jerry[194] hell!"
What was it all for?
The rattle of the snake of war,
The graveyard of the truth,
The bilge of guts upon the ground,
The bloody eucharist of youth.
Ruddy Jerry attacked our line,
First we knew it, the yellow cloud[195]
Drifting desultorily on the wind
Across the torn-up fields,
Where good men died who never sinned,
Some god-awful miasma, a spirit out of hell,
The like I never saw, nor ever shall,
And now I lie in blood-stained bed
Somewhere to the south,

---

[193] 'Just keep on doing the same thing, keep hurling men and materiel at the enemy, and eventually you'll win.' This was how the British generals fought the First World War.

[194] Slang for 'German'.

[195] Mustard gas.

As a nurse spoons morphine
In my wheezing mouth,
Driven mad by the burning and the pain,
Listening to the moans of men,
The cries of the insane.
For God's sake, find a decent man[196],
Take pleasure in your kids,
Enjoy your summers in the sun
And forget me if you can.
My life is over, and I'll never be the same,
I would have been your lover
But now I'm just a broken reed,
Pitiful and lame.
Only the strong survive here,
Courage matters less than luck,
This is not a world for the gentle and the good,
My love,
But the Gatling[197] and the military truck,
And the summer we spent at Heyward

---

[196] Unlike today, in that time, a woman's security depended on a good marriage. The independent career woman was a person of the future!

[197] A multi-barrelled, rotating gun operated by a hand crank that could fire 200 rounds per minute. It was invented in 1862, during the American Civil War, by Richard Jordan Gatling.

Is all I have left of you,
That last idyllic season
Remembered by the few.

Notes

The First World War erupted on 28th July 1914, making 1913 the last full summer of peace. The Edwardian era had passed in May 1910 when Edward VII had died, and with him the transition from the Victorian age, and there was a sense in which Britain was moving into a world of uncertainty. The recently unified and industrialised Germany was flexing its muscles, challenging the established colonial powers; the mutual network of alliances that arose from Great Power rivalry pulled the world into the first global war. *1913* draws a contrast between that last summer of peace and the year of war, a mechanised war that no one was prepared for, and tells the story through one man who goes away to do his duty and ends up gassed and knowing he will never marry the girl he loved. In particular, I draw attention to the false sense of security that enveloped British society at the time, and how that security was rudely shattered.

Perhaps the piece of music that most evokes the lost world of Edwardian England is Elgar's *Cello Concerto*, composed in 1919, the year after the war, very different to the jingoistic *Pomp and Circumstance* march, and heart-reddeningly elegiac in tone. The Jacqueline du Pré version is rated the best, tragic in itself as du Pré was diagnosed with MS at the tender age of 27.

Heyward is a fictional manor house inspired by the sun-filled days I spent with my parents visiting National Trust houses during the long summer vacations out of school. It was inspired by Winston Churchill's home Chartwell which has a stepped gable and even a trellis running up one facing wall, but the stepped gable is nineteenth century in origin and certainly not Jacobean, although some of the brickwork in the original house goes back to Tudor, and certainly Jacobean, times. That said, Jacobean architecture did employ intricate gables, from the stepped gable commonly seen in the tall, narrow houses of Amsterdam, Bruges and Ghent, to a combination of curves interposed with steps, and the chequered corner effect is very much Jacobean.

Note, stylistically, how the rhyming structure changes from the initial scene set in the summer of 1913 to the experience of war in 1914. The initial descriptions of Heyward are sparse in rhyme and more leisurely than the second half of the poem where the rhyming becomes concentrated to increase tension and the momentum of the poem.

Death of a Writer

I wrote out my heart
Till naught was left to write,
And became an empty vessel
With a bottle in the night,
And the world whirled around me
Without a care,
And no one in the world
Knew I was there.
So I put on the player
To a 60's band
And danced in the lamplight
With a gun in my hand.
I choked back the tears
As I spun and I sang,
And a lifetime of failure
Went out with a bang.

Notes

Failure, or fear of failure, is a ghost that haunts most writers. Either the stream of inspiration will dry up and one will never write again, or reviewers will trash your book or simply no one will like what you've written. Writers can be very anxious people. They are also notoriously critical of their own work, often crossing out pages they've spent a day writing or making last minute changes during publication and driving their proof-readers mad. I hold up my hand to this. Sometimes, it is just the stress of living on one's emotions all the time that makes one fall off the seat. That is assuming that one gets published at all. There is not a writer on earth who has not had a rejection slip from a publisher, and publishers and agents are notoriously unsympathetic to new writers, preferring the easy money from existing ones. For the most part, publishers are extremely risk averse and don't want to take a gamble on a writer who doesn't have a provenance.

This poem was written in a fit of depression on a day when the waves metaphorically had gone over my head and suddenly my mind was filled with images of putting a gun to my head (fortunately gun laws over here are tight), but I was able to articulate my suicidal thoughts in a stream of language and imagery so I came to write it out instead of actually do it. Do not underestimate the importance of being able to verbalise one's feelings. Try this: whenever you feel like the bottom has dropped out of your world, sit down and imagine yourself as a character in a story or poem and write yourself. Describe in that story your character's thoughts and feelings and how you as your character struggle to resolve them. Personally, I have poured all my emotions into my poetry over the last thirty-five years, and I would say without hesitation that poetry is single-handedly responsible for preserving my mental health.

The attentive reader will note the deliberate placing of this poem at the end of the fourth temporal section of the book. All the other poems in the collection are arranged alphabetically within their sections, except this. *Death of a Writer* is arranged *out* of alphabetic sequence to convey the metaphor of a 'disordered' mind. It is the last poem in the last temporal section because death really is *the end*, and it is juxtaposed with the *first* poem in this section, *A Solitary Man*, because the solitary man is more vulnerable to depression and suicide than a happily married man with a family.

A
Poem
for
Christmas

Love at Midnight
(A traditional Victorian poem for Christmas)

'Twas late on Christmas Eve
As the frost began to bite,
I took my glass of brandy
And I began to write,
And as the flames burned merrily
And logs crackled in the grate,
A wrote my love a letter
For my hope would not abate.

But I poured out my heart
In every drop of ink,
In every curve of letter
Naught but Lucy did I think,
And then I breathed upon it,
With perfume did I lace,
And thereon signed my name
And dreamed of Lucy's face.

Then I betook me to the door
As carollers walked the streets,
And listened to the sound of bells,

Cries of greetings and of treats,
When of a sudden, a wind swept in,
Pushed past me like a ghost,
It swirled about my room
And took my letter I would post.

Up into the air it went
Through the falling snow,
High among the rooftops
And the houses all aglow.
Up and over chimneys,
Past gardens wreathed in white,
Over church and churchyard,
Till it was lost from sight.

Then after it I ran,
My hat blown off my head,
Through the snow banked up in drifts,
Pursuing my letter as it fled,
But catch it I could never do,
Nor knew which way it blew,
But returned in misery to my house,
Sure my dreams would ne'er come true.

It blew into the orphanage
Where it stuck upon the glass
And all the boys that read it cried
And wished it came to pass.
It blew into the market square
And flattened on the wall,
And all the folk who read it
My love for Lucy did enthral.

It blew into the chancel
As the priest set out the wine
And when he read it, his eyes lit up
For he knew that love of mine.
From the priest's hand 'twas snatched again
And whirled along the nave,
Birled[198] out through the church's door
Faster than he could save.

My Lucy rode in her carriage
That she took to Midnight Mass,
Pulled by two black horses,
Its lamps of burnished brass.
Wrapped up snug and cosy

---

[198] 'Birl' means 'to whirl' or 'spin'.

In her bonnet and her furs,
All was silent on that eve
But the barking of the curs.

Nervously looking at her watch
And fearing to be late,
She wound the carriage window down,
Her driver to berate.
Past the lichened[199] lychgate[200],
Through the black night teared with white,
My letter blew in through the carriage door
And on her lap it did alight.

When she read it, tears welled up,
And love burned in her breast,
And as the church lights came in sight
Her passion gave no rest.
"Driver!" she cried, "Hurry to the gate!"
Then wide she flung the door,
Straight she ran in to the priest

---

[199] Lichen is a slow-growing plant that forms a low crusty growth on rocks, walls, and trees. It is variously orange, dark green or grey.

[200] The lych gate is the gate of the dead through which a body is transported to the consecrated ground of a churchyard.

And his kindness did implore.

She showed the priest my letter,
But he just raised an eye,
"This letter I have seen," he said,
 "And love must never die!"
We must bring him to this church,
There must be no delay,
For you two shall be wed this night,
Wed on Christmas Day.

The priest, he sent the rector
To rouse me from my bed,
And at the sound of knocking,
I turned my sleepy head,
And in the doorway he did stand
In greatcoat and a scarf,
"Make haste, young man, your bride awaits!"
And he began to laugh.

And so my letter blew its way
All around the town,
And among the folk that winter night
Was not a single frown,
But faces did light up with joy

And to the church they streamed,
Wrapped in cloaks with lanterns high
That swung and shone and gleamed,

And as I staggered through the door
Brushing snow from off my cloak,
The crowd got up and all did cheer
And the priest stood up and spoke.
"Do you, Thomas, take this girl,
Young Lucy, as your bride?
For your letter says as much,
And your feelings cannot hide."
Silence fell upon the nave,
And the censer ceased its swing,
Then I ran and took her hand
And the choir began to sing.

And we were wed that Christmas Day
Upon the midnight hour
As candles blazed all through the church
And the snow outside did shower,
And oft I think some secret hand
Did our happiness bring to be,
On the day that Christ was born
And lights decked out the tree.

Notes

Written at Christmas 2021, after the festivities were over, I awakened in the early hours with the schema for this poem already forming in my mind, and it had already begun to compose itself as I was bustling about making breakfast, for I had to grab post-it stickers to write the lines down before I lost them. Wouldn't it be wonderful if someone's dreams were granted, and a love letter thought lost was, by miraculous intervention, united with the woman it was destined for? Unashamedly cheesy and sentimental, I think it perfectly fits the Christmas theme of love, hope and wishes fulfilled. Although it doesn't happen now, it was, in actuality, a tradition in the medieval Church to marry couples on Christmas Day, but in those times couples would be married at the church door, which is the origin of porches in ancient churches (see Chaucer's *Wife of Bath's Tale*).

Liturgical
Poems
and
Prayers

Introduction

Throughout my life, two influences have always pulled at my heart: the Craft (for which read the Witchcraft tradition) and Christian mysticism, embodied by such luminaries at St Teresa of Avila and St Thérèse of Lisieux. I do not consider these traditions as opposites. I enjoy the rawness and earthiness of the Craft and I enjoy the gentle spirituality of Christian mysticism. They are two traditions, each emphasising a different aspect of Spirit: the one extolling the rushing tide of the Life Force in Nature, and the other the gentle illumination of the mind and awakening of the heart through the descent of Grace. I have had profound experiences within both traditions. So, one might say that I have a Christian heart but a pagan soul.

What is it like to live with two such seemingly contradictory influences? Picture a baby buggy with two toddlers; you get the sibling rivalry. The one kicks the other's shin, the second thumps the first. In truth, though, no one is composed of merely a single formative influence. I am blessed to have grown up in both traditions and it has made me a more open-minded and tolerant person as a result. I have had a lifetime to contemplate the nature of Faith, and now, finally, I think I understand. It's been a journey. I was never force-fed religion and I do not force it on others. Ultimately, one's understanding of Faith is one's own. But I do make a clear distinction between Faith that is based on rational theology, and what I call Intuited Faith: a faith based on an indefinable understanding that there is a metaphysical reality that transcends us and is beyond the capacity of Reason or Science to comprehend. It may be vague and ragged around the edges, but that's okay.

I will say in conclusion, that there is no *right* faith. What is important is to have *some* structure of higher meaning, whatever you choose that to be. I liken faith to buying a suit: you can buy one off the shelf or you can have one made especially for you; the one made for you is always a better fit. Most religions are 'one size fits all' affairs, but in reality, each person makes their own peace with Divinity.

I HAVE FAITH THAT THERE IS A DIMENSION OF EXISTENCE, WITH WHICH WE ARE CONNECTED THROUGH MIND, NOT ACCESSIBLE BY OBSERVATION OR REASON BUT SOLELY THROUGH THE OPENING OF INNER PERCEPTION.

Of the poems, *The Bondage of Love* is written in the style of a medieval devotional in the spirit of the Franciscan Order, in which the aspirant aspires to a total identification between themselves and Divinity, humanised as Christ in whom the Spirit expresses itself perfectly through Man. It is hard to explain to someone who has never experienced it, but it wrote itself virtually word for word whilst in a state of deep meditation. Of the following, the *Salve Prayer* is of a similar provenance. They contrast with the *Hymn to Adonai* which is avowedly Jewish with borrowings from the Qabalah, and the *Prayer to the Supreme Being* which is more modern and emphasises the nature of Divinity as pure Being. The final prayer, the *Prayer of Unburdening*, invites the aspirant to look within and place all guilt and regret on the altar of forgiveness.

The Bondage of Love

The Lord binds me that I can do only His will.
He binds my hands that I can do only His work.
He binds my fingers that I can write only His words.
He binds my feet that I can walk only in His
    ways.
He binds my lips that I can speak only His name.
He binds my eyes that I can see only His glory.
He binds my thoughts that I can think only of Him.

I have no body but the body of Christ.
I have no face but the face of the Beloved.
I have no heart save His that beats within me,
For I am His messenger.

I offer my humanity unto Him, and He returneth
    it to me.
I am a statue, cold and hard. He breaketh me.
He taketh my heart of stone and giveth me the
    heart of a man.
Above me the dove of peace, and about me His
    grace falls like rain.

I am a falcon,
And He the falconer;
At His word, I fly betwixt the heavens and the earth,
Yet shall I always return to His glove.

I rest like a dove in His hand;
He does not crush me, nor do me harm,
I trust in His love and in His goodness.

I am a torch in the garden where He walks,
For He setteth me on fire
And I burn with His love.

I am a wineskin,
And He filleth me with wine,
And in my drunkenness I call His name.

I am a field of gold for my Lord to tread;
Flowers spring up where He has passed
And their scent is the odour of sanctity.

He sayeth, "Mine is the Kingdom",
And I sayeth, "I am its foundation and its
    cornerstone".

He sayeth, "I am the power and the glory",
And I sayeth, "I am a tent for thy brilliance".

He is my Master and my Mistress,
My Lover and my Guide.
He is the companion of my days,
My crook and my staff
Never shall I leave His side in Life or in Death.

Hymn to Adonai

Adonai,

Who art the Unfolding Light,

The Power and Intelligence that floweth through
    all things,

Who art the flooding and the ebbing of the tide,

The budding of the flower and the rotting of the
    stem,

Whose Name is written in thunder and in flash;

Thou Titanic Power

Seated in Majesty,

Christ at Thy right hand,

Samael [201] at Thy left,

And before Thy Temple

The Pillars of Mercy and of Wrath.

Our hands reach up to Thee,

And our tears fall upon the Earth.

Witness our orisons,

---

[201] Samael, often confused with Satan, but also the Archangel of
Mars, is the wrathful aspect of the Holy Spirit, as Christ is the
aspect of Divine Love.

Anoint us with the incense of Thy breath,
Touch our heads with flame
And bestow upon us
The Grace of the Holy Spirit.

Prayer to the Supreme Being

Oh thou Limitless Light of Existence
That hath neither name nor attribute,
Who art a roaring and a silence,
The roll of thunder on a summer's day
And the promise of a rainbow,
And who brought forth Being
Through which Thy presence flows
Like a mighty river in flood.
Oh Limitless Light,
Thou art beauty and terror,
The softness of rain and the hardness of ice.
Through the Will to Be
Thou wrought all things,
And all things are contained in Thee,
Perfect Mind unfolding into Existence,
The Word that moves across the page,
The Book that writes itself.
Does not the flower turn its head to the Sun?
Do not the birds sing the breaking of the dawn?
If Thou hadst a name I would speak it,
But all that liveth speakest Thy name.
Oh Limitless Light,

Help us seek unity
In the midst of separateness,
And put aside illusion and falsehood
That we may express Thy Light and Grace and
   Majesty
Though our minds and hearts.

Salve Prayer

Adonai, Lord of Thrones, Blessed of my Heart,
Who art the Life of all things,
Receive me!

Salve, Salve, Salve[202]

Adonai, Light of Light, Light upon Light,
Spirit that moveth over the face of the waters,
Bless me!

Salve, Salve, Salve

Dove of Grace, be upon me,
Dove of Grace, be within me,
Dove of Grace, open my heart.

Salve, Salve, Salve

---

[202] Salve means 'Hail!' In Latin

Christ, Star of the Firmament,
Whose raiments are of the Sun,
Open unto Me the path to the City of God[203]

Salve, Salve, Salve

---

[203] The City of God or the Kingdom of God refers to an inner state of spiritual illumination. "The kingdom of God is within you." (Luke 17:20-21)

Prayer of Unburdening

I offer unto Thee my hatred that it shall be
transmuted into love.
I offer unto Thee my violence that it shall be
transmuted into kindness.
I offer unto Thee my rage that it shall be
transmuted into joy.
I offer unto Thee every sin, falsehood and
abomination that I shall have new life.
I lay upon Thine altar the worst of me and the
best of me.
I offer up these things to the Great Silence that
they may be dissolved in Beauty and Light.
For in thee, the storm ceases, the winds drop and
the waters are stilled, and the blue vault of
Heaven is reflected in the clear waters of the
mind.
Before me thou settest a table in the garden of the
east
Containing many good things,
Food for the soul and victuals for the thirsty,
And all the mysteries of Heaven and Earth thereon,

Whereof I eat of the bread of wisdom and drink of
    the wine of ecstasy,
That I may be made new in Thine image,
And I call upon the Holy Spirit to rest within me.

Additional Poem
by
Adam Holland

The Magical Box

I will put in my box
The shell from a swishing sea,
The dog from a dark alley,
The pupa from a butterfly shaped as a cylinder.

I will put in my box
A drop of snow touching the tip of a tongue,
A spider spinning a web in the golden sun,
A silver moon from the sky.

My box is fashioned from light green emeralds,
Its hinges are a scorpion's claws,
The corners are made of platinum inlaid with
    rubies.

I shall travel in my box
To Mars and beyond,
And swim with dolphins in the deep blue sea.

Notes

This poem was written by my partner's son, Adam, during his junior school years at Motcombe in Eastbourne. I was immediately struck by its visionary quality and determined that it needed to be preserved for posterity. It is reproduced here by permission.

A Candle
Before the Sun

Discursive Essays
On Faith and Being

Discursive Essay on the Nature of Divinity
Exploring themes from *Priapus*

The evolution of religious thought from the polytheism of paganism to the monotheism of Judaism and thence Christianity (which also incorporated the philosophic monotheism of Plato) didn't change the fundamental idea of God as a creative entity, and both these religions (as well as Islam) adhere to the belief that God made the heavens and the earth, including all life. The result is a curiously static view of the universe as something unchanging: everything that is has always been, even though we know it has not and that it constantly changes. In this model, God is regarded as eternal and immutable, existing outside of space and time, and before 'he' can create anything, must therefore create space and time. The theological objection to creationism is that the very act of creation changes the creator, so if God creates the universe, 'he' cannot remain eternal and immutable. Let us say, I write a book (this one is a good start): I am not the same person after I have written it as I was before. I have gained in confidence and experience, my style has evolved, I have enhanced my knowledge by looking things up, and I have stimulated my imagination and thought processes. So, it follows that God cannot be the same god after creating the world as 'he' was before. Equally, to claim the 'perfection' of God implies either a prior state of imperfection (since perfection is part of a process that leads to something becoming 'perfect') or the *possibility* of imperfection.

This dilemma was addressed in Platonism by having an intermediate being – the Demiurge – 'translate' the ideas of God (as the Monad) into actual physical form. The Demiurge takes the ideas of the Monad, and the Monad remains the Monad. The equivalent in Christianity is the Holy Spirit, which is also present in Judaism as the *Ruach ha-Kodesh*. In Christianity, the Holy Spirit is perceived in subtly different ways. The early Christians equated the Holy Spirit with the Greek idea of *pneuma* or 'breath': the animating principle of Spirit. The Holy Spirit, however, is also viewed in the Gospel of John as the 'Word' which makes the heavens and the earth and governs the laws of nature, roughly cognate with the Greek *logos* as 'universal mind' or principle of Being. Although these two representations of the Holy Spirit sound quite different, they share an affinity with the symbolic language employed to describe them: the Breath (*pneuma*) expresses itself as the Word (*logos*); if we want to take the analogy further, we can say that the Word in turn gives birth to the Book (*biblion* in Greek – hence 'bible' – or *sepharim* in Hebrew) as the 'received Word' or revelation of God to Man. The Jewish conception of the *Ruach ha-Kodesh* is again somewhat different: as the indwelling presence of God in the world who is the source of prophesy and confers the grace of the Spirit on the faithful, and in this way is very similar to the idea of the Shekhinah as the 'dwelling' or 'settling' of God upon the holy. The experience of the blessing of the Holy Spirit was said to be like a wind that came with fire and light, sometimes accompanied by the tinkling of bells. In Ezekiel 3:12, it is stated, "the spirit took me up, and I heard behind me a voice of a great rushing," and an example from the New Testament would be the descent of the Holy Spirit on the Apostles at Pentecost in Acts 2:1, which is also referred to as the *parousia* or 'presence':

When the day of Pentecost came, they were all together in one place. Suddenly a sound like the blowing of a violent wind came from heaven and filled the whole house where they were sitting. They saw what seemed to be tongues of fire that separated and came to rest on each of them. All of them were filled with the Holy Spirit and began to speak in other tongues as the Spirit enabled them.

Jesus' somewhat oblique comment in John 3:8 "the wind bloweth where it listeth" is likewise a reference to the Holy Spirit descending on some but not on others. Thus, the Holy Spirit, can be said, depending on one's interpretation, to persist in three modes of being: as the pure energy and consciousness of Spirit, as the numinous 'distributed' consciousness of the universe (that Anaxagoras called 'universal mind') and as the 'messenger' who speaks to the receptive through dream and revelation and bestows its grace upon the faithful. As the consciousness of the universe, the Holy Spirit partakes of the Greek *pnuema* or universal animating principle, the *logos* of Philo of Alexandria and the Neoplatonists and the *anima mundi* or 'world soul' of the Stoics.

Thus, in both Judaism and Christianity, Divinity has a twin aspect as transcendent (existing outside of time and space) and as immanent (a power of divinity that is present in existence). In Latin, these are distinguished by the terms *Deus* meaning 'God', and *Numen* meaning that force which permeates all things, as in 'numinous'. The burning bush in Exodus 3:1-15 out of which the voice of the Angel of the Lord speaks to Moses is a perfect metaphor for the numinous spirit behind the forms of life; the flame that does not consume. Yet there is still a problem of how the insubstantial interfaces with the physical, which would, theoretically, require an intermediate dimension whereby Spirit interfaces with matter. Further, for Spirit to interface with matter at all, or even create the energetic framework on which matter is based, Spirit would itself have to be a form of energy in its own right, albeit *not an energy of the physical world.*

I take the view that 'God' or 'Spirit', rather than a discrete creative entity, is the combined energy and consciousness of Existence, the purest expression of the 'Will to Be', which progressively unfolds through Nature, continually experimenting with new forms of life, each living thing possessing its own 'will to be', expressing itself through nervous systems of increasing complexity until it achieves self-awareness through its own creation. It is intelligent, but far from being the intelligence of a single creative entity, it is rather diffused throughout all things; it is *Numen* as opposed to *Deus*. Where does this primal 'will to be' come from? In the Holy Qabalah, it is said that such a desire 'to be' arose within the Limitless Light[204] (the Ain Soph Aur) which then divided: one portion of that Light emanating into Being, the other remaining pure and unchanged in what we might term Negative Existence. We can therefore posit that God or Divinity has two aspects: that which remains unchangeable beyond space and time, and that which, as Spirit, emanates into Being as a force of Life and Consciousness, achieving awareness of itself through existence.

In my studies of the mystical traditions of various faiths, I was attracted to the study of the Jewish Qabalah. For me, the idea of 'God' as the primal 'Will to Be' is suggested by the name said to

---

[204] Light' is used as a metaphor. Outside causal reality there is neither light nor darkness.

have been revealed to Moses in Exodus 3:14: *Ehieh asher Ehieh*, 'I am that I am' (or simply *Ehieh*, 'I am'[205]), that is, pure being without attribute; that which cannot be defined in terms other than itself. *Ehieh*. It sounds like the outpouring of breath, doesn't it? Indeed, it cannot be said to be a name at all but an existential statement: I AM. From this root statement, Existence itself unfolds poetically as the breath of life. I AM CREATION. I AM EXISTENCE. I AM BEING. This Primal Will to Be, from which Being itself arises, and which we can justifiably equate with 'Spirit', can manifest both as the enlightenment of the mind and the rushing tide of the life force. It is not entity, nor is it in origin self-aware, and it is certainly not moral, but it attains experience of itself through its own unfolding into existence. I call it the 'Threefold Will': to Be (express itself through existence), to know itself, and in turn be known.

I achieved this understanding over many years of study and reflection, to the extent that the conventional way that Divinity is understood in

---

[205] The 'I am' phrases in the Gospel of John are used by Jesus to identify himself with God.

institutional religion began to seem antiquated and medieval. I concluded, in the spirit of iconoclasm, the following:

God is not a person (and thus no human qualities can be ascribed to Divinity)
God is not a king[206]
God is not a lawyer (for the making of laws belongs to princes and parliaments)[207]
God is not a judge
God is neither good nor evil
God is not a moral arbiter (since morality is a societal concept)[208]
God is not on anyone's side
God doesn't have a chosen people
God doesn't have a country

---

[206] "The kingdom of God is within you." (Luke 17:20-21)

[207] There is no such thing as Divine Law. The making of law is a product of collective intelligence in which competing interests are harmonised with the public good. The Civil Rights Act was not given to us by a finger pointing out of the sky.

[208] The metaphysical concept of good and evil is fundamentally different from the human concept of good and evil. Metaphysical or spiritual good can best be defined as *the potential of the Spirit to realise itself through life*, with spiritual evil being the opposite: a counter-creational, counter-evolutionary force that is antithetical to life and existence.

God does not support the Republican party

God is not an emergency rescue service

Nor does God require to be worshipped, since God is not an oriental potentate; Divinity commands reverence since it is the very root of our being, but our attitude should be one of humility without subservience. I will state categorically that *the objective of a life of faith is communion with Divinity as the totality of Being and not worship of it as an entity external to the Self.* In this, I find myself in agreement with Meister Eckhart who proposed (very reasonably) that God is not a being but Being itself and therefore cannot be conceived of in terms any human can understand. It follows therefore that one cannot worship God since only *a being* can be worshipped; Being itself cannot.

Bad things happen to good people. God is not a superhero in red underpants and blue tights who flies in to stop the school bus going over the side of the bridge. Equally, prayer is not a substitute for human action (or at least until human action has exhausted itself). The question 'why would a loving God allow bad things to happen to good people?' rests on the delusion of God as a discrete self-aware and morally conscious entity who micromanages every aspect of existence; yet it is unrealistic to expect that a being who existed alone outside of time and space before anything was created would possess any traits that properly belong to membership of a complex society, such as, love, empathy, morality, or even self-awareness, let alone the making of laws. After all, how does one reconcile the savagery of Nature with the morality of God? How does one reconcile the idea of an all-powerful god who micromanages everything with the principle of free will and mathematical probability? Are we saying that people who die tragically are being 'punished' for not believing in God (itself a despicable idea)? The reason why bad things happen to good people is because God is not a moral entity (otherwise, the Holocaust would never have happened, nor any other atrocity or natural disaster) but rather a collective intelligence that permeates and manifests through Being, from the lowest molecule of DNA to the most advanced mind, achieving self-awareness through the evolving consciousness of Man. The Spirit evolves through Man, and Man evolves toward God. A high charge is thereby placed upon humanity to raise itself to the dignity of the Spirit, of which Man is the foremost expression. Man is not a mere subject or 'creature' of Divinity, but an active participant in the making of Existence. *Man is the completion of God.*

It is time we stopped the silly business of anthropomorphising Divinity. Rather, it is Man who humanises God. It is Man who legislates. It is Man who makes moral decisions through his own capacity for reason. It is Man who judges Man. It is Man who loves. It is Man who creates just and unjust societies. It is Man who has stewardship over the earth, and God isn't going to rush in and save us when it all goes wrong. It's called responsibility.

Given that it is easier to say what God is not than what God is, what then is God? From a personal view, God is the seed, Nature and Man are the Tree, and the tree contains the essence of the seed. Man is the realisation of self-awareness of 'Being in Existence', and I think that because our core being is Spirit, there is a primal relationship of love that binds Man with Divinity but transcends (and is different from) human love. I have touched this energy during meditation, have felt it course through me and clinch me in its rapture, so I speak from experience. Love is there.

Even if one rejects the Church's idea of God (as I do, suborned as it is to infantile medievalism), remember that you and I, and all of us, are part of a reality greater than ourselves, and understanding this is the root of faith; for just as we belong to Nature, and Nature belongs to Being (not a scientific, but a philosophical concept), so Being also is part of a greater metaphysical reality that is unknowable to the intellect, but intuited by the soul.

ALL RELIGIOUS TRADITIONS CONTAIN WISDOM AND STUPIDITY IN EQUAL MEASURE AND THE ART OF UNDERSTANDING IS TO TEASE OUT THE ONE FROM THE OTHER.

Discursive Essay on the Idea of the Soul

Exploring themes from *Passing*

Dying consciously is a theme that is common to the Egyptian and Tibetan Books of the Dead, and to the Greek Mystery cults where, at death, the Orphic[209] celebrant would be given a choice to drink of the Fountain of Eternal Life or the Fountain of Sleep and Forgetfulness, and this metaphor also appears in Jesus' conversation with the Samaritan woman at Jacob's Well in the Fourth Gospel (John 4:7-15) – to drink of the well water (ordinary human consciousness bounded by dimensional reality as symbolised by the walls of the well) or of the Living

---

[209] Orphism was a reformed version of the earlier Dionysian religion, which likened the mythic lyre-player, Orpheus (who was torn apart by wild animals), with the infant Dionysus who had been torn apart and consumed by the Titans (forces of Chaos and powers of earth), for which offence Zeus incinerated the Titans with a thunderbolt. From the ashes of Dionysus humanity was born, thus having a dual nature: a body derived from the Titans and a Divine spark or soul derived from Dionysus. Initiates underwent the ritual purification of Teletē which involved symbolically reliving the suffering and death of Dionysus and would, after death, spend eternity with the god (much as Christians today identify with the suffering Jesus – the parallels are unmistakeable).

Water of pure boundless Spirit– as though it had been lifted directly from the Greek Mysteries.

When I say 'dying consciously', I mean the unification of all the components of the individuate consciousness under Will as a precursor to becoming a vessel of Spirit both during life and after physical death, at which we become a part of the greater consciousness of Divinity. While we are all born with the potential for a soul, the soul is something I believe we have to *create*. Think of it this way: we are all *of* Divinity, but most of us are not aligned *with* Divinity; we do not have our faces turned towards it. Our consciousness is *of* Spirit but, because it is *individuated* consciousness turned outward to the world, it is *cut off* from the Great Sea of Spirit like a lake cut off from the stream that feeds it. A further metaphor: Man is the mirror wherein Divinity reveals itself, but if the mirror is clouded or dirty, the light of Divinity is imperfectly reflected in us. While Christian theology, in my view, wrongly attributes this caesura to Original Sin, really it is about *forgetfulness* of our Divine origin, forgetfulness of the Source of our Being, and this is one important aspect in which the Greek Mysteries differed from Christianity. *The criterion for functioning in a dimensional world is that the non-dimensional is veiled from us.* There is an allusion to this in that evocative phrase from the Fourth Gospel (John 1:5): "And the light shineth in the darkness; and the darkness comprehended it not." The idea of the divine Soul trapped in the darkness of blindness and ignorance is expressed most appositely in Psalm 82:

> They do not know or understand;
> They wander in the darkness;
> All the foundations of the earth are shaken.
> I have said, 'You are gods;
> You are all sons of the Most High.'
> But like mortals you will die,
> And like rulers you will fall.

"You are gods in as much as you are born of Spirit, but you are oblivious to your birth right. You flounder in the darkness and ultimately you will die as mortals." Most of us are driven this way and that by our emotions and unconscious impulses. The average person isn't a single coherent consciousness but a set of different personas at war with each other. Our unconscious motivations are out of

synch with our conscious aspirations, and there is a yawning gulf between the person we believe ourselves to be and the person we truly are. This is why Christ expends so much space in the Sermon on the Mount on the difference between inner motivation and outward action; it wasn't so much to do with being consistent than with the integrity of the soul. If we do not attain to a single unified Self then our consciousness is so fragmented that, at death, it splits apart into its component elements of personality (what I term the 'fragmentation of the soul') that can remain earthbound. This teaching is encoded within the synoptic gospels in Matthew 12:25, part of the Sermon on the Mount:

> Every kingdom divided against itself is brought to desolation, and every city or house divided against itself shall not stand.

What is being spoken of is the integrity of the soul as a single coherent entity that can survive the trauma of physical death by becoming a vessel of Spirit, uniting human consciousness with Divine consciousness. In short, we are concerned with the idea of 'wholeness', a word that is closely related to 'holiness', as both words derive from the Old English *hālig* and the German *heilig,* and the inference is that *before we become whole in death, we must become whole in life.* There is an echo of this in the story of the biblical flood in Genesis which is really an allegory or teaching story. The ark represents the soul that is built and fortified to withstand the deluge of death, and the animals contained within it represent the unified components of the personality in a single vessel. [210]

Of course, the foregoing begs the question of what the soul is. Is the soul something we are born with? Does it enter the body at birth (Plato) or are we born with it (Aristotle), or (my personal view) is it something we are born with a potential for but must *create*? Is it something we can lose (or worse, sell)? Is it just one thing or are there gradations of

---

[210] The antecedents of the deluge story are found in the Sumerian *Epic of Gilgamesh* and the Akkadian/Babylonian *Atrahasis*. Noah is referred to as Utnapishtim in *Gilgamesh* and as Atrahasis in the latter work. In the myths, the god Enlil determines to send a flood to kill all humans, but the god Enki warns Atrahasis/ Utnapishtim of the plan. Atrahasis/Utnapishtim then builds a boat and saves his family and animals. He and his wife are subsequently deified by Enlil and this is the secret of immortality he passes on to Gilgamesh. In *Genesis*, however, Noah is not deified.

soul? What is its relation to Spirit or Divinity? Can it survive physical death?

Greek philosophy made a distinction between *psyche* and *pneuma*, with *pneuma* representing the immortal and universal principle of Spirit (literally 'breath of life') while *psyche* referenced the human soul, although Aristotle conceived of three *psyches*: vegetal, animal and rational. These terms, *pneuma* and *psyche*, have a dual aspect, however, as both animating principle and energy of consciousness. Thus, the Hebrew *ruach*, translating as 'wind' or 'breath', is used contextually for both spirit and soul: *ruach ha qodesh* as the Holy Spirit and *ruach* as the soul, confirming the idea that soul is a derivation of Spirit. While, as the internalised expression of Spirit, soul supports the energy matrix of the body, *psyche* or 'soul' is most often said to represent the principle of mind as the organised expression of consciousness, although the intellect was known in Greek philosophy by the name *nous*. Jung, however, distinguished between *psyche* and *soul*. For him, *psyche* represented the entirety of human consciousness (including the Conscious and the Unconscious) whereas soul denoted the personality or mind, or put a better way, the soul as the *individuated* aspect of the *psyche*.[211]

Life and consciousness, consciousness and life: are they not inseparable? Can we conceive of consciousness without life or life without the possibility of consciousness, even when that consciousness is so primitive that mind has yet to make an appearance on the evolutionary stage? Biology studies the forms of life: the metabolism of the cell, the intricate double helix of DNA, but the forms of life are surely not life itself. The hearts beats, the organism digests, cells replicate, nerves register pleasure and pain: but these are the functions of life and not life itself. We know the mechanics of life, but *what is life an expression of?* For assuredly, all Life is an expression of something hidden from the view of the observer, like a stream flowing beneath a glacier. Life and Nature, these words are intangibles; they have an 'otherness' that defies the curt description of the lexicographer. We say, "Nature *designed* things this way or that way," or "Nature decided to evolve

---

[211] Jung, C.G. (1971). *Psychological Types*, Collected Works, Volume 6, Princeton, N.J.: Princeton University Press.

this way or that way," as though we are dealing with a living force, something numinous that lies concealed beneath the surface appearance of the organism, only for science to deny this very premise. But peel back those surface realities and what is beneath it all? Something designs, something experiments. *What* experiments? Surely not an old man with a long white beard who invented giraffes on a draughtsboard. No, intelligent design is not an argument for God as entity, a single all-powerful creator, but rather a distributed intelligence, a force or power that permeates all things: something we can call 'Being', the action of Spirit at work behind the scenes of the visible measurable universe; that creates the energy matrices on which physical life is fleshed out, that imbues life with the raw energy of consciousness that dances among the tangles of delicate neurons which become the scaffold of mind.

It would seem sensible to regard *pneuma* as a transcendent all-pervasive energy of conjoined life-force and consciousness which expresses itself through the human organism as *psyche,* the basis of mind. It follows that the stronger and more coherent the mind, the stronger and more coherent the soul. Yet because the soul gazes outward on existence and comes to believe in the material world as reality, it loses contact with the source of consciousness from which it arises. That source, *pneuma,* can be posited as an energy that transcends space and time, with its roots in the acausal (non-physical) universe, manifesting through organic nervous systems in the causal (physical) universe in order to express itself: the more complex the nervous system, the more refined the expression of Consciousness through Mind. While biological science would argue for a purely physiological origin of consciousness[212], and would even dispute the possession of it by primitive life forms, we can ask what would be the point of a universe devoid of Consciousness, that could never be beheld by any sentient being? Objectively it would exist, of course, but it would not be 'real', since reality is defined as *existence actualised by mind.* Rather, the universe would occupy a kind of 'dreamtime' during which it is validated by nothing. Thus, Roger Penrose, Emeritus Professor of Physics at Cambridge writes, "Any universe that can be observed must, as a logical necessity,

---

[212] A purely physiological explanation of consciousness would have to explain the capacity for abstract thought which occurs in the absence of any physiological stimulus.

be capable of supporting conscious mentality, since consciousness is precisely what plays the ultimate role of 'observer'. This fundamental requirement could well provide constraints of the universe's physical laws, or physical parameters, in order that conscious mentality can (and will) exist."[213]

Supporting the acausal origin of consciousness as a property of Existence, findings in the science of parapsychology hint at the ability of consciousness to behave like a quantum phenomenon, defying physical laws, or more specifically, for causal mind to interface in some way with the acausal universe. The value of parapsychology for our argument lies not in proving the existence of ghosts but in fundamentally changing our view of the nature of reality. Experiments in parapsychology (supported by thousands of cases of anecdotal evidence and eyewitness accounts, which mainstream science arrogantly rejects out of hand) suggest that the consciousness of an individual can be projected from the body,[214] an individual can be 'possessed'

---

[213] Penrose, Roger (2004). *The Road to Reality*. Jonathan Cape, London, p.1030.

[214] In my day-to-day work, I have had extraordinary conversations with people, but one in particular stands out. A gentleman

by the consciousness of another, a mind can be read by others, someone can experience the trauma of a person close to them from several thousand miles away in a manner suggestive of quantum linkage, or experience the premonition of a disaster, and even that the consciousness of a person can remain earthbound after their death. Indeed, I am convinced that strong emotions such as love can create connections or linkages between people on a quantum level of mind such that a 'web' of connections can exist, traversing the distinctions of past, present and future, space, time and distance, intriguingly similar to the Norse and Anglo-Saxon idea of the 'web of wyrd' or fate. To summarise, then, I view Man as existing at the junction between the causal and acausal universes, with the acausal expressing itself through causal consciousness, which in some gifted individuals manifests as the

---

named 'Michael' related how he suffered a cardiac arrest on the operating table and found himself looking down at his own body. The weirdest thing about the story, however, is that while he was hovering between life and death, he heard a female voice ask him, "Do you want to die now, Michael?" He replied "No" and found himself back in his body. I believe that what he heard was either his 'oversoul' or guardian angel, or what we call a 'guide of the dead'.

ability to express consciousness in a quantum way or even demonstrate the 'gifts of the Spirit' described in accounts of the great mystics. I therefore posit the existence of some hitherto unknown neuronal-quantum interface which allows the acausal energy of consciousness to work through organic nervous systems, and, in a reverse way, for the human mind to gain access to acausal consciousness, often referred to as 'the Sight' or 'acausal perception'; it is no coincidence then that the chakras (latifas in Sufism) correspond with the major nerve plexi of the body. The prophesy of the wise woman and the revelation of the Christian mystic therefore have their roots in the same gift of acausal perception, and the idea of the one coming from the Devil and the other from God are surely false.

I might add at this juncture that humanity is unique amongst all beings in Nature in possessing the ability not only to access their own subconscious mind but to connect through deep mind to the acausal universe.

There is a suggestion of this acausal origin of consciousness in the Eden myth (wholly misunderstood by Christians) in which the serpent encourages Havah (Eve) to eat of the fruit of self-awareness and pass it to her husband Adam, thus removing Man from the instinctual animal state (and thus as a 'creature' of God). The key to understanding the myth is that Adam and Eve are not people at all but principles. In the myth, 'God' represents that aspect of Divinity that creates the material world. The serpent is a *cthonic*[215] symbol representing the 'other side' of Existence (acausal universe) and thus the source of the raw energy of Consciousness or Spirit which makes us "as gods", i.e. possessing free will and the power to imagine and create: not at all the Satan of subsequent Christian interpretation, nor a counter-cosmic force of evil, but the 'dark' or hidden face of Divinity.[216] The name Havah

---

[215] Pertaining to the underworld.

[216] During the 6th to 4th centuries BC, a heretical sect originated in Zoroastrianism called Zurvanism, which was an attempt to ameliorate the dualism between Ohrmazd (Ahura Mazda, the principle of Light and Creation) and Ahriman (the principle of darkness and chaos). Zurvan represented a third primal state of Eternal Time (actually timelessness or acausality) which gives birth to the twin forces of Light and Darkness (as God in *Genesis* separates the light and the darkness). For our purposes, Zurvan is depicted as an anthropoid figure with a lion's head and a serpent twining up the body. The lion's head represents the bright creative aspect of divinity which brings forth the universe while the serpent denotes the Other Side of Existence, the shadow universe which is the source of the energy of Life and Consciousness without which the universe of Matter would

(properly Chavah) in Hebrew translates as the verb 'to breathe', related to the verb *chayah*, 'to live or give life', which renders Havah the equivalent of *Ruach* (the ensouling and animating principle, literally 'breath of life'), in contrast with Adam, the physical body (derived from *Adamah* meaning 'earth'), and the fruit of the serpent symbolises the soul's connection with the primal energy of acausal consciousness, which is Spirit.

---

be inert. In modern language, we would describe these universes as the causal (pertaining to time and space and obeying the laws of physics) and the acausal (transcending time and space and operating more like quantum phenomena). *It is the opening of the mind to this acausal universe that brings the gifts of psychism.* The classic image of Zurvan was appropriated by the Gnosticism of the first centuries after Jesus to describe the lion-headed serpent (minus the anthropoid body), otherwise known as Yaldabaoth, the Gnostic demiurge or intermediate creator who takes the divine ideas and moulds them into physical form (an idea taken from Plato) but who, in Gnostic thought, desires the worship that is due to God. A hint of the Zurvan cult is suggested in the *Book of Genesis* in which, following the death of Abel, a new child, Seth, is born to Adam and Eve, one who will transcend the duality represented by Qayin (Cain) and Abel. For those with eyes to see, there is a recurring theme in the *Book of Genesis* of the 'Bright Twin' and the Dark Twin': Qayin and Abel, Isaac and Ishmael, Jacob and Esau, (one good, the other bad or unruly) and my personal belief is that these are motifs for the original principles of Light and Darkness in Zoroastrianism: Ahura Mazda and Ahriman.

Thus, the so-called Fall of Man was mythically a fall from the animal state in which we became ensouled beings with the spark of Divinity within us while at the same time blind to the *source* of our Being; we ate of the Tree of Good and Evil (self-awareness and free will) but the fruit of the Tree of Life (Divine Consciousness and eternal life in the Spirit) eludes us; instead, suspended between the animal and the divine, we walk the existentialist desert of the soul in search of meaning. *"Foxes have holes and birds have nests, but the Son of Man has nowhere to place his head"* (Matthew 8:20). Unlike birds and beasts, we have no natural place in Nature (because of free will), but neither have we found our place within the wider framework of Existence; we persist in a state of existential *angst*, neither the sand nor the sea.

As individuals, we are like flowers that bloom, seed and die; yet as humanity, we are as roots intertwined deep below the earth, and as such are we rooted in acausal Being, the numinous power behind phenomenological Nature.

In the foregoing essay, I spoke of my personal interpretation of Divinity as the raw energy of consciousness that acquires awareness of itself through experience of life in the physical world. One might say that there is no God traditionally conceived of as entity, but only Spirit which expresses itself through life and acquires sentience through experience of being: all our memories, all our knowledge, all our life experience returns to it when we die, but we cannot cross over until we have achieved wholeness of being. I aver that human consciousness derives from Spirit but is qualitatively different: Existence is One but there is a polarity in the expression of energy between Nature on the one hand and pure Spirit on the other. The consciousness of Man traverses this axis, expressing itself through Nature and the physical world or aspiring to a life of communion with Spirit.

Given that, as said before, the soul or 'psyche' denotes both mind and the energetic form sustaining the physical body, I believe that the self-awareness we develop in life can engender a coherent soul with the potential to survive the disintegrating effect of death. In the terms of classical theosophy, the 'soul' could be considered as the amalgam of what is known as the 'etheric body', or energy matrix, and 'mental body' or mind. Thus the soul is not 'one thing' but multi-layered and we see this in many unrelated traditions. Just as the Greeks distinguished between *pneuma* (lifeforce) and *psyche* (mind, personality), in ancient Egyptian religion, the *ka* denoted the lifeforce while the *ba* represented the personality: joined together after death they formed a divine spark called the *akhu*. In Haitian vodou, the *gros bon ange* is the energy matrix of the body supporting vital functions while the *ti non ange* represents mind and personality. I posit that a concentration of spiritual energy, in tandem with the training of consciousness, has an accelerating effect both on mind and etheric body, enabling the resultant soul to retain its coherence after physical death, allowing it to persist within the greater consciousness of God or Spirit; a nodal point in the web of universal mind. As God (or Spirit) is the Lord of Lights, so each person who dies *to* God becomes a light *in* God. The converse is the disordered soul at war with itself, torn apart by its own contradictions, that fragments at death, some fragments remaining earthbound energies, while others (as incomplete souls) being re-absorbed back into the great sea of consciousness in perpetual sleep.

The training of Mind and development of a coherent spiritually aware soul, and that soul's return to the acausal, constitutes a kind of 'respiration' between the acausal and causal universes, the unseen and the seen. The state in-between, in Byzantine and Patristic literature, is described as the Middle State of the Soul, that twilight between the death of the physical body and its final 'crossing over' into the 'Other Side' of Existence. This is often portrayed as a kind of dream state, and is the period when prayers are spoken to guide the soul to cross over peacefully. It is also the period when the soul is most likely to visit dead relatives with whom it held a special attachment ('crisis apparitions' in parapsychology), and the period when the soul is most vulnerable to necromancers who would seek answers from it. I posit that during this time, the soul persists in a quantum state prior to passing into the dimension of pure Spirit, suggesting that the quantum universe is really an intermediate dimension mediating between the physical universe and pure Spirit. Given that this state persists from between three to seven days, all brain activity would presume to have ended and yet we have anecdotal evidence of the existence of a soul that can be seen by some.

Not all souls pass over peacefully, and some don't pass over at all. They live in a state of torment as quantum entities, wanting to return to the life they have lost. In Jewish demonology, these are known as *dybuks*. They can be especially dangerous as they can possess the living and even try to enter the foetus of the unborn child in order to be reborn.

Illuminism vs Salvationism

By and large, there are two approaches to the idea of the survival of the soul after death as a coherent consciousness, and I call these Illuminism and Salvationism. They are not mutually exclusive, however, since both are premised on the idea that how one lives one's life depends on one's outcome after death.

Illuminism is a form of mysticism whereby the soul – and by extension consciousness – is opened to the power and consciousness of Spirit *during life*, in the knowledge that the soul will persist in an exalted state after death. This exalted state may assume a number of forms: persistence as a self-aware soul as *part* of the totality of Divinity, or *unification* of the soul with Divinity – a state of complete oneness that is sometimes referred to as 'annihilation in God'. The latter is more common in eastern mysticism (Sufism, Buddhism) than in Christianity where the idea of the soul 'dwelling' *with* God is more prevalent. Illuminism utilises a combination of different methods to achieve the opening of the soul to Spirit, but these are not 'techniques' so much as a total lifestyle. Mysticism within the framework of the Church commonly took the form of a mystical identification with the 'radiant Jesus' (the resurrected Christ as opposed to the suffering Jesus[217]) as 'opener of the door to the heart', augmented by fasting, meditation and prayer in which the aspirant 'empties' themselves (kenosis) so they can be filled by the higher consciousness of the Spirit, based on the idea that it is the Self which stands in the way of God as a pebble can block out the sun. There is, however, a well-established tradition of Christian illuminism outside the Church, characterised by Rosicrucianism and Martinism which both evolved out of speculative freemasonry fused with a Christianised version of the Qabalah. In addition to mystical identification

---

[217] This difference of emphasis is why Latter-Day Saints and Jehovah's Witnesses do not wear a crucifix.

with Christ and meditation, these traditions practice theurgy: the drawing down of divine power using the Divine Names. Thirdly, a tradition of illuminism is evinced in writings of independent theologians, in particular the Catholic mysticism of Meister Eckhart and the Protestant mysticism of Jacob Boehme (Böhme). Both men were charged with heresy by the powers of the time: proof that *the greatest enemy of faith is a dull mind*. What all the great mystics have in common is that they received visions from an early age: Jacob Boehme, for instance, had a mystical experience triggered by the reflection of a shaft of sunlight glancing off a pewter dish. These mystics were 'called to faith' by a power beyond our (and their) comprehension, which lends credence to my remarks below that some of us are 'born to Spirit' while others are not.

Salvationism in the Christian tradition, by contrast emphasises a theological rather than mystical approach to salvation based on the salvific power of Christ. Central to this approach is the premise that we are already saved through Jesus' sacrifice, but it is only through 'accepting' Jesus (commonly expressed as belief or faith) that we partake of that salvation. Salvation in this view is exclusively an afterlife experience in which we are resurrected after death in a spiritualised body. This is the dominant theology of mainstream Church-based Christianity and is largely antithetical to illuminism. However, this remark must be qualified since many of the great Christian saints achieved illumination within this same salvationist paradigm.

So, to summarise, while illuminism is quintessentially a mystical approach, Salvationism is theologically driven, but they are not mutually exclusive: Salvationism does not exclude illumination of the soul during life as the lives of the saints attest to. This said, Salvationism does not *require* illumination during life; for the average Christian, belief in Jesus assures salvation in Heaven after death with no mystical experience or alteration of perceptual awareness during life. Another way to think of the difference is that Illuminism is associated with initiatic systems (closed fraternities and sororities) while Salvationism is more commonly associated with congregational religion (open churches, synagogues and mosques).

The hierarchy of the soul

In Jewish Qabalistic mysticism, there are five levels of the soul, each corresponding with one of the four worlds of the Tree of Life, with the fifth and final one transcending them all. All these states of the soul are actual or potential in everyone, but the higher ones are dormant in most. The *Nephesh* is the instinctual self, containing all our basic instincts, and corresponds with the life force. The *Ruach* is the seat of the higher emotions, while the *Neshamah* is the seat of higher reason. The fourth, *Chaya*, is a transcendent state of perfect alignment with Divine Being: the individuate consciousness is retained but the person becomes a channel for Divine Will and Power. The final state, *Yechida*, is effectively a state of union with God in which the individuate consciousness is merged with Divinity.

In Islam, there is no clear distinction between soul and spirit; rather there are three gradations of soul or *nafs*: the instinctual soul (nafs *ammarah),* conscience *(nafs lawwamah)* and the reformed soul that is aligned with God *(nafs mutma'innah).* The soul is born with the body but it also contains the *ruh* which is implanted in it by the Divine; broadly, the *ruh* is the Spirit of God that draws a person to God. The Shiite mystic Mulla Sadra (1571–1640) subscribed to the idea of the evolution of the soul from vegetative (basic functions) through to animal (instinctual), progressing to rational and, in some spiritually trained individuals, culminating in the transcendent soul. Thus, the soul (*nafs*) is that in a person which *learns*, while the *ruh* is that which *links* the soul with Divinity, which we might call the 'Divine spark' within the soul.

Christian mysticism does not have such a finely tuned schema of soul development as that present in the Holy Qabalah or mystical Islam. The closest Christian mysticism has come to such a schema is St Teresa of Avila's *Interior Castle* which likened the soul to entering a circular castle whose outer rooms represented the coarser aspects of the soul and in whose centre dwelt the Divine Presence. The title comes from John 14:2: "In my father's house are many mansions," these referring to the 'mansions' of the soul. This is interesting because while in 'official' Church theology, a person is either 'saved' or 'not saved', in as much as they identify with Christ, the idea of 'sanctity' implies *degrees* of closeness to Divinity. The word 'saint' does not define someone who is 'saved', as someone who is 'saved' does not necessarily become a saint. Rather the word 'saint' describes someone whose closeness to Divinity results in them displaying the gifts of the Spirit during life and after death.

I would interject here that while we are all born with a potential for achieving illumination, there are essentially three *types* of people: those born to Spirit (and with an innate intuitive connection with Spirit), those born to Nature, and those born somewhere in between.[218] It is those born closest to Spirit who often receive a spiritual 'calling', in that they are naturally drawn to those things of a spiritual or mystical nature. This is so because

---

[218] While those 'born to Nature' tend to be physically robust and hearty, those 'born to Spirit' tend to be neurasthenic, underdeveloped and suffer frequent bouts of illness. It is thought that the etheric body isn't as closely tied to the physical body as in most people, and it is as though the psychic faculties steal the physical energy that the body needs to function. This is common to all saints and mystics, but read St Teresa of Avila's autobiography for a first-hand account. It should be noted that one of the functions of the etheric body is as a shield to block out sense perception of the acausal and the discarnate entities that dwell in it. Thus, those with a thinner or weaker etheric body are naturally open to acausal perception. Additionally, one consequence of either voluntary or involuntary (as during sleep) astral projection is that one becomes visible to astral entities, and this in itself may be a gateway to cases of 'possession'.

all of us possess a connection with Divinity in the deepest part of our Psyche (or Deep Self) that for the most part lies dormant until it is awakened. The phrase in John 3:6 "That which is born of flesh is flesh; that which is born of Spirit is Spirit" is almost gnostic in its expressed dualism between Nature and Spirit. Nature and Spirit return to their own states after death but in life it is the soul that holds the balance between the two. Nonetheless, there are souls for whom the gravitational attraction to Spirit is stronger than to Nature and these are the souls that are 'born to Spirit'. Bearing this in mind, one argument that has plagued Christian theology is the dichotomy between a 'democratic' view of salvation where everyone who 'receives' Jesus becomes a 'son/child of God' and an 'elect' ideology whereby certain souls are already 'pledged' to God (Predestination), which is a feature of Reformation Calvinism.

I also believe, but cannot prove, that Man inexorably evolves *back* toward Divinity: that just as there is an outward expansive current in which life and nature unfold into existence, so there is also a return current whereby the consciousness expressed through life works its way *back* to Divinity (or fulfils its inherent spiritual potential), increasing in complexity and self-awareness until Divinity is perfectly expressed through Matter. I believe (but cannot prove) that, in addition to the Darwinian laws of natural selection and survival of the fittest, there is another law driving the long-term trajectory of evolution from the simple to the complex: the pressure of consciousness expressing itself through life. Indeed, I would argue that human evolution has now entered a post-Darwinian phase in which the evolution of mind has accelerated exponentially faster than the evolution of the body, engendering the development of self-awareness and the ability of humans to access their own subconscious, which is the gateway to the greater consciousness of Spirit. The post-Darwinian thesis, in essence, states that human evolution cannot be understood through physiology alone but through the interconnected evolution of mind, spirituality and society.

Sons of God

A person whose soul is sufficiently evolved becomes a spiritual intermediary, equivalent to the Judaic idea of a 'Son of God': the archetypal Man of Spirit whose soul is perfectly aligned with Divinity, thus abnegating the state of sin defined as separation from Divinity. Theologically, the 'state of sin' is not a moral problem but an existential one: it is the condition of alienation from the source of one's being, which in turn engenders the 'act of sin' defined as an offence against Being and expressed as violence, greed, arrogance, deficiency of empathy and exploitation of each other and the natural world. 'Son of God' was not a title peculiar to Jesus but to anyone whose soul was in perfect harmony with Divine Being, in which human will and Divine Will (expressed as spiritual potential) were at one. A 'Son of God' is one who has made of themselves a vessel for the Spirit of God (*Ruach ha Qodesh*). Essentially, the title 'Son' means 'partaking of the *nature* of the Father (i.e., God)', and so can refer to one whose mind is illumined by the Spirit without necessarily *being* God in the flesh. It cannot therefore be said that Jesus was *the* Son of God but rather *a* Son of God, although, over time, the title came to refer explicitly to Jesus as Christ.

The 'Son of Man', however, was a completely different concept. Originally, the Son of Man was a heavenly judge who, at the end times, would "come with the clouds of Heaven" to judge Mankind. It thus belongs to the apocalyptic tradition in Judaism, first mentioned as a vision in the Book of Daniel 7:13, and is evoked by Jesus in prediction of the coming apocalypse in Mark 26:64: "Jesus said unto him, 'Thou hast said; nevertheless I say unto you, hereafter shall ye see the Son of Man sitting at the right hand of Power, and coming in the clouds of heaven,'" and there is a similar passage drawn from the same source in Luke 21:27 and in Matthew 24:30. There is no suggestion here that Jesus is identifying himself with the Son of Man, but in John 5:25-27, we find Jesus explicitly making just such an identification: "For as the Father has life in Himself, so He has granted the Son to have life in Himself, and has given Him authority to execute judgment also, because He *is* the Son of Man." Thus, the titles Son of God and Son of Man gradually came to refer to the same person in the figure of Christ.

The question for us is in what way the Christian idea of a 'son of God' differed from the Judaic. This is not entirely easy. While Jesus becomes cemented as the Son of God, the New Testament promises to make those who 'accept' him 'sons of God'. Thus, in John 1:12-13, the Son of God gives those who receive him the power to be 'sons of God', which is redolent of Psalm 82. John repeats the phrase in John 10:34: "Jesus answered them [the Pharisees], 'Is it not written in your Law, 'I said, you are gods'?'" Is this an illuminist or a salvationist statement? Is John implying that Jesus will 'open' his followers to make them 'holy vessels' in their lifetimes, or is he stating that they will become 'sons of God' after death? Thus Galatians 3:26 has: "For ye are all the children of God by faith in Christ Jesus. For as many of you as have been baptized into Christ have put on Christ," which is to say, the Sons/Children of God who have 'put on' (accepted/identified with) Christ in life acquire spiritual bodies after death; they exist 'in Christ' as part of a kind of a 'Christ consciousness'. On the other hand, Hebrews 2:11 has, "For both he that sanctifieth and they who are sanctified are all of one: for which cause he is not ashamed to call them brethren..." which implies an illuminist view: that Jesus represents a state of sanctification attainable by all; we cannot *be* Jesus but we can attain to 'knowledge of God *through* him as a state of exaltation in the Spirit. Then there is that telling phrase of John the Baptist in Matthew 3:11: "I indeed baptize you with water unto repentance: but he that cometh after me is mightier than I, whose shoes I am not worthy to bear: he shall baptize you with the Holy Ghost, and with fire," reiterated in Luke 3:16.[219] A distinction is hereby presented between mere baptism for sin (more properly 'spiritual renewal' since it was a once-only event) and baptism with the 'fire' of the Holy Spirit. What does this phrase mean? Does it imply that Jesus deviated from the other apocalyptic holy men like John in psychically opening his disciples to the power of the Spirit? Did exaltation of the soul in this life precede exaltation in the next? Those familiar with Sufism will know that the Sufi sheikhs would ceremonially 'open' the initiate (or *murid*) through transmission of the *barakah* (blessing or grace), transferred from one sheikh to another through the chain of succession from the Prophet. There is a dim reflection of this in the transmission of the grace of Jesus through the Apostolic succession in the Catholic Church involving the laying on of the hand during the ordination of priests. Another explanation, however, may lie in St. Paul's two-step theology of salvation in which

---

[219] Interestingly, there is not a single account of Jesus performing water baptism in the gospels, although there is evidence that he delegated this task to his disciples.

one dies to one's old self at baptism but is 'raised up' in Christ after death (literally reborn in the Spirit).

All of this begs the questions: What is salvation? What am I saved from? What would a soul look like when it is saved? What happens to it when it not saved? And how do I know I have been saved? Does salvation refer to becoming a 'whole' person in this life or does it refer to what happens to us after death (Illuminism vs Salvationism)? I think that both propositions are true: that the way we develop as souls in this life affects what happens to us after physical death, and that therefore 'salvation' refers to our experience in both worlds.

The Christian view of salvation

Jesus was a visionary but left no writing behind him. As a natural mystic, theology would have been unimportant to him since it was experience of the Spirit that mattered. St Paul, by contrast, was a system builder, and it was St. Paul who created the foundational theology of Christianity, such that some wits have dubbed the religion 'Paulianity'. St Paul experienced a powerful vision of Jesus on the road to Damascus, recounted in Acts 9, that set him on a mission to spread the word of Jesus, but he had to relate that revelatory experience (his Jewish side) to his rational self (his Hellenic side), which meant creating a rational theology of who Jesus was, what his mission was and why he died... and he was not the only one asking those questions.

For the Jews, salvation comes from the Law; it is not that the law saves them, they are saved *because* of the Law. The whole thrust of Jesus' teaching was the internalisation of the Jewish law (Torah) until it became a part of the self; one became the *living* law. That was not the view of St. Paul who pointedly said, "The Law cannot save you" (Romans 7:13-24)[220]. For St. Paul, who I don't think really understood Jesus at all, the Jewish Law was a mere system of unthinking conformity; people obeyed the law out of fear of sanction, but it didn't really change them. For St. Paul, it is mystical experience of God through

---

[220] Contrast with Jesus in Matthew 5:17: "Think not that I am come to abolish the law or the prophets. I am come not to destroy but to fulfil." This is one example of the divergence between St. Paul and Jesus. There is an element of common ground, however, in that Jesus emphasised the *spirit* of the Law as opposed to its letter.

His Son Jesus Christ (the descent of grace[221]) that awakens and fundamentally changes us, and so our path to salvation (if one is a Christian) is through identification with Christ, but how does identifying with Christ save us?

The three forms of identification with Christ

Identification with Christ is expressed in Christianity in three ways: mystical, theological and humanistic.

Mystical identification with Christ implies that, through entering the consciousness of Christ, one enters into the consciousness of God. The anthropomorphic figure of Christ or 'radiant Jesus' bridges the gulf between the human and Divine and provides a medium for divine power to flow into the mind of the supplicant. What if the historical Jesus wasn't *physically* God but was only a *vessel* for the Spirit of God – does that make a difference? Academic biblical scholarship has, in the last few decades, cast doubt on many of the assumptions

---

[221] Nothing really descends. The expression refers to a subjective experience of an inner state of sanctity which in Arabic is called *barakah.*

of the gospels, highlighting a rift between the historical Jesus and the divine Jesus. At risk of upsetting entrenched views, it is of very little practical consequence whether Jesus was possessed of the Holy Spirit or whether he was physically 'God made flesh'; in both senses he is a conduit of divine power and love and a vital link in the chain of grace between God and Man. I rest that Divinity is so far removed from human intellect and imagination that it is virtually impossible to relate to without an intermediate figure, who in Christianity is Jesus as Christ. Mystical communion with Christ opens the heart and mind to the transcendent power of Spirit that expresses itself through Being. Yet, what do we do with that experience when we come down from it? Does it engender a permanent change in our consciousness? Then again, can we trust our visionary experiences which are invariably clothed in the religious/cultural tradition in which we are immersed? How do we tell the difference between a vision sent by the Spirit and a projection of our own Unconscious and is there a dividing line at all or one seamless continuity between greater spiritual reality and the human mind? Indeed, such intense spiritual experience can also work *the other way*: it

can unbalance us and drive us into mania, hence
the many false messiahs of the biblical period and
self-styled modern prophets and cult leaders. Then
there are the fanatics for whom faith assumes the
form of mental illness. Are they saved? Well, they
seem to think they are. I think that the opening
of the heart and mind to Spirit is a necessary first
step in breaching the rift between human and
divine consciousness, but it is not the totality of
the concept of salvation. Without mental training
and self-discipline, the experience can overpower
the emotions and result in imbalance.

Theological identification with Christ is framed
in terms of rational theology rather than mysticism,
and it follows the argument that Jesus as Christ
died to free us from sin and so, by 'believing' in him,
we are saved from the Original Sin of disobedience
that let the power of evil into the world. This 'taint'
which St Paul and St. Augustine held that all 'born
of woman' possess was held to operate as a brake
on true free will[222], and prevents our return to the

---

[222] Augustine speaks of the 'illusion' of free will: that we believe
we have the judgement to choose, when we are really driven
by our worst impulses. Think of it as the difference between
'volition' and 'free will'. If I throw a brick through a shop window

'Adamic' state of spiritual innocence; hence the rite of baptism which was said to 'wash away' Original Sin through the 'living water' of the Spirit and the subsequent adult rite of Confirmation. The theology of Original Sin assumes that we uncritically believe in the Eden myth as literal truth as opposed to allegory, which I personally don't, and it also assumes that sin is heritable, which I don't, but even when 'cleansed' of Original Sin, we can still abuse free will and sin again; we can still turn from the Light, for which we are dependent on Christ for forgiveness. This theology is predicated therefore on the 'acceptance' of Christ throughout life. The entirety of the Christian theology of salvation is thus based on forgiveness of sin, but while forgiveness confers a kind of wholeness and frees us to move on with our lives, it is surely the *beginning* of salvation and not salvation itself. Each time we perform a duplicitous or violent act we not only offend the individual, but we offend Existence and we also offend our own soul, and so we must ask forgiveness of Existence in order to recover our wholeness, but

---

in a fit of temper, that is volition, but I could not be considered to be operating under free will.

surely this is but *one step* toward leaving the 'State of Sin', our alienation from Divinity and the source of our own being which sees us floundering like a blind man in fog.

Thirdly, there is the *humanistic* interpretation of salvation: that identification with Christ means striving to attain the ideal of the Perfected Man which Christ embodied, in which Christ represents the potential for spiritual awareness and ethical living that we all have. This interpretation does not require us to believe in Jesus as a divine being: it is the very humanness of Jesus that speaks to our own humanness for we know that he travailed and won, and if he can transcend his merely human nature then so can we. For the most part, Jesus' ethical teachings are contained in the Sermon on the Mount (Matthew 5-7) and form the basis of Christian morality, but if we abstract them from the framework of Christian theology what we are left with is humanism. They offer a reinterpretation of Jewish law in which outward action must be brought in line with inner motivation and the spirit of the act transcends the act itself.

Jesus' ethical teachings must, however, be placed within the context of his own apocalyptic world view.

There is a sense in everything Jesus says and does that time is running out; the Kingdom of God is about to come, and everyone had better get ready for it. In practice that meant justifying oneself inwardly: obeying the Jewish law not just according to its letter but adhering to its spirit.

In conclusion, we can say that none of the three ways of identification with Christ are complete in themselves. Theological identification with Christ, for example, is inadequate without the mystical and the humanistic.

Heaven and Hell

The idea of Heaven and Hell originated not from mainstream Jewish thought (which held that the dead inhabited an underworld realm called *Sheol,* similar to the Greek *Hades*) but from Jewish apocalypticism. For St Paul, himself an apocalyptic, the fruit of forgiveness is resurrection on the Day of Judgment in which we enter the Kingdom of God: this is the so-called Eschaton which is not so much the end of the world but the end of the duality of Spirit and Matter in which the acausal and causal universes collapse into a single spiritual reality. In this world view, souls which have hitherto remained dormant will be judged and will either enter Heaven or be consigned to Hell. As the expectation of the Kingdom of God on earth receded further into the remote future, the idea of Heaven and Hell as alternative destinations after death gained greater traction.

If salvation is going to Heaven, what and where is Heaven, and what do we have to do to get there? In the Middle Ages, the wealthy endowed monasteries, cathedrals, and universities to redeem their souls. This was in direct contrast to St. Paul's teaching, amplified by Augustine, that neither good works nor moral action could save one: only faith in Jesus saved one because, by his death, he cancelled the debt of sin that Man had occurred through disobedience to God. The Protestant Reformation, with its theology of *salvation by faith alone*, therefore, represents a regression to an earlier Augustinian theology rather than an innovation in Christian thought.

One can imagine a priest explaining to a family member the idea of resurrection and final judgment, which might go something like this: "Actually, Mrs Smith, your mother hasn't been taken into the arms of the loving God. She is stuck in limbo for several thousand years until God decides to dissolve the universe, after which she will have to go through a judicial process, but I need to warn you that if she didn't accept Jesus, things could go badly wrong for her."

I take the view that Heaven and Hell are not places at all but states of being, i.e., states of spiritual development *that extend into the afterlife experience.* Gregory of Nyssa wrote that "the most painful torment in Hell is regret" and Luther spoke of "the Hell of conscience". Some souls become locked into a state of warring components as their contradictions tear them apart; others are riven by regret, and still other souls lapse into a state of unconsciousness or sleep (the original meaning of the Jewish *Sheol*). Some people live in their own personal hell right now. For the illuminist, the choice is not between heaven and hell but between reintegration with the Divine or disintegration.

The return to innocence

The idea of salvation is consonant with the idea of some manner of experience or reckoning that changes us, so we may rightly ask what causes such a seismic shift in our perception that we are no longer the person we were? One thing is for certain: it does not come from a religious authority telling us to believe in God. The path of institutionalised religion simply breeds mass unthinking conformity, but after years of believing what we are told to believe, we remain the same person under the skin. Historically, institutional religion has utterly failed to reform human behaviour. More likely, what puts us on the path to change is variously a sudden inexplicable sense of being 'called' to faith (an *awakening* if you like), a personal crisis arousing feelings of guilt or regret, or a sudden flash of insight that our lives are not working, and occasionally it really can be a revelatory dream or mystical vision... all the more interesting when it occurs in someone who would not have described themselves as a religious believer, in which case it is pertinent to ask '*what* calls us?' When we metaphorically perform the *volte face* that changes our course in life, we may not think of it as a *spiritual* experience, but it is, even when it is not a *religious* one. When we start putting our lives back together, and become more sensitive, more informed, more *clear*, then it is a spiritual experience. When we develop a sense of personal integrity, when we are clear about our motives, when we reject the falsehoods of the world, when we consider the ethical consequences of our actions and we do not allow others to use us for their own agendas, it is a spiritual awakening. When we hire a life coach instead of a priest, it is still a spiritual experience because it involves a return to 'wholeness' and therefore it is 'holy'.

For me, one of the core themes in Christianity is a return to innocence as a necessary precursor to openness to spiritual experience, irrespective of whether one subscribes to the whole 'God sent his only beloved Son to redeem us from sin through his own sacrifice' theology. It is a process of 'simplification' where we remove the meaningless to reveal the meaningful, as the Franciscans have it. Thus 'spiritual poverty' misses the mark; it is not spiritual poverty but 'spiritual simplicity' that redeems us: becoming aware of the contradictions that divide us, ordering our priorities, living by a simple code that respects our fellow man or woman, only taking from life what we need, understanding the connectedness of all life and existence, living consciously, making ethical decisions based on empathy, and putting ourselves in the place of another, never doing anything that offends our conscience and our innate sense of right and wrong. Innocence is not a moral state, but a state of being: a state of perceptual openness and curiosity that only one who has escaped the prison of culture possesses[223]. When we gaze in wonderment at the beauty of the world, when we cease to want and to possess and to exploit, when we rejoice in the joy of *being* itself, then we achieve innocence, and in the silent space we create, around which everything revolves, we can touch the most Divine part of ourselves and experience that Divinity through our own self-aware consciousness. As Divinity is a unity, whole and indivisible, so do we aspire to that same unity and innocence of Self; the unity of the soul draws us closer to the unity of God or Spirit.

---

[223] Just as culture creates a framework for living, so it also creates a prison of the mind and is inherently divisive. Literally, *culture is the enemy of thought*, and we can only truly think once we have transcended the tyranny of culture.

To be saved, then, is to become one's own light *and* a light unto others.

Many of us come to the realisation that, somewhere along the line, we lost our innocence; we have become worldly and we play the game by the rules set out by the world. Jesus frames it as, "Except ye change and become as little children, ye shall not enter the Kingdom of Heaven" (Matthew 18:3).[224] The truth is, we can never recover the naïve innocence of childhood, but we can acquire what I call an 'informed innocence', an innocence which guides us to right action and would never lead us to harm anyone. I call it 'becoming clean'. Yet I think that what Jesus was also talking about was the capacity to spiritually 'see'.[225] Critically, a child can see what adults can't; they are open and receptive and haven't been 'programmed' by the adult version of reality. [226] They see without analysing *what* they

---

[224] There is a tacit admission in this passage that the adults screw up the world, not the kids.

[225] I am informed by my partner Fatna, who comes from near the Somali/Kenya border, that certain African tribes marked a triangle of three dots on a baby's forehead to keep the third eye open for as long as possible.

[226] Hence almost all reported visitations of the Virgin Mary, as at Fatima and Lourdes, have been to children. Heretical as

see; there is no filter to inner reality, and this is the second meaning of 'innocence': an openness and receptiveness to experience and to possibility; a curiosity about what lies beyond our own small lives. In a sense, a return to innocence is a 'coming home' to our core nature as beings of Spirit.

Becoming more 'whole', self-aware and responsible (more *innocent*) is a step toward the integration of all the components of the psyche which culminates

---

it sounds, I do not believe this to be the historical mother of Jesus but a 'holy daemon' or thought form created by centuries of veneration that has achieved independent existence, and she will tell you that she is the Mother of God or the Mother of the Word. This should not be taken to mean she is not 'real'; she is *very* real but in the quantum rather than physical universe. She is a construct of mind, an anthropomorphic representation of a spiritual principle fashioned from the universal energy of consciousness consequent on centuries of faith. We do not see her as she truly is for her reality is beyond human conception. She can foresee future events, she visits whomsoever she pleases, and she can end your suffering and guide you through the gates of death into the next world if you supplicate her to do so. Daemons/daimons (wholly different from demons), as understood by occultists, are anthropomorphic thought forms that act as intermediaries between Man and the formlessness of the spiritual world. As such, there is little functional difference between a modern Catholic setting up a votive altar to the Virgin Mary and a pagan priestess setting up an altar to the goddess Isis or the goddess Hekate in the Greco-Roman world. The principle remains the same. We create an anthropomorphic 'shell' for Spirit to inhabit and communicate with us.

in touching the core of 'Spirit' within our own being, and we carry this wholeness with us *into the very experience of death*. We cannot open ourselves to the Spirit if we are conflicted within and blind to our own ways, as oil or wine cannot be poured into an impure vessel. The path of spirituality is to understand that every violent, selfish or deceitful action leaves a stain on the soul, a darkening of its light. It is to understand that we are all children of the Spirit and to hurt another is to hurt oneself.

Just as the Law does not save us, neither does moralistic-based religion: what Jesus taught was not public or cultural morality but an empathetic morality based on a feeling relationship with our fellow man and woman; a perfect synthesis of rational ethics and empathy, uniting reason with the higher emotions. Reason alone may be betrayed by self-interest while empathy alone does not guarantee that we will think clearly. Jesus also understood that morality, untempered by kindness, compassion and empathy, becomes a source of tyranny in its own right, and that is when one gets toxic Catholicism and toxic Calvinism, a book-burning, fundamentalist cancel-culture of grim-faced priests and tight-lipped nuns policing a creed founded on sin and guilt, whose watchword is "Thou shalt not...".[227]

To summarise, it is not theology, law or morality that fundamentally change us, but an awakening or crisis that makes us re-evaluate our lives and sets us on a course to reclaim the innocence we had forsaken and pursue a spiritual path that reconnects the soul with higher metaphysical (acausal) reality. Once we change, we become a 'new person' and are no longer hostage to the past. How, then, do we pursue that path?

Dissecting the Pauline theology of salvation

The Pauline theology of salvation, expressed simply, states that a rift between Man and God was created due to the disobedience of Adam, the first created man, necessitating God to redeem the sin of Man by sacrificing his 'Son' Jesus, with the consequence that we share in that salvation by faith in Jesus. St.

---

[227] The passage "Blessed be those who are persecuted for righteousness sake" (Matthew 5: 10-12) has a double meaning: "Blessed be those who are persecuted *for* being righteous" and "Blessed be those who are persecuted *by* the righteous."

Paul's elaborate theology is predicated on a number of assumptions, namely: the Eden myth as literal truth, the status of Jesus as a pre-existent divine being, the idea that Jesus died for us, the nature of sin with particular reference to Original Sin, and the doctrine that salvation is achieved *through faith alone*. Any of these, if found to be flawed, nullifies the Pauline theology of salvation.

The Eden myth and its importance to St. Paul's theology

In the Eden myth (Genesis 2-3), there are two trees, the Tree of Knowledge of Good and Evil and the Tree of Life, from which the first man and woman must not eat. God tells Adam and Eve (Havah) that to eat of the fruit of the Tree of Knowledge is to die. The serpent tells Eve that, instead, "your eyes shall be opened and ye shall be as Gods, knowing good and evil." Eve shares the fruit with Adam and they develop awareness of their own nakedness. In other words, they leave the realm of Nature and acquire free will and self-awareness. Before they can eat of the Tree of Life and live forever, God drives them

581

out of Eden and a cherub with a flaming sword bars the way. The Gnostics of the early Christian era asked a pertinent question: why would God withhold knowledge from Man? They interpreted the serpent as the true giver of knowledge and God as the wicked demiurge who would deprive Mankind of spiritual knowledge.

It is unclear whether Adam and Eve exist in a spiritual state and, having eaten of the fruit of knowledge, they fall into an earthly material state; this seems unlikely as Adam clearly represents 'earth' and thus matter. Yet we find St. Paul asserting that the deception of Adam introduced 'death' into the world. Perhaps he thought that because the physical and spiritual existed in perfect balance, Adam and Eve were at once physical and immortal, or at least had immortal spiritual 'bodies' and the disobedience against God created a rift between the physical and the spiritual in Man. Another interpretation (and one that I favour) is that Adam and Eve 'fall' from being 'creatures' of God to possessing free will (that is, they leave the instinctual state but in so doing lose their connection with Divinity).

St. Paul, like Jesus, was an apocalyptic, and the apocalyptics held to a dualistic dichotomy between good and evil, light and darkness. This dualistic theology had originated during and after the Babylonian captivity of the sixth century B.C. in which certain Jewish groups were exposed to Zoroastrian ideas. St Paul adhered to the idea of a malign force in Existence, and he is among the first writers to expound a theory of evil, although he refrains from telling us the origin of such a power of evil. The temptation of Eve by the serpent in the Eden myth and her deception of Adam constituted the first disobedience from which Original Sin arose, which became part of human nature, being passed down through their progeny. It is, one might say, 'part of our DNA'. This malign force did not come into being *because* of the first disobedience, as it already existed, but it was held to enter the universe or 'creation' *because* of Man's disobedience; sin is like a dark thread that wove itself into Existence until it cannot be unpicked therefrom. Accordingly, God, realising that Man is powerless to raise himself from sin, 'redeemed' the Original Sin of Adam by sacrificing his own son Jesus (who is also God), thereby repaying the debt of sin; that is, Jesus is ransomed for Man's sin. Original Sin is washed clean by baptism but belief in Jesus is essential for salvation by resurrection. Thus, baptism in the 'living water' of the Spirit and resurrection at the end of time are polar ends of the process of salvation. In St. Paul's terms, we 'die' to Jesus at baptism but are 'raised' in Jesus in spiritualised bodies at the coming of the Kingdom of God. In modern comprehensible terms, baptism marks the death of the old self while being 'born from above' (in John's phrase) marks the birth of the new self. They are both baptisms, in a way, but one is a baptism in water and the other is a baptism in the Holy Spirit (Matthew 3:11; Luke 3:16). Thus, *the death and resurrection of the individual mirrors the original death and resurrection of Jesus.* Crucially, in this theology, baptism itself does not guarantee salvation (merely the end of Original Sin and the restoration of free will) but only belief in Jesus guarantees salvation. St. Paul's theology of salvation therefore says that since Jesus redeemed our sin, we can only share in that salvation by belief (or more correctly *faith*) in Jesus.

The substance of this argument is set out in Romans 5 and 1 Corinthians 15. In all these passages, St. Paul portrays Jesus as the 'second Adam' or the 'new Adam'. What was undone by Adam is put right by Jesus. Hence the *logos* or 'Word' in the Gospel of John, which incarnates in the flesh as Jesus, is often referred to as Adam Kadmon: the pure, untainted Adam. Thus Romans 5:12-21:

> [12] Wherefore, as by one man sin entered into the world, and death by sin; and so death passed upon all men, for that all have sinned:

> [13] (For until the law sin was in the world: but sin is not imputed when there is no law.

> [14] Nevertheless death reigned from Adam to Moses, even over them that had not sinned after the similitude of Adam's transgression, who is the figure of him that was to come.

> [15] But not as the offence, so also is the free gift. For if through the offence of one many be dead, much more the grace of God, and the gift by grace, which is by one man, Jesus Christ, hath abounded unto many.

¹⁶ And not as it was by one that sinned, so is the gift: for the judgment was by one to condemnation, but the free gift is of many offences unto justification.

¹⁷ For if by one man's offence death reigned by one; much more they which receive abundance of grace and of the gift of righteousness shall reign in life by one, Jesus Christ.)

¹⁸ Therefore as by the offence of one judgment came upon all men to condemnation; even so by the righteousness of one the free gift came upon all men unto justification of life.

¹⁹ For as by one man's disobedience many were made sinners, so by the obedience of one shall many be made righteous.

²⁰ Moreover the law entered, that the offence might abound. But where sin abounded, grace did much more abound:

[21] That as sin hath reigned unto death, even so might grace reign through righteousness unto eternal life by Jesus Christ our Lord.

And 1 Corinthians 15:45-47:

[45] And so it is written, The first man Adam was made a living soul; the last Adam was made a quickening spirit.

[46] Howbeit that was not first which is spiritual, but that which is natural; and afterward that which is spiritual.

[47] The first man is of the earth, earthy; the second man is the Lord from heaven.

It is through belief in Christ that the rift in Existence is healed allowing man to be justified with God. It is a deceptively simple but flawed theology, and also a curiously transactional one that treats sin as a kind of heavenly balance sheet in which God, like the merchant of Venice, demands his pound of flesh. Moreover, the entire theology is predicated on the weakness of Man; it assumes that we are dependent on a divine being to do the heavy lifting for us, and all we must do is 'believe'. Conversely, there is a well-established initiatic tradition within Christian Illuminism, Jewish Qabala and Islamic Sufism that demands of its students years of hard work and dedication to open their hearts and minds to Spirit – an initiatic tradition based on the agency of the student and not merely on the salvific power of a divine being.

Clearly, St. Paul believed in the Edenic story as part of scripture. To say, however, that he made a distinction between the historical and the mythic, would be to retroactively apply a modern mindset to that of two thousand years ago; there simply wasn't such a distinction as in that time the mythic commingled freely with the historical and, being a 'magical universe', there was no barrier between the supernatural and the natural. 'Truth' was based on 'received tradition', either scriptural or oral, in the absence of a culture of critical thought. From our modern perspective, we can trace the Eden myth all the way back to Sumeria from which the myth of the Deluge also came.

The origin of the myth lies in the Sumerian Gilgamesh epic, and the origin of the serpent is the god Ningishzida, Lord of the Underworld, who is depicted with serpents rising from his shoulders. Ningishzida is called the Lord of the Tree of Truth after Nin meaning Lord and is-zi-da meaning Tree of Truth. He also has the function of guarding the eastern gate of heaven together with Dumuzzi who is the guardian of the Tree of Life. In *Genesis*, 'God' guards both trees and the serpent is depicted as an adversarial underworld entity intent on corrupting Mankind. Additionally, it is God's own cherub that guards the eastern gate of Heaven and not the 'other god' Ningishzida. So, we have the possibility that Ningishzida offered the couple the fruits of *his* tree but Dumuzzi denied them the fruits of the other tree.

Today, with the exception of a few diehard fundamentalists, there is a consensus even within the Church that the Eden myth is an allegory of the rift between the spiritual and the physical that speaks of the disconnect with the root of our own being. If we accept that the Eden story is an allegory, does St Paul's elaborate theology collapse? Yes and no. There would be no ransoming of Jesus for the sins of Mankind, but I think we would come away with a more informed idea that malevolence does not enter the universe in a once-only *aha* moment, but slips through whenever humans turn away from love, life and being, when they cease to strive for the good; and I think we also come away with the truism that at particular periods of history, certain people are born with exceptional gifts and exceptional humanity who remind us to 'stay on the yellow brick road'. Looking beneath the surface of St Paul's theology, one may find an allegory for the Holy Spirit 'reaching out' to the soul in the darkness of Nature (crucifying itself on the cross of Matter, if you will) in which we are given the strength and meaning necessary to die to our instinctual human self and metaphorically be reborn. Thus, Jesus, as Everyman, dies to the merely human to be resurrected as the new Adam who is the mirror of God in the physical universe. Just as Jesus is the new Adam, so the Virgin Mary is the new Eve; rather than tempting him with the forbidden fruit proffered by the serpent, the grace of the Spirit flows through her into her child. In this drama, it is Judas who becomes a lower analogue of the serpent in Eden: just as the serpent betrays Adam (through Havah or Eve), so Judas betrays Jesus, but the cosmic betrayal is reversed in Jesus' resurrection and Judas (the defeated serpent) hangs himself in shame. Each person who wishes to rise to the fullest potential of their humanity must pass through their own Calvary. Surely the lesson of the Eden myth is that Man must fall from being a mere creature of Nature in order to embrace Divinity through his own self-conscious awareness: the true meaning of the parable of the prodigal son in Luke 15:11-32. We *had* to fall in order to rise again as something new and wonderful: beings with the capacity to 'touch' Divinity and as active participants in the Divine drama instead of mere 'creatures'.

The status of Jesus: exaltation from below or salvation from above?

The esoteric teachings that Jesus taught his disciples[228] were lost when the locus of early

---

[228] "He answered them, 'The mystery of the kingdom of God has been granted to you. But to those outside everything comes in parables,'" (Mark 4:11). When the new religion of Christianity spread throughout the Greek and Roman world, it was established as an 'open' religion, but the gospels make it

Christianity shifted from Palestine to the Greek world, and the Jerusalem Church of James (Jesus' brother) ceased to exist after the Roman destruction of the Temple in 70 A.D. This left the emergent religion of Christianity with an evolving theology and belief system but without a praxis. A tradition of Christian mysticism had to be built from the bottom up, and at the core of it was the mystical identification with Jesus as the Word or *Logos* who 'dwelt with God and was God'. This was not, however, the original view held of Jesus, and some of the earliest views about Jesus recorded in the synoptic gospels of Matthew, Mark and Luke are at variance with the later theology of Jesus' divinity expressed in the Fourth Gospel (of John). This is important, because if we adopt a view of salvation based on the Divinity of Jesus, we must also be aware of how Christian theology changed during the first three centuries of the Christian era up to the Council of Nicaea in 325. In the early Christian era, certainly in the first century, we cannot speak of a

---

clear that not everything was revealed by Jesus, and the Jesus movement had more in common with an initiatic system.

single Christianity at all but a family of competing Christianities.

It was Jesus' death that began the long period of theological speculation about him: What was his nature? Was he a holy man? Was he a prophet? Was he the Messiah? What was the meaning of his life? What happened to him after his death? Was he sent by God or was he just an itinerant preacher (and there were many of those)? When Jesus died, many early Christians claimed that he had been exalted to divine – read 'angelic' – status at his death (much as the prophets Enoch and Elijah had been 'translated' into Heaven), and this became known as an 'exaltation' Christology.

There was a belief current at the time among the Jewish apocalyptics (likely taken from Persian Zoroastrian sources[229] following the Babylonian Captivity) that everyone had an angelic counterpart (*Fravashi* in Zoroastrianism) and an Adversary (variously described in the apocalyptic literature

---

[229] A hint of Persian influence on the life of Jesus is the journey of the Magi to Bethlehem to witness the birth of the *Saoshyant*, the Saviour of the World, 'the one who will make existence bright'. The star is, of course, not a real star (as Biblical literalists would have it, since stars don't hover over villages) but a messianic symbol implying divine destiny.

as Azazel or Samael). The goal of the mystic was
to rebut the temptations of the Adversary (as per
Jesus' temptation in the desert, in Matthew 4:1-
11 and Luke 4:1-13) and ascend to unification with
their angelic Over Self; in this wise, the prophet
Enoch was said to have become the archangel
Metatron at his ascent. At this juncture, it is
germane to speak of two rival priestly lines in
Judaism: the Levitical priesthood descended from
Aaron, Moses' brother, referred to as Kohanim,
and the Sethian priesthood that followed the
quasi-mythical line of Enoch through Melchizidek.
Characteristic of this second line is the practice of
a proto-Qabalic mysticism derived from primitive
shamanistic soul travel (with its roots in northern
Israel) called the Maaseh Merkavah ('Work of the
Chariot') or Hekhalot ('palace') mysticism whereby
the soul of the prophet ascended as a fiery chariot
of the soul through the seven spheres or heavens.
The seventh heaven contained seven palaces, of
which the topmost palace contained the Throne
of God, guarded by angels and encircled by flames

and lightning.[230] There are hints of this practice in the First Book of Enoch, in Isaiah's Temple vision (Isaiah 6), in Ezekiel's vision of the chariot of God drawn and powered by angels (Ezekiel 1:4-28), and in the ascent of Elijah into heaven in a fiery chariot at his physical death (2 Kings 2): "And it came to pass, as they still went on, and talked, that, behold, there appeared a chariot of fire, and horses of fire, and parted them both asunder; and Elijah went up by a whirlwind into heaven" (v.11). In *Enoch* 1, for instance, the prophet ascends to the highest sphere of heaven to intercede with God on behalf of the fallen angels. The culmination was the transfiguration of the prophet at his death into an angelic being... "And Enoch walked with God: and he was not; for God took him" (Genesis 5:24). The practice, however, could also unbalance the mind resulting in messianic delusion[231] and this was

---

[230] There is a parallel with the Tantric practice of the Kundalini energy ascending from the base of the spine up through the seven chakras to achieve union with the Supreme Self or Atman.

[231] As an example, take Abraham Abulafia, founder of the school of Prophetic Qabala in Zaragoza, Spain. In 1280, Abulafia set off to Rome to convert the Pope, Nicholas III, to Judaism. On hearing of his coming, the Pope screamed "Burn the fanatic!" (as popes did in those days). The stake had already been erected

the root of many of the prohibitions placed upon its study. It is interesting that in Hebrews 7:13-17, Jesus is referred to as "a priest in the order of Melchizidek", meaning that he would not qualify for the regular Kohanite priesthood, but practiced an alternate form of mysticism. This may go some way to explaining Jesus' antipathy to the Temple priesthood. Moreover, we know that the Qumran priesthood[232] and the itinerant holy men (like John the Baptist) who followed the Fourth Philosophy[233] of dualism, apocalypticism, messianism, spiritual purity, Jewish nationalism and armed resistance to Rome, regarded themselves as belonging to the line

---

inside the city gate to receive Abulafia, but fortuitously Nicholas III died suddenly just before Abulafia reached the citadel. Divine intervention or coincidence?

[232] The roots of Jewish radicalism lie far back in Babylon after that nation's conquest by Cyrus the Great of Persia in 539 BC, ending the Babylonian Captivity, after which they imbibed elements of Zoroastrianism such as a dualism between Light/ Good and Dark/Evil, the belief in the coming of a Messiah who would remake the world (the *saoshyant*), and an angelology derived from the *Fravashis* (spiritual guardian or genius of each individual) and *Yazatas* (celestial angels).

[233] From the Jewish historian Josephus, the first three philosophies were the Sadducees (the priests of the Temple), the Pharisees (antecedents of the Rabbinic tradition) and the Essenes (quietist mystics).

of the Melchizidekian priesthood and the Enochian tradition, hence the Enochian literature and other Jewish mystical texts found at Nag Hammadi in 1945. The Holy Land itself constituted a spiritual map with the arid desert of the south culminating in the Dead Sea denoting the 'existential desert of the soul' while the Galilee (formerly Israel and before then Canaan) being the 'Land of Milk and Honey' or heavenly paradise with the sacred Mount Herman at its northernmost extreme. The River Jordan that flowed between the two represented the river of life (the descent of grace *from* God and the path of ascent *to* God) and this was why the radical Jewish sects practiced water baptism in the Jordan, realigning the soul with the 'living waters' of the Spirit. During its descent, the Jordan dilates into the Sea of Galilee, to which Nazareth is adjacent, symbolically representing the Spirit of God (*Ruach ha Qodesh*) upon whose waters Jesus walks. The city of Jerusalem represented the soul (the 'city set upon a hill' in the Sermon on the Mount) holding the balance between the forces of Spirit and Nature, Life and Death as represented in the hexagram. In this schema, Jesus is the prophet from the North (the sacred land) sent down to redeem the soul of Israel (Jerusalem). This spiritual topography is reflected in the middle pillar of the medieval Qabalistic Tree of Life.

How much the writers of the synoptic gospels (being Greek Christians) understood of this dual lineage is uncertain, but the Transfiguration (Matthew 17:1-9; Mark 9:2-10; Luke 9:28-36) gives us a glimpse. It portrays a radiant Jesus, aflame with Spirit, atop a 'high place' (probably Mount Tabor) in the company of Moses and Elijah, a tableau theologically intended to convey the idea that Jesus was the seal of the Law of Moses and of the Prophets, but it is the association with Elijah that interests us, as Elijah's ascent in a fiery chariot is a folk memory of the Merkabah tradition. I suspect that the Transfiguration scene is intended in some way to depict Jesus as uniting the two priestly traditions in himself. For our purposes, however, the Transfiguration presages Jesus' own angelic 'exaltation'.

To some other early Christians, however, Jesus was a man into whom the Spirit of God had entered, enabling him to perform 'the works of God'.[234] This is known as an 'adoption' Christology, on the basis that Jesus was the *adopted* Son of God, and is the dominant Christology of the synoptic gospels written around 65-90 A.D. In Mark 1:9-11, the earliest gospel, the Holy Spirit descends on Jesus as a dove at his baptism by John the Baptist and thus proceeds to work through him. There is no virgin birth and no suggestion that Jesus is actually God incarnate: if he were, he would not have required baptism! The Holy Spirit enters Jesus at his conception in Matthew 1:30 and Luke 1:35 but there is no suggestion that Jesus is *physically* God as in the Nicene and Athanasian creeds, merely that Jesus is born a man with the *Spirit of God* within him.[235] Moreover, in Luke's account, both

---

[234] In the Old Testament context, the Holy Spirit did not simply bestow the grace of illumination but could intercede in physical existence, through elect individuals, causing changes in matter such as the power to heal.

[235] Matthew 1:18: "Now the birth of Jesus the Messiah took place in this way. When his mother Mary had been engaged to Joseph, but before they lived together, she was found to be with child from the Holy Spirit."

Matthew 1:20: "…do not be afraid to take Mary as your wife, for the child conceived in her is from the Holy Spirit."

Luke 1:35: "The angel said to her, "The Holy Spirit will come upon you, and the power of the Most High will overshadow you;

Jesus and John the Baptist are born by Immaculate Conception[236] and the Holy Spirit works through *both*; John was 'demoted' by subsequent Christian apologists in favour of Jesus.

Jesus is the unearthly child, the Man of Destiny, the Chosen of God, symbolised by the star. He is the 'one who will make existence bright', and through his sacrifice he will achieve his own spiritual apotheosis, becoming 'one with God'.

Further supporting this interpretation, in Luke 2: 36-38, the infant Jesus is recognised as one 'marked by God' by the prophetess Anna, of the tribe of Asher, daughter of Phanuel. Phanuel (or Phenuel) is not the name of her father, however, but of an angel whose name means 'face of God' and to whom Anna has been dedicated. It is a prosaic way of saying that Jesus was favoured by the Angel of the Lord. This is the same Peniel with whom Jacob wrestles in Genesis 32:30, while Asher was the eighth of Jacob's twelve sons. Asher represents the lost northern Israelite tradition and, for Luke, Jesus is the new Jacob who

---

therefore the child to be born will be holy; he will be called Son of God."

[236] Luke 1:36-37.

will restore the nation of Israel in anticipation of the coming Kingdom of God.

There are passages in the gospels which portray Jesus as a mystic wielding the power of the Holy Spirit. One such is Mark 8: 22-26 in which Jesus heals a blind man by mixing earth and spittle and applying the poultice to his eyes. Key to understanding this is that spittle contains his divine 'virtue', the Spirit of God that moves through him. The passage is given below:

> And he cometh to Bethsaida; and they bring a blind man unto him, and besought him to touch him. And he took the blind man by the hand, and led him out of the town; and when he had spit on his eyes, and put his hands upon him, he asked him if he saw ought. And he looked up, and said, I see men as trees, walking. After that he put his hands again upon his eyes, and made him look up: and he was restored, and saw every man clearly. And he sent him away to his house, saying, Neither go into the town, nor tell it to any in the town.

The passage was known to the writer of John who added it to his gospel, but the premise is entirely different: in the context of Mark, it is the Holy Spirit working through Jesus that performs the miracle whereas in John it is Jesus' own divinity. There are other differences also: whereas in Mark, the man begins to see gradually, in John the healing is virtually spontaneous. The following quote is from John 3:1-7.

Now as Jesus passed by, He saw a man who was blind from birth. And His disciples asked Him, saying, "Rabbi, who sinned, this man or his parents, that he was born blind?" Jesus answered, "Neither this man nor his parents sinned, but that the works of God should be revealed in him. I must work the works of Him who sent Me while it is day; the night is coming when no one can work.[237] As long

---

[237] The writer of John is more interested in symbolism than theological coherence. Of course, Jesus as the Son of God *could* work miracles at night, but as the 'Light of the World' he was symbolically associated with the Sun; besides which, it was important for John's gospel that Jesus be *seen* to work miracles which no one would at night. Perversely, in the prophetic age, the Holy Spirit was said to descend upon the holy *at night.*

as I am in the world, I am the light of the world." When He had said these things, He spat on the ground and made clay with the saliva, and He anointed the eyes of the blind man with the clay. And He said to him, "Go, wash in the pool of Siloam". So he went and washed, and came back seeing.

What follows is an altercation between Jesus and the Pharisee about spiritual blindness; indeed, both the passages from Mark and John can be interpreted symbolically as stories about spiritual blindness. Although performed in the name of God, this episode nonetheless represents, in my personal view, an intrusion of pre-Judaic shamanism among the Jewish mystics and thence into early Christianity, in which Jesus is both priest and shaman, magician and holy man. There is a ring of authenticity about this episode, suggesting that it comes from a very early personal eyewitness account of Jesus in which Jesus was regarded as a wandering 'holy man', magician, healer and exorcist in common with other such persons we know about, such as Honi the Circle Maker. It seems oddly out of place in John, whose version of Jesus as the incarnation of the Logos would not have required his hero to mess around with spittle and dust like a Siberian shaman or African witch doctor.

Jesus' 'virtue' is a power that he embodies as a quality (or hypostasis[238]) of the divine power that flows within him. It is at once part of him and also independent of him. An outstanding example supporting this theory comes from Luke 8:43-47 when his robe (not him personally) is touched by a woman in the street where he is walking with his disciples:

And a woman having an issue of blood twelve years, which had spent all her living upon physicians, neither could be healed of any, came behind him, and touched the border of his garment: and immediately her issue of blood stanched. And Jesus said, "Who touched me?" When all denied, Peter and they that were with him said, "Master, the multitude throng thee and press thee, and sayest thou, Who touched me?" And Jesus

---

[238] When we speak of the 'wisdom of God', for example, wisdom is both a property of God and a thing in itself. This is a hypostatis.

said, "Somebody hath touched me, for I perceive that virtue is gone out of me." And when the woman saw that she was not hid, she came trembling, and falling down before him, she declared unto him before all the people for what cause she had touched him, and how she was healed immediately.

Clearly, Jesus' 'virtue' passes into (and abides in) everything he wears or touches, which is to say it is transmissible; it is in his bodily fluids, it is in his clothes. There is an echo of this belief that a person's 'virtue' passes into their clothing in the practice of unmarried women touching a bride's dress. The quasi-independent action of Jesus' healing power suggests that he is the channel for the Spirit of God rather than being divine in himself. In the Fourth Gospel (of John), however, written near the end of the first century, the theology has shifted to an 'incarnation' Christology whereby Jesus is now a pre-existent divine being (the Word or *Logos*) incarnated in the flesh. He has now become the Son of Man, but the Son of Man is no longer a cosmic judge but a redeemer of

Humanity.[239] "Anyone who has seen me has seen the Father. How can you say, 'Show us the Father'? Don't you believe that I am in the Father, and that the Father is in me? The words I say to you I do not speak on my own authority. Rather, it is the Father, living in me, who is doing his work" (John 14:9-10). Passages such as these are reinforced by the so-called 'I am' statements that pepper John's gospel, and of these there are seven instances (eight if one includes Jesus' response to Pilate at his trial).[240] These derive from Exodus 3:13-14 in which God reveals his name to Moses: *Ehieh asher Ehieh*, "I am that I am"; in other words a statement of pure Being rather than a name as such.

---

[239] For those who are interested in further investigating the differing theologies of early Christianity, I highly recommend the writings of Bart Ehrman, which assess Jesus from a historical rather than a faith-based perspective.

[240] The occurrences of the 'I am' statements are as follows:
I am the Bread of Life (John 6:35)
I am the Light of the World (John 8:12)
I am the Door (John 10:9)
I am the Good Shepherd (John 10:11,14)
I am the Resurrection and the Life (John 11:25)
I am the Way and the Truth and the Life (John 14:6)
I am the Vine (John 15:1,5)
Then there is John 18:37 at Jesus' trial: "Pilate therefore said unto him, Art thou a king then? Jesus answered, Thou sayest that I am a king."

¹³ And Moses said unto God, Behold, when I come unto the children of Israel, and shall say unto them, The God of your fathers hath sent me unto you; and they shall say to me, What is his name? what shall I say unto them?

¹⁴ And God said unto Moses, I Am That I Am: and he said, Thus shalt thou say unto the children of Israel, I Am hath sent me unto you.

The writer of John inserts these 'I am' sayings as ciphers or concealed messages into the text of his gospel so that only Christian followers will understand that Jesus is identifying himself with God.

The high point of the Gospel of John is Jesus' raising of Lazarus in John 11 which is so contrived that it cannot be considered historical truth, especially when Jesus could have healed Lazarus while he was still alive but instead chooses to delay his journey, letting him die so he can resurrect him in a show of power! The scene is a spin-off on the parable of the rich man and Lazarus in

Luke 16:19-31 in which the rich man, cast down into hell, implores Abraham to send Lazarus to warn his family that this will be their fate too, to which Abraham replies, "If they do not listen to Moses and the Prophets, they will not be convinced even if someone rises from the dead", which is the objective of John's set piece: to convince readers that resurrection is possible and therefore prepare the way for Jesus' own resurrection. 'We know it can be done so is it so far-fetched if Jesus also rises from the dead?' There is also an attempt in this passage to draw a comparison with the prophet Elijah who raises from the dead the son of the widow of Zarephath in 1 Kings 17:21-22. When I first read this passage, however, it carried the suggestion not of an actual resurrection but of an initiation ceremony in which Lazarus, dressed in grave clothes and kept in a tomb for four days, is released by Jesus to be symbolically reborn; we know such practices were undertaken in the Greek Mysteries where the tomb assumed the role of a dream incubation chamber allowing the astral body of the initiate to separate out from the physical.

In John 2:13-22, Jesus, after having turned the money changers out of the Temple (a scene that doesn't occur until just before the trial in the synoptic gospels), foretells his own resurrection:

> Jesus answered and said unto them, Destroy this temple, and in three days I will raise it up. Then said the Jews, Forty and six years was this temple in building, and wilt thou rear it up in three days? But he spake of the temple of his body.

But this passage says more than it actually does about the nature of Jesus' mission. In the 2018 film *Mary Magdalene*, directed by Garth Davis, Jesus attacks the priests as they are slaughtering the lambs for Passover, and challenges them with the question "Have their hearts been altered when they leave this place?" It is an apposite question directed at the nature of religion itself. If religion doesn't effect a permanent change in consciousness (if it is simply empty ritual) what good is it? Thus, the shift in emphasis from the physical temple to the body as temple marks a transition from a sacrificial religion to an inner mysticism that might be deemed the 'Protestantisation of Judaism'.

John therefore gives us what is termed a 'high Christology' (Jesus as a pre-existent aspect of God who emanates or incarnates into physical existence) as opposed to the 'low Christology' of the synoptic gospels (Jesus as a human being in whom the Spirit of God enters either at his baptism (Mark) or at birth (Matthew and Luke) and is raised to Divine status at his death.

The theological underpinning of the gospel of John is set out in the very first chapter. It reads like a catechism and may indeed have been an early Christian catechism that the writer of John decided to use as the introduction to his – or her – gospel.

[1] In the beginning was the Word, and the Word was with God, and the Word was God.

[2] The same was in the beginning with God.

[3] All things were made by him; and without him was not any thing made that was made.

[4] In him was life; and the life was the light of men.

[5] And the light shineth in darkness; and the darkness comprehended it not.

[6] There was a man sent from God, whose name was John.

[7] The same came for a witness, to bear witness of the Light, that all men through him might believe.

[8] He was not that Light, but was sent to bear witness of that Light.

[9] That was the true Light, which lighteth every man that cometh into the world.

[10] He was in the world, and the world was made by him, and the world knew him not.

[11] He came unto his own, and his own received him not.

[12] But as many as received him, to them gave he power to become the sons of God, even to them that believe on his name:

[13] Which were born, not of blood, nor of the will of the flesh, nor of the will of man, but of God.

[14] And the Word was made flesh, and dwelt among us, (and we beheld his glory, the glory as of the only begotten son of the Father) full of grace and truth.

Whereas *Matthew* havers uncertainly between the Judaic and Greek worlds, John is firmly planted in the Greek world. The term *logos* as used by the writer of the Gospel of John is substantially different from the term *logos* as used by the pre-Socratics, by Plato and later expounded by Philo of Alexandria. In its Platonic form, the *logos* is the Divine Mind or Divine Reason, the sum of all the ideas that are destined to become Matter. Plato distinguishes between 'perfect form' and 'imperfect matter'. The *logos* therefore bears some similarity with the Demiurge who mediates between the Monad (God) and Matter, bringing into being the Divine Ideas, although the later Gnostics held a negative view of the Demiurge as a false god. Given that the universe follows rational laws, it follows that the Divine mind that conceived it must also be rational, and given also that human reason is a fragment of Divine reason, the logos must be comprehensible through rational philosophy (a very different view from the later religion of Christianity in which Divinity cannot be known rationally but only intuitively through the heart). The writer of John has taken this Platonic idea of the Logos and given it a theological twist so that, in John 1, the *logos* is still an emanation of God but its mission is a salvific one: it incarnates in the flesh as Jesus to redeem Mankind. This was a development of the Greek view of *logos* as the 'knowable' aspect of the Monad; in Greek philosophy, the *logos* could be apprehended through mind and through the physical universe it created. John takes this one step further: we come to 'know' God through Jesus Christ.

I confess that the incarnation theology has never made much sense to me, not least because, in its original sense, the Logos doesn't just incarnate into a single man but 'moves' through many men and women in many ages, who all inspire and move us forward. The theological objection to John is that if everything exists within the *logos* and the *logos* exists in everything, there is simply no necessity for the *logos* to incarnate in a single person. Since the time of the Prophets, Divinity had made itself known through the visionary or intuitive faculty of those receptive to it. The idea of God incarnating in a person is alien both to Judaism and to Platonism. There is also the question of 'why now'? After several thousand years of human history, why does God decide to send a saviour? In first century Christianity, there was a very good reason: the coming of the Eschaton, although given the prevalent belief in the coming of the Kingdom of God, there is no sense of its imminence in John.

John conceives Jesus as a pre-existent divine being that is *part* of God and he adapts the existing word *logos* (expressed as 'the Word') to describe that being. The Gospel of John, however, was written when the dominant paradigm was a binary relationship between God and the Holy Spirit (the transcendent and immanent aspects of the godhead). The use of *logos* or 'Word' is therefore broader than simply the Holy Spirit. The Word makes the world (John 1:3 and 10), which is a function of the Holy Spirit, but it also incarnates in the flesh as Jesus, which is a function of the pre-existent

Christ ('the Son' in trinitarian terms). Clearly, then, the functions of the Holy Spirit and the Son are bound together in the concept of the Word. Although a form of proto-trinitarianism appears in the first century *Didache,* it would not be until the second to third century under Tertullian that the doctrine of the Trinity would fully delineate the functions of the Holy Spirit and the Son (mindful that metaphysical reality doesn't obligingly change to accommodate the diktats of the Church). John's theology is developed further in Jesus' night-time conversation with Nicodemus, the Pharisaic leader, in John 3:1-21. I shall quote verses 1-8:

[1] There was a man of the Pharisees, named Nicodemus, a ruler of the Jews:

[2] The same came to Jesus by night, and said unto him, Rabbi, we know that thou art a teacher come from God: for no man can do these miracles that thou doest, except God be with him.

³ Jesus answered and said unto him, Verily, verily, I say unto thee, Except a man be born again, he cannot see the kingdom of God.

⁴ Nicodemus saith unto him, How can a man be born when he is old? can he enter the second time into his mother's womb, and be born?

⁵ Jesus answered, Verily, verily, I say unto thee, Except a man be born of water and of the Spirit, he cannot enter into the kingdom of God.

⁶ That which is born of the flesh is flesh; and that which is born of the Spirit is spirit.

⁷ Marvel not that I said unto thee, Ye must be born again.

⁸ The wind bloweth where it listeth, and thou hearest the sound thereof, but canst not tell whence it cometh, and whither it goeth: so is every one that is born of the Spirit.

[9] Nicodemus answered and said unto him, How can these things be?

[10] Jesus answered and said unto him, Art thou a master of Israel, and knowest not these things?

[11] Verily, verily, I say unto thee, We speak that we do know, and testify that we have seen; and ye receive not our witness.

[12] If I have told you earthly things, and ye believe not, how shall ye believe, if I tell you of heavenly things?

[13] And no man hath ascended up to heaven, but he that came down from heaven, even the Son of Man which is in heaven.

[14] And as Moses lifted up the serpent in the wilderness, even so must the Son of Man be lifted up:

[15] That whosoever believeth in him should not perish but have eternal life.

¹⁶ For God so loved the world, that he gave his only begotten Son, that whosoever believeth in him should not perish, but have everlasting life.

¹⁷ For God sent not his Son into the world to condemn the world; but that the world through him might be saved.

In a play on words that only works in Greek (thus raising doubts of the encounter's historicity since Jesus would have spoken Aramaic), Jesus uses the word *anothen* to mean both 'above' and 'again': "Except a man be born *from above*, he cannot see the kingdom of God". Hence Nicodemus' confusion. Being born 'from above' means 'being born of the Spirit', and that in turn means not merely being baptised (symbolic immersion in 'the living water') but accepting the power of the Spirit into the soul. Hence John is rephrasing a passage found in Matthew 3:11 that has John the Baptist declare: "I baptize you with water for repentance, but he who is coming after me is mightier than I, whose sandals I am not worthy to carry. He will baptize you with the Holy Spirit and fire". The passage is also found in Luke 3:16. The one who opens the door to salvation is Jesus who, as the pre-existent *logos*, 'comes down from heaven', and since Jesus will not always be around to personally 'baptise with fire' (for which read 'initiate' or 'open a person to the Spirit') through his sacrifice he opens a path to salvation that anyone who accepts him will share in that salvation.

We both gained something and lost something from this incarnation theology. What we gained was a beautifully symmetrical idea that, through Jesus, Man came to understand what it is to be God and God came to understand what it is to be human. What it also did, however, was to elevate Jesus' Divine aspect at the expense of his humanity. We are saved 'through him' as a divine being but we cannot 'become him'. He doesn't have to overcome his weaknesses because he doesn't have any, and so we cannot relate to him as a complex person. He is tempted but we know he will not succumb. He is crucified but we know he will transcend death. As God clothed in the likeness of flesh, he is forever beyond our reach. I vividly remember back in 1988 when Martin Scorsese's film adaptation of Nikos Kazantzakis' novel *The Last Temptation of Christ* came out on release and the furore that surrounded it: nuns and evangelicals protesting outside cinemas, the Greek Orthodox Church excommunicating the author and the Catholic Church banning the book... and yet they all completely missed the point. Given that Jesus (as per the Nicene and Athanasian creeds) was "fully divine and fully human", how natural was it for his human side to rebel and want to live the life of a normal man? The whole sad affair advertised to all the intractability of the religious mind. These protesters were so inured to religious orthodoxy, their small minds couldn't accept that there might be a contradiction between Jesus' human and divine natures.

Why did Jesus die?

The Gospel of John marks the culmination of a theological development that elevated Jesus to divine status, and that elevation to divine status required early Christians to explain *why* he died. The Jewish Messiah wasn't supposed to die. Born from the Davidic line, he would lead the nation of

Israel (which in Jesus' time had shrunk to Judea, since the ten northern tribes had been dispersed by the Assyrians centuries before) to victory over its enemies and restore the rightful worship of God. So, the Messiah was something of a holy warrior: both king and religious leader. To answer the question 'How could the Messiah die?', people reasoned that if God had *allowed* the Messiah to die, he must have died *for them*. Conveniently, Christians looked to the prophesy of the Suffering Servant of Isaiah 53 who suffers for his righteousness (but is not the Messiah of the Jewish tradition) and so the theology of the suffering Christ was born.

Further, Christians systematically mined the Old Testament or Tanakh for other prophesies of Jesus' birth in an egregiously dishonest manner; specifically, the birth narratives in Matthew and Luke were written to fit the prophesies of Micah 5:2 and Isaiah 7:14 (Jesus' birth in Bethlehem of Judah, and the birth of a saviour called Immanuel to 'a young woman', wrongly interpreted as a 'virgin'[241]). They were dishonest because prophesies

---

[241] In Isaiah 7, Jerusalem is being threatened by the Aramites and Israelites (the northern tribes). The prophet declares to King Ahaz that Aram and Israel would not be successful in conquering

are always concerned with things that are likely to happen *in the near future* based on affairs at the time they are made, not hundreds of years ahead. The gospel authors thus set out to construct what one might deem a foundational myth: that Jesus is the fulfilment of prophesy, that Jesus is the Jewish Messiah born of the line of David, and that Christianity is the natural successor to Judaism. Hence Matthew and Luke set out to create genealogies for Jesus that pass through the Davidic line and have him born in Bethlehem in

---

Jerusalem for "the Lord himself shall give you a sign; Behold, a virgin shall conceive, and bear a son, and shall call his name Immanuel. Butter and honey shall he eat, that he may know to refuse the evil, and choose the good. For before the child shall know to refuse the evil, and choose the good, the land that thou abhorrest shall be forsaken of both her kings" (Isaiah 7:14-16). Basically, Isaiah is saying that in the space of time it takes a young woman to bear a child, and before that child can make a moral choice, the Aramites and Israelites will be no more. No more is actually said of the mysterious child and there is no indication that it is a prophesy of the Messiah. The Hebrew used for 'young woman' is *almah* whereas the proper word for 'virgin' is *bethulah*. Nonetheless, when the Greek Septuagint was being compiled, *almah* was mistranslated as *parthenos*, meaning 'virgin', which found its way into the Latin Vulgate as *virgo* (although in Latin *virgo intacta* is the proper word for a virgin). The prophesy of Isaiah formed the basis of the virgin birth in Matthew (1:18-25) and Luke (1:26-38) but it is clear that the Septuagint was used as the basis for these passages rather than the original Hebrew.

Judah, which was the birthplace of David, when he is more likely to have been born in Bethlehem in Galilee just next door to Nazareth; there were *two* towns called Bethlehem. Given also that Herod had destroyed the genealogical records in the Temple so no usurper to claim descent from David, it is difficult to see how those genealogies could have been constructed. The truth is that theologically and historically Christianity derives from the apocalyptic sect (known as the Fourth Philosophy) within Judaism and not from mainstream Rabbinic Judaism, which would cast doubt on Jesus' descent through the Davidic line, although there probably were Pharisees sympathetic to Jesus as witnessed by Nicodemus' night-time conversation with Jesus in John. These remarks aside, the figure of Jesus that we see in the synoptic gospels (particularly Matthew[242]) is a conflation of the Jewish Messiah

---

[242] Matthew (who is believed to have been a Jewish Christian) wants two irreconcilable things: he wants the Jewish Messiah who will bring about the Kingdom of God on earth and he wants the Christian Saviour (based on the Suffering Servant of Isaiah) who will redeem the sin of Man through his sacrifice in a manner wholly antithetical to Jewish tradition. It is as though he were trying to reconcile the Jewish and Christian elements of his identity which are at war with each other. One gains the sense that he is conflating the Messiah and the Suffering Servant

and the Suffering Servant, a compound figure who bears little or no relation to the historical Jesus.

The Pauline rationale for Jesus' death is fundamentally at odds with the original Suffering Servant narrative of Isaiah 53, briefly touched upon above. First, it becomes clear from a reading of the text that the Suffering servant doesn't die:

If He renders Himself *as* a guilt offering,
He will see *His* offspring,
He will prolong *His* days,
And the good pleasure of the Lord will prosper in His hand. (Isaiah 53:10)

Secondly, his suffering is intended as proof of faith or 'virtue', allowing him to intercede with God on behalf of Mankind, which makes him less of a sacrificial offering than a divine intercessor:

---

into a single figure, and I think one reason for the confusion is that Matthew draws into his gospel older sources (such as Matthew 19:28) that portray Jesus in a very different light to the Christian idea of 'saviour'.

Yet He Himself bore the sin of many,
And interceded for the wrongdoers.
(*Isaiah 53:12*)

In other words, he is not sacrificing himself to repay a debt of disobedience to God and he is certainly not redeeming the Original Sin of Adam which would have been anathema to the Jewish faith. Instead, he is restoring the connection between God and Man through a demonstration of faith. Indeed, the theme of the divine intercessor is more in keeping with the Enochian tradition than the Pauline.

The problem of Original Sin

We have seen that although St. Paul asserted that Jesus died to redeem Mankind from the Original Sin of Adam, the ceremonial washing away of sin through baptism does not of itself confer salvation since we can sin again through free will. The doctrine of Original Sin was promoted by St. Augustine of Hippo (354-430) but in his time it was not universally accepted. Specifically, the Welsh monk Pelagius (355-420) critiqued Augustine's theology on two grounds: first, that original sin did not taint human nature, and humans by divine grace have free will to achieve human perfection; and second, that it was unjust to punish one person for the sins of another and therefore infants are born blameless. Unfortunately, it was Augustine's power of persuasion within the Church that won the day and Pelagius' thought was condemned as heretical at the Council of Carthage in 418. Pelagius was hounded out of the Church and the whole episode reflects badly on Augustine who, basically, was intolerant of anyone criticising his version of theology. As with St. Paul, it was 'my way or the highway'.

For the record, Judaism has no concept of Original Sin, and the concept did not even exist in the apocalyptic Fourth Philosophy, so Jesus (being Jewish) would likely have been appalled by the idea; it isn't even touched on by Jesus in the gospels. At the end of the day, it is, like St. Paul's entire theology of salvation, a construct of the intellect whose deserved place is to be consigned to the encyclopaedia of failed ideas.

Being an astute observer of human nature, I cannot honestly countenance that baptism makes any difference at all to the behaviour of the average human, and humans are just as selfish and greedy after baptism as they were before. If Church leaders cannot see that then they don't get out as much as they should. If there is a predisposition for stupidity, violence, greed, selfishness and arrogance, it is because those traits have always existed in Man ever since we came down from the trees. In evolutionary terms, we resemble a cross between the chimp and the bonobo with the best and the worst of each. If there is Original Sin, it the curse of our own hominid ancestry.

It remains, however, that we are rooted in a higher reality in which we have our being, and it is our blindness to our origin as beings of Spirit that is the *state* of sin from which the *act* of sin (that which offends Being) derives. We are saved when we reject the ape and embark on the journey to recover our own spiritual nature.

Are we justified by faith alone?

Returning to St. Paul, belief in Jesus as the physical incarnation of God and saviour of humanity from

Sin became the central tenet of salvation, expressed in John 11:25-26: "...I am the resurrection and the life: he that believeth in me, though he were dead, yet shall he live, and whosoever liveth and believeth in me shall never die." This is known as St. Paul's doctrine of *justification by faith alone*. Jesus took the hit for us, so all we have to do is have faith in him (meaning 'to become one in him') in order to share in that salvation. What if one doesn't subscribe to St. Paul's transactional theology of sin and redemption? Well, I think that faith is a much broader concept than theology, and in many respects transcends individual theologies, and basing my faith on a rational theology never made much sense to me, let alone St. Paul's bizarre theology in which Jesus is ransomed for Man's sin. I certainly don't believe that salvation is dependent on a single theology, or indeed, is dependent on belief in Christ without the necessity of personal self-awareness and moral effort. I shall now discuss my reasons for thinking this.

We have this word 'belief' in John 11:25-26, but belief in itself does not change a person's core nature, because belief is an intellectual abstraction. I can believe the moon is made of green cheese but it doesn't change the nature of the moon. I can believe the earth is flat but it doesn't change the nature of the earth. I can believe that Jesus was the incarnation of God on earth, but what happens if he was just a man through whom the power of the Sacred flowed and not a pre-existent divine being (and we have seen that many other interpretations of Jesus occur in the gospels)? If I *believe* in Jesus, how am I changed? What change of inner state takes place? How does my perception alter? In what new way do I come to understand? Is belief in Jesus simply a promissory note redeemable when I die, or is it transformative in life? *One can believe whatever one wants but one remains the same person under the skin.* A better choice of word would be *faith*, because faith of the soul is very different from intellectual belief. Faith translates as *trust*, and for St. Paul, faith was "the substance of things hoped for, evidence of things not seen" (Hebrews 11:1), specifically, trust in Jesus' sacrifice to redeem Man from sin. More broadly, though, it can be construed as trust in the living presence of Divinity, with which we are all connected through the Deep Self, and in the capacity of the Holy Spirit to move us to a higher form of love. I have a rather different take on faith, not as theology, but as the *intuited* awareness of a higher order of reality that we cannot rationally define, an order that we are part of and have a purpose in. More, faith is for me an *opening* of the Self to that intuited Divine presence; a reaching out with the spiritual imagination to the Spirit that reaches out to us (an 'imaginative engagement' with supernal reality, if you will) as we struggle to understand it 'from the inside'. Furthermore, I have faith that the experience of that higher metaphysical reality is transformative and engenders a perceptual alteration. I trust in a higher metaphysical reality, but I don't feel the necessity to define that intuited faith in terms of a rational theology. Faith is not something we are given; it is something we are *called to*, and even when faith *is* handed down to us, we must make it our own. Succinctly, faith begins with a quest for meaning in existence, either because of an inner awakening or personal crisis, and that quest is prompted by an intuited understanding that we are part of a greater metaphysical reality that is beyond understanding by conventional science, because it can neither be observed nor quantified. We might say that spiritual experience is fundamentally different from scientific method in that the subject-object dichotomy of science is dissolved and faith in a spiritual realm beyond the physical, with which we are connected through deep consciousness, is a necessary precursor to entering into it. Faith is something that is lived and experienced, and not something that can be studied. It is 'intuited knowledge', because there are many ways of knowing and science is only one of them. Further, while science can *explain* the universe, it cannot ascribe *meaning* to it, relating the individual to Existence, since meaning is *created* and belongs not to science but to philosophy and faith; as humans, we are wired to seek out meaning, in whatever form that may take. There will always be faith because we cannot live without it.

Faith also has the connotation of *identification*. There is a monastic precept that says, "They who trust in the flesh shall perish with the flesh." We are saved or condemned by what we identify with. In the orthodox Christian sense, in having faith in Christ we are identifying with Christ as the human face of Divinity, but in the mystical sense we are identifying with the Divine principle *in ourselves*, that which transcends flesh, thus giving us a focus that makes Divinity more accessible to us. Even if we don't subscribe to the Christian theology of incarnation, we can still identify with Jesus as a Man of Spirit or Perfected Man – the living image of what we can become. In identifying with Christ or Divinity in the abstract, we are also expressing a relationship with Divinity, but critically we don't need to define Divinity rationally in order to relate to it because our knowledge of Divinity is intuited; it is hard-wired into us.

In Christian mysticism, identification with Christ as Spirit forms an important meditation exercise in aligning the soul with Divinity and activating the principle of Spirit within the soul (because Christ represents the Divine indwelling presence[243]) *but it only works in conjunction with control of the emotional Self, the development of empathy and self-awareness, and the opening of the Self to a higher consciousness through prayer and meditation.* It is the opening of spiritual perception, our knowledge of acausal Being, in concert with discipline and self-awareness, that assures the creation of a coherent

---

[243] "Christ is in you" (see *Colossians 1-29*).

soul.[244] *The soul is the ark we build to survive the deluge of death.* Thus, in no sense can it be said that mere 'belief' in Christ (or even God) 'saves' us. Even when we acquire faith in its deepest sense and openness to the power of Spirit within us, we must *do something* with it. We must invite the power of Spirit to open its doors to us, we must perform certain meditational and mantric practices that increase the ascent of spiritual energy in the body, diverting the energy of Being away from its expression through nature and reproduction into the mind, and we must concentrate that energy through Will and self-awareness until we become a single integral spiritual being: the realisation of Divinity in the flesh (which simultaneously transcends the flesh) in which we bridge the physical and acausal universes. Aleister Crowley called it 'Love under Will'. This work is what I call 'the work of faith': the creation of a coherent soul that is aware, empathetic, disciplined, and whose spiritual imagination is alive to the possibility of Divinity, and in my view this

---

[244] To open the mind to acausal reality without the mental discipline to make sense of what we experience would lead to madness.

work of faith is antithetical to St. Paul's theology of salvation by faith *alone*.

The work of faith, too, involves *striving*: striving to comprehend the Divinity which is within us and beyond us, as something that is intuited but eludes the grasp of the intellect, and this is very different from a cut and dried, neatly gift-wrapped theology. There is a mental struggle involved: the more we seek Divinity, the more the Divine principle reveals itself. The work of faith is also *vigilance*: a state of watchfulness where we continually assess our thoughts and actions as, for example, in the examination of conscience. Before we can become fitting vessels of the Holy Spirit, we must become pure and uncorrupted: *we must recover our innocence*. Both of these principles of faith (Strife and Vigilance) are key aspects of Islamic thought (the 'inner jihad') but are poorly understood in the Christianised West where Belief has assumed the greater importance thanks to Augustine, Luther and Calvin. Belief alone will not change you, and theology never saved anyone. Rather than viewing faith as 'belief', we would do better to speak of faith as a 'work': the 'work of faith' is to recover the innocence of the soul. It is self-awareness and self-honesty that free us from the past, and it is innocence and the capacity for love that save us. In short, then, the path of faith is to fulfil the promise of our own humanity.

St. Paul's theology of salvation by faith alone eschews moral action for faith. Neither religious law nor moral law will redeem us, but only faith in Jesus. It all sounds rather callous: nothing you do makes any difference to your possibility of being 'saved'. As remarked above, the entire theology could be construed as predicated on the weakness of Man; Man is so weak, he can't raise himself up by his bootstraps but is dependent on a Divine being to save him, and I think this is a valid criticism – faith is nothing without mental and spiritual discipline which implies *strength*. I believe that St. Paul was right in his view that moral and religious law do not fundamentally change us, but wrong in his idea that we are saved purely by faith without the personal work of self-development. Indeed, the idea of justification by faith alone is explicitly contradicted by James 2:17, *"Even so faith, if it hath not works, is dead, being alone."* In fairness to St. Paul, however, I think he viewed moral action as an expression of consciousness rather than 'law';

rather than denying the necessity of moral action, he viewed moral action as the *expression* of a state of inner justification or 'right alignment'. If we are tainted, then our moral action will be tainted; in other words, *the spirit of the act transcends the act itself*. Put another way, it is the state of spiritual being that saves us, not specific actions, and our actions reflect our state of being. This is revealed in his letter to the church in Corinth (*1 Corinthians*) in which he set out what today we call *The Way of Love*. I am going to quote the entire passage, not merely for the beauty of the writing, but also so that the reader can understand Paul's view of the relationship between love, humanity and faith. It goes like this:

> [1] Though I speak with the tongues of men and of angels, and have not charity, I am become as sounding brass, or a tinkling cymbal.

> [2] And though I have the gift of prophecy, and understand all mysteries, and all knowledge; and though I have all faith, so that I could

remove mountains, and have not charity, I am nothing.

[3] And though I bestow all my goods to feed the poor, and though I give my body to be burned, and have not charity, it profiteth me nothing.

[4] Charity suffereth long, and is kind; charity envieth not; charity vaunteth not itself, is not puffed up,

[5] Doth not behave itself unseemly, seeketh not her own, is not easily provoked, thinketh no evil;

[6] Rejoiceth not in iniquity, but rejoiceth in the truth;

[7] Beareth all things, believeth all things, hopeth all things, endureth all things.

[8] Charity never faileth: but whether there be prophecies, they shall fail; whether there be

tongues, they shall cease; whether there be knowledge, it shall vanish away.

9 For we know in part, and we prophesy in part.

10 But when that which is perfect is come, then that which is in part shall be done away.

11 When I was a child, I spake as a child, I understood as a child, I thought as a child: but when I became a man, I put away childish things.

12 For now we see through a glass, darkly; but then face to face: now I know in part; but then shall I know even as also I am known.

13 And now abideth faith, hope, charity, these three; but the greatest of these is charity.

1 Corinthians 13

If I have faith but have not love, I am nothing. Love is an expression of innocence, and the attainment of innocence is the work of faith; but if we profess faith but have no innocence then we have fallen short of our measure. Put another way, while faith is our struggle to understand the metaphysical reality of which we are a part, and to align ourselves with the Divine principle within our own being, *it is our innocence that is the foundation of that work*. So, St. Paul is doing two things here: he is elevating love (and thus innocence) above mere faith, and he is also making a statement *about* faith. Faith is provisional, not an end in itself: once we see clearly ("face to face"), and we acquire true spiritual knowledge, faith drops away. We *know*; we don't need to *believe* any more. The logic of this is that faith, being provisional, cannot be truth, since truth is absolute knowledge, and (the contradiction in St. Paul's theology) if faith is not absolute truth, then it cannot of itself save us; all it can do is open the door to experience of higher reality. Faith, for St. Paul, is this principle of *striving* to understand: at first we see through a glass darkly and then face to face, and it is symbolised in Jesus' healing of the blind man in Mark 8:22-26 who begins to see gradually, but is just an allegory for spiritual understanding. There is an echo of Plato's 'shadows on the cave wall' here, in his *Republic*: the idea that the reality we see is but a pale reflection of its true reality, but the passage also needs to be understood within the original meaning of the word *apocalypse* in Greek, which is 'to unveil' or 'to reveal'. Just as there is an apocalypse at the end of Time, so the culmination of faith is our own *personal* apocalypse in which we "see face to face". Then there is that wonderful phrase, ...*then I shall know fully, even as I am fully known*, which implies a coming together of Man and Divinity in mutual knowledge and recognition; Man understands God and God understands Man. It is the completion of a cycle.

Faith is an inkling, a glimpse: a shimmering of the curtain between the worlds, the small quiet voice urging us to 'come and see'. It is a way, but we are not given the map. It is what we do with that glimpse that saves us; the inner voice invites an answer.

Conclusion

To summarise, I make a fine distinction between Faith (as intuited understanding of Divinity or Spirit or Higher Metaphysical Reality, or whatever one wants to call it) and history, scripture and theology. I do not place my faith in purported historical events like the Virgin Birth or the Resurrection which have a probability of being proven false and almost certainly are; for me, these are symbolic and not literal events. I do not place my faith in scriptures that have been copied and re-copied, with words put into the mouth of Jesus to justify the author's theological views; nor do I place my faith in rational theologies which are creations of the intellect: attempts to rationally interpret Jesus' life and mission, but in their pleasing symmetry may bear no relation to the truth. *"The wind bloweth where it listeth, and thou hearest the sound thereof, but canst not tell whence it cometh, and whither it goeth: so is every one that is born of the Spirit."* (John 3:8) This is probably the most profound definition of faith ever written: faith as something that is felt and heard through the heart, but we cannot say where it comes from, nor on whom it will settle. There is an aspect of Divinity that reaches out to us but the true nature of Divinity is dark. For me, faith rests on an intuited knowledge and understanding of Divinity (*gnosis*[245]) even though it cannot be rendered in intellectual or scientific terms.

I do not subscribe to the incarnation theology in Christianity, nor do I subscribe to the idea that Jesus was ransomed by God for Man's sin; I resolutely reject Original Sin as I refuse to believe that we are born tainted. But rejecting that theology does not lessen my personal faith. I understand Jesus for what he was: a mystic and a teacher, but one among many. A teacher equips the student with the knowledge to take control of their life; he doesn't make the student dependent on him. A teacher opens the door, but it is the student who walks through. I can *relate* to that Jesus in a way that I can't relate to Jesus the Divine Being; someone we can never *become*. For me, Jesus was *a* son of God, not because he was literally *the* Son of God but because he partook of the *nature* of God, as being a vessel for the power of Spirit, and he gave his life to help others realise Divinity within themselves. In simple terms, the human Jesus represents what every person has

---

[245] Greek for 'knowledge' but typically used in relation to 'spiritual knowledge and understanding'.

the potential to be. He is Everyman. I therefore draw a firm line between the mystical Jesus and the historical Jesus. For me, the mystical Jesus is an anthropomorphic expression of the divine principle, and specifically the divine principle in Man and in this way is integral to mystical identification with Spirit. This is not to say the mystical Jesus or the Virgin Mary do not have their own 'reality' as 'holy daimons' (*agathodaemon*): thought forms created by hundreds of years of faith that exist on a quantum level and act as spiritual intermediaries between the human and the Divine.[246] Alternatively, Jung would have regarded them as aspects of the Collective Unconscious.

For me, salvation is the empowering of the soul with the energy and consciousness of Spirit in conjunction with a process of inner rectification and training of the mind, in which it is wedded with its own spiritual nature in a *hieros gamos*, making it a single coherent entity within the greater consciousness of God or Spirit: the Adamic state...

---

[246] The Tinkerbelle effect, named after the eponymous fairy in *Peter Pan*, holds that entities created by thought depend on people's belief in their existence with the implication of thought as energy.

heaven not as a place but as a state of being. The converse, hell, is the fragmentation of the soul into its component parts where those parts are at war with themselves. I think of salvation not as a payoff in the next world for being a moralistic rule follower but as a process of awakening and transformation in *this* life. This is where it all happens, not when we're already dead. This life is the alchemical alemb where we come to understand our nature as beings of Spirit and Spirit comes to understand itself through us.

It is when religion focuses on belief in and worship of God to the exclusion of the inner work of self-awareness, emotional control and critical thought that we get religious wars and identity politics. Faith is *not* an expression of cultural identity but a work of inner transformation. Faith is *not* about worship of God: it is about our connectedness with the source of our Being and with each other. Any religion that advocates worship of God but does not make its adherents kinder and more empathetic people is a failed religion.

**I AM DEFINED NOT BY WHAT I BELIEVE
BUT BY WHAT I AM AND WHAT I ASPIRE TO BE**

Discursive Essay on the Sacred Marriage and the Eucharist
Exploring themes from The Song of the Shekhinah

The divine marriage or *hieros gamos* represents the union of the feminine soul with the masculine spirit, and this is behind many of Christ's allusions to the wedding feast, and in a broader sense the marriage of humanity with God (See Matthew 22:1-14, the parable of the wedding feast and symbolism of the wedding garment as denoting worthiness; Matthew 25:1-13, the parable of the wise and foolish virgins with its symbolism on nourishing the light of the soul; John 2:1-11, the marriage feast at Cana in which Jesus transforms water into wine; John 3:29 "He that hath the bride is the bridegroom"). The marriage at Cana (occurring only in John) is particularly interesting because neither the bride nor groom are named, suggesting its allegorical nature. Both the marriage feast at Cana and the feeding of the 5,000 (Matthew 14:13-21; Mark 6:31-44; Luke 9:12-17; John 6:1-14) contain symbolism which appears later in the Eucharist, first instituted at the Last Supper, which prompts us to ask the question: is the Eucharist a symbolic marriage feast?

Secret symbolism of the Eucharist as a marriage feast

The Eucharist (meaning 'thanksgiving' in Greek) was a simple meal of bread, fish and wine eaten in fellowship; in early Christianity, it was known as an *agape* or love feast, which conveys the idea of a consummation with the sacred. There is a painting of it adorning the wall of the Crypt of Lucina in the Catacombs of St. Callixtus, Rome, clearly showing an arrangement of bread and fish. I would argue that the Eucharist does not symbolically represent just one thing but rather constitutes a complex of symbolism, among which is the symbolic marriage of soul and Spirit. If we take the symbolism of the Cana feast, the feeding of the 5000 and the Last Supper as a collective, we can infer the following:

Bread   Bread is a symbol not just of physical nourishment but of the life that proceeds from the Spirit which is absorbed into and becomes part of one's very flesh. To translate into the modern idiom, the bread symbolises the principle of pure Being that sustains us. Hence the expression in Matthew 4:4, "Man does not live by bread alone, but by every word that proceeds out of the mouth of God," and John 6:33, "For the bread of God is he [the One] which cometh down from heaven and giveth life unto the world." So, here we have an identification between bread and the Divine *logos* or Word: that aspect of Divinity that projects itself into existence to reveal itself to the soul through Jesus, or, in the case of the Fourth Gospel (of John), literally assumes human form in the person of Christ. Thus, in John, Jesus is not simply a channel for divine power; he is *literally* God made flesh, whereas in the synoptic gospels of Mark, Matthew and Luke he is possessed of the indwelling Spirit of God but in every other respect human. Being a circular flatbread of the Levantine type, bread represents eternity. Its symbolism derives from the manna that fell from Heaven to nourish the Israelites on their journey in the desert, which is itself a metaphor for the descent of divine grace, and formed the basis for the shew bread displayed on a table in the Temple in Jerusalem. Even the name Bethlehem is redolent with symbolism, as Beth Lehem translates as 'House of Bread' and thus symbolically 'House of the Spirit'. Thus, read with insight, Jesus is born in the House of the Spirit.

Wine   Wine is a symbol of spiritual ecstasy. The goblet into which it is poured symbolises the receptive soul. Wine is the product of transformation of a base material (grape juice) into something that elevates the senses (wine) thus denoting the exaltation of the consciousness of the soul through the action of the Holy Spirit; wine is no longer just grape juice but something *new*. This is precisely what is being enacted at the allegorical marriage feast at Cana. Further, the grape is the fruit of the vine, and the vine, although it appears gnarled and dead, shoots forth new leaves each year. The life of the vine is the secret knowledge carried in the blood: the knowledge of our own divine origin. Note also the hidden Dionysian symbolism embedded in the wine: to be inebriated is to be possessed by the god's spirit. Wine, however, also symbolises blood, and, in Judaism, blood represents the life force which belongs to God. The Hebrews took this from the Sumerians (and Babylonians) where, in the *Enuma Elish* and *Atrahasis* creation myths, the first man was created from clay by the goddess Nintu (also known as Bēlet-ilī) intermixed with the blood of a slain god (note the parallel with the slain Jesus who 'redeems' Man in his own image).[247] With reference to the Passover, just as bread symbolises the manna that sustained the Israelites in the desert, so wine also symbolises the blood that was painted on the doorposts of the Israelites to ward off the Angel of Death as a propitiatory sacrifice: the event that initiates the Exodus out of Egypt and the allegorical journey to the Promised Land symbolising the soul's journey back towards God.

Fish In Greek, the words *Iesous Khristos, Theou Huios, Soter* ('Jesus Christ, Son of God, Saviour') spell out the acronym Icthys meaning 'fish', hence the fish became a symbol of the meeting places of the early Christians, but the fish symbol is more than a mere cipher. First, the name Jesus (Aramaic *Yeshua* and Hebrew *Yeheshua*) is derived from

---

[247] Sumerian mythology provided the Hebrews with most of their foundational myths, including the Creation, the Garden of Eden and the Flood. The Sumerian antecedent of Noah is Atrahasis. The original Adversary of Man was Enlil. In the *Epic of Gilgamesh*, the eponymous hero is not only semi-divine but the son of a carpenter.

Joshua who led the Israelites into the promised land of Canaan. Joshua was called 'Son of Nun' and in Paleo-Hebrew the letter Nun is represented by a fish. Secondly, the fish symbol is formed from the intersection of two circles forming an ellipse known as a *vesica piscis*[248]. The *vesica piscis* symbolises unity behind duality, the common Source behind the appearance of form. It also symbolises Man and Woman (or body and soul) as both having their origin in Spirit. Thirdly, the fish (exemplified by the salmon) returns to its spawning ground and thus conveys the mystical idea of returning to one's source.

Bread is thus a masculine symbol of the descent of Spirit. Wine is a feminine symbol of the consciousness of the soul transformed through the action of the Spirit. The fish symbolises the active principle (Christ) who brings about the marriage of the two in a *hieros gamos* or sacred marriage. Thus, Christ serves as *hierophant* or High Priest in the marriage of Spirit and Soul. This was a marriage that was celebrated in life through the drawing down of the Holy Spirit into the physical

---

[248] 'Belly of the fish' in Latin.

body and is thus radically antithetical to later Christian ideas of salvation in Heaven as a reward for moral conformity on earth. The mysticism of the Eucharist has nothing to do with social morality or moral conformity; it is about a change in the nature of the Self: the alignment of the soul with divinity. On a further level, the bread and the wine relate to the Exodus and the mystical journey of the soul back to God. As stated, the wine is symbolic of the blood painted on the doorposts of the Israelites to ward off the Angel of Death, thus liberating them from bondage in Egypt (for which read 'bondage in the realm of Matter'), while the bread is the manna that falls from heaven to sustain them on their way through the desert to the allegorical Promised Land. This symbolism ties the bread and the wine to the Eucharistic meal held at Passover (whose translation of 'thanksgiving' refers to 'liberation through the grace of the Spirit'). It was only later that the Eucharist acquired its sacrificial imagery as the body and blood of Christ.

The wedding feast and the exodus are really complementarities, which is the reason why they share the same Eucharistic symbolism. Jesus' teachings concern themselves both with the individual soul's reunion with Spirit (the mystical wedding) and with the journey of humanity *as a whole* – or in the narrowest sense, the Jewish nation – back toward God (the journey to the Promised Land). Hence the mustard seed as a metaphor of the Kingdom of God (Luke 13:18-19), representing the germination of the Spirit in the heart of the individual Soul, and simultaneously, the flowering of faith among humanity.

The communion rite pre-dates Christianity and Judaism. The consumption of a sacred cake or wafer was part of the worship of Ishtar and Asherah (the Jewish goddess in the days before patriarchy), and also appears as a sacrament in Mithraism which had many features in common with Christianity including a sacred meal, the struggle between good and evil, a belief in heaven and hell and a close association with the cult of *Sol Invicta* (the Unconquered Sun) which had December 25th as its sacred holiday. While in early pre-Pauline Christianity, the Eucharist began as a meal celebrating fellowship (and we still use the expression 'to break bread' with someone), by the time the synoptic gospels were written (around 65-90 A.D.), it had become ritualised as part of a cosmic drama. In the gospels, written *after* Paul's letters[249], it anticipates the Passion of Jesus, and its imagery is overtly sacrificial: Jesus offers up his body and blood to his disciples *figuratively* as bread and wine for the forgiveness of the sins of Mankind (although the early Church, into medieval times, insisted on a literal transubstantiation). But it is important to understand that the symbolism of the Eucharist transcends the later sacrificial theology. First, the bread and the wine represent the physical body of Man existing in perfect harmony with the numinous presence of the Divine, which we term 'Spirit', and this can be traced all the way back to the Sumerian creation myth[250] in which the gods chose one of their own to sacrifice his body and blood to ensoul the first man.

---

[249] The books of the New Testament are historically in the wrong order. St. Paul's letters should come before the gospels and the Gospel of Mark should come before Matthew, as both Matthew and Luke were based on it. The reason why they are arranged in their present order is because they constitute a narrative.

[250] Christianity owes much to the myths that preceded it. The reason why Christianity spread so quickly throughout the Greek world was because the myths of the demigod (Hercules, Dionysus, Apollonius of Tyana) and the dying and resurrected god (Attis, Adonis, Osiris) were already present in myth and culture. It is no coincidence that the cult of the Virgin Mary was grafted onto the pre-existent cult of Isis.

Ea opened his mouth and said to his fellow gods: "On the first, the seventh and the fifteenth of the month I will institute a cleansing rite, a bath. Let one god be slaughtered *and the gods be thereby cleansed* [my italics]. With his flesh and his blood let Bēlet-ilī [Nintu] mix some clay, so that god and man are mixed together in the clay. In future time we may hear the drumbeat [= the heart], from the flesh of a god let the spirit be produced. It shall reveal its sign in a living being, a sign not to be forgotten, the spirit!"

This passage is eerily prescient of the sacrifice of Jesus' body and blood to his disciples. Note that is not just the blood of a god that is kneaded into the clay of Man but the blood *and* flesh of the sacrificed God, and this is important for understanding Jesus' reference to his flesh and his blood given unto Man for the redemption of sin. The origin myth, however, is very different from the Christian interpretation. In its original Sumerian context, humans are created and endowed with souls to spare the work of the lesser gods, not to redeem Mankind from sin; but irrespective of its original context, the story conveys the mythic truth that the human soul is Divine in origin. In this way, the dramaturgy of the Last Supper *offers our divinity back to us.* "This is who you are, you've just forgotten." I believe that a fragment of the myth was familiar to the Jewish community during the Babylonian Captivity in the sixth century B.C. and found its way, via the apocalyptic sects[251], into the unconventional imagery of the Last Supper which is so alien to Rabbinic Judaism. This is not so improbable when one considers that the Creation, Eden and Deluge myths entered the Jewish collective mind as reinterpretations of earlier Sumerian myths during the same period, being written down in the

---

[251] It is likely that these sects (collectively known as 'the Fourth Philosophy') remained in Babylon after the conquest of Babylon by Cyrus the Great in 539 B.C. which signalled the end of the fifty-year Babylonian Captivity, where they imbibed elements of Zoroastrian dualism. Following the conquest of Persia by Alexander the Great in 331 B.C., they returned to Judah where they participated in the Maccabean Revolt (167-160 B.C.) against Greek Seleucid overlordship, but split from the Maccabeans when Simon Thassi ('the wicked priest'), brother of Judas Maccabeus, combined the High Priesthood and kingship in his own hand and founded the Hasmonean dynasty in 141 B.C. Thereafter, they retreated into the desert to await the coming apocalypse that would remove first the Hasmoneans, then Herod and the subsequent Roman occupation.

Book of Genesis in the post-exilic era. History aside, the symbolism of the Eucharist stands on its own terms as a means of spiritual awakening, entirely independent of the later Christian theology of Jesus ransomed for the original sin of Man.

The Eucharistic meal, therefore, represents a 'sacred marriage' between 'Spirit' and flesh, or rather Spirit and soul, in which soul is the individualised, outward-looking aspect of Spirit which has lost connection with its origin in pure undifferentiated Spirit. In this wise, the Eucharistic meal amounts to an extreme identification of the soul with God, in which the soul aligns itself with the primal energy and consciousness of the Source. The bread and the wine are likened symbolically to the 'metaphysical body of God' (the Macrocosm or Adam Kadmon as the Heavenly Man)[252] before

---

[252] Philo of Alexandria (a Jewish philosopher who combined Jewish mysticism with Platonism) claimed that Adam Kadmon, the Divine Adam, was the 'spiritual man', created in the image of God and untainted by corruption. Adam Kadmon is associated with the *logos* (the immanent aspect of God in a similar way to the Holy Spirit) which in Pauline Christianity incarnates in the flesh as Jesus. Thus, in sacrificing his body and blood to his disciples, Jesus, as the expression of the *logos*, is presenting them with 'spiritual food': the symbolic body and blood of the Heavenly Man that they may become in his likeness.

being taken into the physical body (Microcosm or Body Mind as we would say today) where the *alchymical marriage*[253] is consummated. Moreover, as ritual objects, the bread and wine would have been blessed and, once taken into the body, the divine energy they were imbued with would have been assimilated as a 'spiritualisation of the flesh'. This is what transforms the Eucharist into a *hieros gamos* or sacred marriage, although the marriage symbolism is obscured by the later Christian sacrificial imagery of the rite. Poetically, Divinity desires to be known. It ever seeks out its Bride (the Soul who is lost in the darkness of Matter and forgetfulness), desiring union with her, whispering to her in the fastness of the night. It sacrifices itself eternally through its pouring out of divine grace, not for forgiveness of any specific sin, but rather to redeem the soul trapped in the illusion of matter. Thus, the wedding and sacrificial imagery is intertwined in the symbolism of the Eucharist.

---

[253] The reader is referred to the early Rosicrucian text *The Alchymical Marriage of Christian Rosencreutz.*

The Passover problem

The Last Supper is of course presented as a Passover *seder* or meal, but there is very little that is recognisable as a traditional Jewish Passover supper which would have consisted of lamb, unleavened bread, wine and bitter herbs. The purpose of Passover (Hebrew *Pesach*) is to recall how the Angel of Death passed over the houses of the Israelites in Egypt whose doorposts had been marked with the *tau*[254] cross in the blood of a lamb. Given that Jesus' Passion occurs around Passover, Jesus is often referred to as the Paschal Lamb, reflecting the theological argument that Jesus sacrificed himself for the sins of humanity. However, the history has been skewed to fit the theology and the symbolism of Jesus as sacrificial lamb does not match the Jewish festival it is assigned to. The original Passover lamb was *not* a sin offering: it was a propitiatory offering (to ward off the Angel of Death) and the subsequent Passover rite commemorates this event as an

---

[254] Tau cross which is our capital letter T: a vertical surmounted by a horizontal with no vertical above it; after the Greek letter *Tau* and the Hebrew *Tav*.

affirmation of faith. The *actual* sin offering occurred at Yom Kippur, the Jewish New Year, when the High Priest entered the Holy of Holies behind the curtain and cleansed the altar with the blood of a bull, while beseeching atonement for the sins of the people, and a 'goat for Azazel' carried the sins of the people out into the desert. Moreover, in John 19:14, Jesus is crucified on the Day of Preparation *before* Passover (which begins at sunset, not midnight), which symbolically coincides with the slaying of the lambs in the Temple, for the sole purpose of making a theological point that Jesus is the Paschal Lamb; John is not therefore writing a literal historical account but is making the facts fit the symbolism he wants to convey.

Given this inconsistency, why do the Last Supper and Passion occur at Passover? The symbolism of the Passover turns on the allegory of the soul's journey back to God from bondage in Egypt, which symbolically represents the realm of Matter or Illusion (and thus Sin, defined as separation from God, or existentially, the source of our being), through the desert representing the dark night of the soul or state of doubt, to the Promised Land symbolising the harmonisation or alignment of the soul with God. The implication is that Jesus, as 'saviour', is the new Moses and, indeed, Jesus takes his name from Joshua who completed the journey. The original inner meaning has been obscured by the 'dead hand' of biblical literalism which is blind to the allegory and symbolism underlying the surface meaning of scripture. What is alien to the Passover imagery, and the original meaning of the Eucharistic meal, however, is the idea of Jesus' sacrifice as an atonement for Man's sin, which was a later theological development occurring toward the end of the first century; in this later narrative, Jesus became identified with the Paschal Lamb, with the Eucharist explicitly evoking the sacrificial imagery of the Passion in which Jesus, as God, physically offers up his flesh and blood for the redemption of Man. In the original Passover story, however, Jesus is the new Moses leading his people on an allegorical journey out of the existential state of alienation from Divinity, but this liberation mysticism did not require Jesus' death. Jesus as the new Moses cannot be Jesus the Paschal Lamb. The symbolism of Passover, however, also turns on *who* gets to be saved, and there is a parallelism between the Israelites saved by the mark of their faith and Jesus' followers who are marked to be saved at the coming Kingdom of God. Early Christianity was grounded in an apocalyptic theology that had largely disappeared by the time the Fourth Gospel (of John) was written around A.D. 90 – 100, since it was obvious that it wasn't going to happen, or at least it was shunted far into the indeterminate future (there is no imminent coming of the Kingdom of God in the Gospel of John). The historical Jesus was an apocalyptic prophet who espoused an extreme dualistic version of Judaism which advocated national spiritual renewal and rejected all foreign influences. On the night of Passover, he and his disciples (the thirteen) are awaiting the advent of God's Kingdom on earth[255],

---

[255] *Malkut Shamayim* in Hebrew, which roughly translates as 'rule or sovereignty of God', and not some otherworldly heaven. At the coming of the kingdom, a feast (the Messianic Banquet) would be celebrated in the presence of Abraham, Isaac and Jacob, as foretold in Isaiah 25:6 and hinted at in Matthew 8:11: "And I say unto you, that many shall come from the east and west, and shall sit down [*recline at table*] with Abraham, and Isaac, and Jacob, in the kingdom of heaven." Isaiah speaks of "a feast of fat things, a feast of wines on the lees, of fat things full of marrow, of wines on the lees well refined." The question for us is, how do we reconcile the Messianic banquet in Matthew with the pre-crucifixion eucharistic meal (also in Matthew) and does the Passover meal in some way anticipate the Messianic feast?

in the form of the Son of Man, a heavenly judge,
'coming upon the clouds' (an image taken from the
Book of Daniel) with Jesus as earthly king reigning
over it and the twelve disciples on twelve thrones
representing the original twelve tribes of Israel
(Matthew 19:28). Together, they are the Elect
and so it is fitting that, when the Kingdom does
come and humanity is judged[256], they are somehow
marked out to be spared just as the Israelites were
spared when the Angel of Death passed over their
houses. Of course, for this to happen, the revival of
faith would have had to have reached a critical mass
while, in reality, Jesus was a minor prophet from
the North who, in the synoptic gospels, only visited
Jerusalem once before his death. Did he cast himself
as the Suffering Servant of Isaiah 53, proving his
worthiness to intercede with God on behalf of
Mankind (much as the prophet Enoch interceded
with God on behalf of the fallen angels in the First
Book of Enoch)? By taking on the sins of Man as
God's righteous servant, did he intend to trigger

---

[256] The dark question is 'what happens to non-Jews?' Is salvation
just for the Jews or does everyone get a shot at it? This was the
major contention between St. Paul and the Jerusalem Church
after Jesus' death.

the Eschaton that would bring about the Kingdom of God on earth? I cannot say, nor can anyone, and quite possibly Jesus did not intend to die (especially if he was going to rule with his twelve disciples as priest king over God's Kingdom[257]), but I do believe

---

[257] Herein lies another contradiction between early and late Christian theology. Jesus' prediction of the coming of the Son of Man upon the clouds (Matthew 24:30 and Luke 21:27), the twelve disciples seated on twelve thrones about the Son of Man (Matthew 19:28) and the Messianic feast (Matthew 8:11) are, scholars believe, all authentic sayings of Jesus which have been woven into the gospel narratives of Matthew and Luke. It is almost certain that Jesus is not talking about the Son of Man as himself since at this stage of theological development, Jesus was not regarded as a pre-existent divine being. Yet, given that he is anticipating the coming of the Kingdom of God on earth, in the eucharistic meal he anticipates his own crucifixion. Is it his crucifixion that brings about the Kingdom of God on earth (which it doesn't)? When the twelve tribes are judging the twelve nations of Israel, where is Jesus, since presumably he would be with his disciples? Is Matthew implying that Jesus will return *in spirit* and inaugurate the Kingdom of God on earth, which he signally doesn't because, after meeting his disciples and showing his wounds, he ascends 'to the Father'. If Jesus intended to witness the new Kingdom of God, and even take a leading role in it, he cannot simultaneously have sacrificed himself as atonement for the sins of Mankind, and so this marks a potential contradiction in the Gospel of Matthew. Jesus' ambition to present himself as priest king over the new Kingdom of God on Earth provides, perhaps, the motive for Judas' betrayal, and the epithet nailed to his cross. Alternatively, he may have intended to suffer on the cross as the Suffering Servant (who suffers for his righteousness *but does not actually die*) as a demonstration of faith, but to be taken down before he died, which is possible given that his legs

that quite early on he fell out with the radical Jewish agenda and broke with John the Baptist, believing, rightly, that only a spiritual regeneration of Israel would bring about the Kingdom of God on earth while a direct military assault against Rome would bring about the wholesale destruction of Jewish culture and religion and the Temple itself, as indeed it did in 70 A.D.

Within a few years after Jesus, the Eucharist lost its eschatological significance. Originally, it was intended to celebrate the end of days and the coming Kingdom of God on earth. This didn't happen and by the time the Gospel of John is written, the Kingdom of God resides not on earth but in the spiritual 'other world' where Jesus is the *heavenly* king: "The kingdom of God is within you" (Luke 17:20-21). Where in early Christianity, Jesus was awaiting the Son of Man to "come upon the clouds", by the time of John's gospel he *is* the Son of Man. Concordantly, the meaning of the Eucharistic feast changed to reflect the continual bestowal of divine grace through the (now transcendent) Christ.

---

were not broken, and the fluid on his lungs released by a spear to the side. He had also arranged to be taken to a private tomb through the intercession of Joseph of Arimathea.

Salvation was no longer a single event at the end of time, but continual and ever-present, and it was defined by belief in, and identification with, Jesus, expressed in the Eucharist.

The Illuminist Tradition

In the tradition of Christian illuminism, which dates from the 16th to 18th centuries, exemplified in the Rosicrucian and Martinist movements, the Eucharist is idealised symbolically as the 'metaphysical body of God' expressed as Adam Kadmon who contains the Qabalistic Tree of Life within him, rejuvenating the soul through partaking of the Spirit that is the source of its being. The flowering of the Spirit on the cross of Matter is represented by the rose blooming at the intersection of the cross and by the *crux serpentis*: the serpent of wisdom coiled about a tau cross, akin to the bronze serpent that Moses raised in the desert in Numbers 21:9, and employed as altar pieces by the Gnostic Ophites and Naasenes.

So, I have a very different take on the Eucharist than the gospels. Interpreting it as a marriage feast presided over by Jesus, in which the disciples symbolically take God into themselves, and thereby enact the marriage symbolism in the gospel of Matthew, is, to me, more apposite, and truer to the original spirit of early Christianity.

Twenty-Two Theses on Faith

I have spent my life on a mental and spiritual journey trying to understand the nature of faith and arrive at a version that is meaningful to me. This I have attempted to do in a critical but sympathetic way. Behind it all is a vague sense that "there is something there" that I cannot rationally or empirically prove nor see any necessity of doing so. Although my background is in the tradition of the Craft of the Wise, which has had its own conflicts with the Christian religion, on principle I am never dismissive of another form of spirituality unless I have studied it. In my researches on Christianity, I came to realise that it possesses a philosophical depth that is often obscured by its surface dogma of sin and redemption. Christianity is a polarising religion, some vehemently rejecting it, others cleaving fanatically to it; sometimes presenting a tolerant aspect, at other times a wrathfully paranoid one. Looking beneath the surface, as one who digs from the earth a valuable artifact lost to history, what would I find?

My fleeting experience of Church-based Chris-
tianity had been a disappointing one. Walk past
any church and one cannot ignore the familiar
clapboards proclaiming 'Jesus loves you' or 'Jesus
saves', formulaic pronouncements that offer
absolutely no exegesis as to how exactly Jesus saves
us or what salvation actually means. This, indeed,
is a persistent problem with priests: they preach
scripture, but they don't explain; they don't look
beyond the surface of the words to their underlying
symbolic meanings. They also tend to be starchy
and vaguely patronising and absolutely hate
being asked questions. They have been taught in
seminary a model of 'command and control' whereby
the priest preaches and the congregation listens.
Quite simply, the decline in Christian congregations
is precisely the failure of the Church to make faith
relevant to the modern mind, and to date the
Church's sole concession to modernity has been
church discos and trendy vicars. Then there was
the experience of sitting in a freezing nave on hard
seats singing either dreadful Victorian dirges or
happy-clappy hymns to 'worship' a god that seemed
utterly remote. Coming from a ritual-based Craft
tradition where everyone is a priest or priestess and

everyone participates, the passivity was crushing; I wanted to be at the front performing the mass! It was this need for involvement, the sense of actually working with spiritual power, of actively participating in ritual invocation of Divine power and grace, that made my experience in the Craft so much more satisfying.

I would look around me at other congregants. Were they Christian because they had a vague belief in God and admired Jesus' ethical teachings or did they believe lock, stock and barrel in Pauline theology? Did they believe Jesus was ransomed for Man's sin? Did they believe in a physical resurrection? Did they believe the Garden of Eden and Adam and Eve were real historical events? Did they ask questions of their faith or just accept it as truth? Did they read books about spirituality and church history, or did they only read the Bible? Did they honestly believe that the theology they were presented had been the teaching of the Church since the year dot? I would aver that most embrace faith from an ill-defined sense of the sacred and Jesus as 'a good bloke' than from adherence to a specific theology, at least in the tolerant Anglican tradition.

Although from a background in the Craft, I realised that while the oblique theology of St. Paul never made much sense to me, there were deeper themes in Christianity that I could relate to such as the 'regeneration of the soul' which is a prominent theme also of the Greek Mysteries, the idea of sin as a state of separation from Divinity, the recovery of innocence as a precursor to spiritually 'seeing', the idea of becoming a 'new' person freed from the shackles of the past, the notion of the Kingdom of God as something that dwells within one, the theme of the solitary Man of Spirit standing against the Men of Power, and (very American) the idea that one good person can change the world. These are all memes that persist in modern spirituality even among those who would not describe themselves as Christian. Perhaps the most enduring meme given to us by Christianity is the idea of 'humanity' as a collective, an idea that transcends nation and tribe and marks a seismic turning point in the evolution of human thought. In fairness, this revolutionary idea in which Humankind develops a concept of itself goes back to Cyrus the Great of Persia in the sixth century B.C. who had abolished slavery and established freedom of religion through the empire, and the idea was current in Rabbinic Judaism from which many of the ethical teachings of Jesus originate, but Christianity was the first 'universal' religion in the West promoting the ideal of 'one humanity-one God' and, as such, an abrupt departure from the former temple-based religions worshipping national gods.

The ideal present within the *religion* of Christianity was not reflected in its institutions, however. Notably, the Church made a pact with the Roman Empire, first as favoured religion under Constantine I and then as official religion under Theodosius I. Conversion became a means of acquiring power and wealth, the Church's ranks were swollen with sons of the nobility and it began to reflect the status quo as 'God-given order' instead of the reformist force it could have been.

I have a problem with the institutionalised expression of religion, and the problem is that as soon as faith becomes institutionalised as religion, it becomes very much a matter of unthinking conformity in which doctrine becomes more important than the search for truth, and the religious institutions themselves succumb to corruption, as the Catholic Church did in the Middle

671

Ages. The needs of the institution take precedence over its foundational principles; after a while, a kind of institutional rot sets in and one gets politics, bureaucracy, careerism, enmity, jealousy, and the politics of division. All institutions – even religious ones, however well-meaning – contain the seeds of their own corruption.

Then there is the appalling history of the Church, and not only the Church but organised religion in general. Religion has gone badly wrong. It has become subsumed into cultural prejudice and identity politics. It has become enslaved to habit. It has utterly and completed failed to change human nature for the good; certainly, the behaviour of our world leaders for whom politics and economics has become divorced not only from common morality but from *humanity*. I have come to realise that faith is something one is called to, and if religion is imposed on an entire population of people who merely pay lip service to it, is it really going to change them? If one prays in the church or mosque and then cheats one's business partner or one's wife the moment one leaves it, what has faith done for you?

Historically, both Christianity and Islam have acquiesced in slavery and exploitation, and the forced acculturation of native peoples, although in the end it was reformist Christianity that abolished the slave trade, and most Muslim nations didn't abolish slavery until the twentieth century, as it became incompatible with the idea of a modern civilised society. Similarly, both Christianity and Islam have sanctioned territorial wars under the banner of religious expansion: the seventh century jihads, the crusades of the eleventh to thirteenth centuries. They have executed heretics. They have persecuted supposed witches. They have promoted sectarianism and religious intolerance. They have repressed women. They have declared war on single mothers. They punish gay and transgendered people for being who they are. Even today, radical Islam is driven by an insecurity complex that blames the West for the chronic poverty and lack of development in the Islamic world, and radical Islamists perpetuate a myth that the West wants to destroy the Islamic faith: for that, they recruit naïve idealistic young men to bomb and massacre westerners, taking innocent lives in the name of a paranoid fantasy.

Institutionalised religion has been hijacked by patriarchal culture. It reflects cultural prejudice instead of challenging it. It promotes blind faith instead of teaching people how to think. It places doctrinal conformity above the pursuit of wisdom. It teaches fear of God instead of love. It preaches worship of an external God instead of the realisation of our own Divinity, and it has failed to make faith relevant to the twenty-first century mind.

There are those for whom 'the Will of God' means anything they want it to mean and use it to justify the most terrible calumnies. In the Middle Ages, both Islam and Christianity justified territorial wars in the name of 'the Will of God'. In the colonial era, Europeans believed that God had 'given' them the new lands of Africa and Latin America to exploit. That same mentality continues unabated today. In Brazil, evangelical Christians advocate expropriating the Amazon rainforest for economic development and the displacement and implied annihilation of the native tribes that inhabit it, because "God gave them the land", and mark my words: in another thirty years there will not be a single Amazonian native left alive, and what was begun by the Spanish and Portuguese five hundred years ago will be completed by Brazil's land-hungry colonialists and the corrupt politicians in their pockets. In Israel, Zionists force Palestinian families off their land to build settlements for Jewish and Christian fundamentalists in the West Bank because "God gave them the land". Islamists persecute Christians and Jews living in Pakistan and Nigeria (and other Muslim nations) because "God gave the land to Muslims". In Myanmar, Rohingya Muslims are pushed off their land by Buddhist nationalists because "the land is Buddhist". It is a complete nonsense to say that a geographical area of land is Christian or Muslim or Jewish or Buddhist or what the hell else it is; faith is not defined by geography and God is not a real estate agent. We carry our faith wherever we live; there is no such thing as 'sacred earth'.

Similarly, in traditional societies, religion is habitually conflated with culture, with religious law being influenced by cultural assumptions, such as food taboos and penalties for infractions of public morals. The reason why Islam, Judaism and Christianity all evolved codes of law is the result of a historical accident, since in antiquity, in an age when society was torn apart by warlords, it was religion that assumed the role of civiliser, uniting society behind a common belief system and code

675

of morals. The question is thus begged: in the age of the nation state, is there a place for religious law codes that belong to a different time? It can at times be difficult for people living in traditional societies to determine what is sanctified by religion and what is received from culture. The foremost example of this is the headscarf or hijab in Islam. The requirement of women to cover their hair was always a cultural one. The veil *pre-dated* Islam and was practiced by all cultures around the Mediterranean and Middle East in antiquity; it was simply a means of protecting the virtue of a woman and reducing the incidence of sexual jealousy and rape with consequent blood feuds in tightly knit tribal societies, yet wearing the veil became incorporated into the religious conventions of those societies. Thus, in Surah 33:60 of the holy Quran we read: "O Prophet! tell your wives and your daughters, and the women of the believers, that they should pull down upon them of their outer cloaks from their heads over their faces. That is more likely that they may thus be recognised and not molested. And Allah is Most Forgiving, Merciful." The veiling of the head was practiced in Judaism and was even advocated by St. Paul: "But

676

every woman that prayeth or prophesieth with her head uncovered dishonoureth her head: for that is even all one as if she were shaven. For if the woman be not covered, let her also be shorn: but if it be a shame for a woman to be shorn or shaven, let her be covered" (1 Corinthians: 11: 5-6).

There is a difference, however, between the veil as an accepted convention, and arguing that it is a symbol of religious identity. The hijab is not a symbol of Islamic identity, any more than the veil was in Judaism or early Christianity. Nor is there any law in Islam that punishes a woman for *not* wearing a veil; and yet we find women being whipped or beaten to death by 'morality police' for not wearing it. Such practices have more to do with repressive Middle Eastern patriarchy than with Islam itself. It is time that men stopped legislating on what women wear: hijabs should be a matter of choice, neither banned in the West nor enforced in the East, and certainly not policed by state thugs. In similar vein, there is no Quranic injunction against the education and employment of women (after all, the Prophet's first wife Khadija ran her own trading business), and yet certain fundamentalist Islamic regimes like the Taliban prohibit the education of girls and obstruct women's careers as 'unislamic'. Clearly, then, in traditional societies the line between culture and religion is blurred, and too often religion makes of itself an apologist for cultural prejudice.

Then there is the power problem. When any religious group acquires power, either through numbers or political organisation, it begins to use that power to bend others to its will (often while inventing a myth of itself as victim). In the United States, right-wing evangelical Christians have infiltrated Republican state legislatures to impose Christian morality on the nation via unworkable abortion laws that prevent mothers from terminating ectopic pregnancies or even allowing surgery for incomplete miscarriages as long as a foetal heartbeat is detected. Christian lawmakers didn't seek medical advice when framing these laws nor did they study the experience of other countries like Ireland who revised their anti-abortion laws because they failed. Not content with this, Christian evangelicals shamelessly surveil, harass and collect data on pregnant women and promote a culture of 'informing'. American evangelicals' partisan attachment to the right-wing of American politics, their god-like worship of Trump, their extreme anti-abortion and anti-gay stance, their demonisation of the Democrat party and the Catholic Church, and their love affair with conspiracy theories has done incalculable harm to the reputation of Christianity in the United States. Behind this behaviour is the belief among Protestant non-conformist sects in America that they have become 'marginalised' by secularism, resulting in an (at times) paranoid 'backs against the wall' mentality, and it is instructive to contrast this with the role of the Anglican Church in Britain and the Catholic Church in France, Spain and Poland etc., which have always been well-integrated into mainstream society. For this reason, Catholics and Anglicans lack the insecurity of Protestant evangelicals: they don't feel the need to advertise their faith or push it onto the rest of society, nor do they, like the farmer in Grant Wood's painting *American Gothic*, gaze with barely concealed hostility on the outside world.

Just as Christian evangelicals have embraced the far right in American politics, so the Russian Orthodox Church has embraced the cause of Russian nationalism, giving its blessing to Russia's nationalistic war of aggression in Ukraine and having the audacity to promise Russian soldiers *that their sins would be forgiven if they died for the state*; the same soldiers who were sent there to shoot, rape, torture and terrorise Ukrainian civilians. The same church has since elevated Putin to the lofty status of Defender of the Fatherland and Chief Exorcist! So Vladimir can now express his new-found religious virtues by bombing people out of their apartment blocks! What a complete perversion of religion that Christianity should ally itself with nationalism and make itself a puppet of the state!

WHEN RELIGION HARNESSES ITSELF TO POWER, IT IS THE END OF RELIGION AND THE BEGINNING OF TYRANNY

Finally, a word should be said about the origins of antisemitism in Christianity. While today, antisemitism flourishes both on the left and right wings of secular politics, and runs like a dark stain through Islam, fanned by the historic grievances of Palestinians, its roots in Christianity go back to the very early days when, toward the end of the first century, Christian and Jewish congregations had begun to separate out into their own places of worship. Whereas, in the synoptic gospels, various religious groups are singled out as persecutors of Jesus (e.g., the Pharisees and Sadducees), in the Gospel of John 'the Jews' become a single amorphous group independent of sectarian affiliation. 'The Jews' are the antagonists of Jesus, always looking for ways of killing him because they do not realise who Jesus is. 'The Jews' are collectively blamed for Jesus' death, when in fact it was the Romans who crucified him (and the only ones who could do so). Hence the Jews were tainted as 'Christ killers' and demonised further in the 'blood libel': the lie that Jews sacrificed Christian babies at Passover and used their blood in the making of unleavened bread. In the Middle Ages, the Jewish diaspora in Europe attracted jealousy as successful entrepreneurs and money lenders outside the feudal system; they were also exempt from the usury laws to which Christians were subject. As a result of Christianising policies in the Holy Roman Empire and the growth of Catholic inquisitions in France and Spain, entire Jewish populations were often massacred or expelled from many western countries, migrating eastwards to Poland, Lithuania and Turkey. Antisemitism became woven into the fabric of German society where it surfaced during the Crusades as bands of Crusaders sacked Jewish villages as they marched through the territories of the Holy Roman Empire on their way to Jerusalem; the most well-known of these are the Rhineland massacres of 1096 during the People's Crusade. Thus, antisemitism was well established for several centuries in Germany before Adolf Hitler embraced the Final Solution, but it was a creation of the Christian Church.

I decided to look beneath the surface and devote my life to understanding what faith really is, and how religion has gone so badly wrong; so badly wrong as to pervert the very principles upon which the ideal of humanity is founded. Accordingly, I arrived at twenty-two[258] theses which reflect my current understanding. Why did I do this? Because, from the 'magical universe' of the Middle Ages, the pendulum has now swung too far in the opposite direction to a form of hyper-rationalism ruled by a scientific orthodoxy that is just as dangerous as religious orthodoxy, in which the average person

---

[258] Mirroring the numbers of sacred letters in the Hebrew alphabet.

believes in nothing they cannot see or touch or has been 'proven' by science. Ironically, a tiny sub-section of Christianity has reacted to this excessively rationalistic culture by retreating into a biblical literalism that views itself as wholly antithetical to science. That too is a religious dead-end.

IF RELIGION DOESN'T CHANGE US, IF OUR HEARTS ARE STILL CLOSED, AND WE ARE STILL THE PEOPLE WE WERE, WHAT GOOD HAS IT DONE AND WHOM DOES IT SERVE?

So, at risk of sounding didactic, here are twenty-two principles which summarise my interpretation of faith and the nature of divinity.

1. Faith is not a matter of belief; it is experiential. It is a work of actualising our connection with Spirit, not as worship of God as *a* being but communion with God as Being. Its purpose is not the worship of Divinity outside us but to bring us closer to the perfection of ourselves as divine beings. Those who say, "Man is but a

creature of God" have not understood that Man is the realisation of Divinity on earth. Those who worship God are doomed to be slaves of God nor ever see the beauty of God within them.

2. Divinity cannot be comprehended through science or through reason but is discerned in the silence of meditation and the inspiration of poetry. It is comprehended not through mathematics but through vision and metaphor; we say, poetically, that Divinity is the Book that writes itself, it is the Flame that does not consume, it is the Veiled Light[259], metaphors that hint at the paradox of self-generated existence, but we cannot say, in rational terms,

---

[259] "Allah is the Light of the heavens and the earth. The Parable of His Light is as if there were a Niche and within it a Lamp: the Lamp enclosed in Glass, the glass as it were a brilliant star, lit from a blessed Tree, an Olive, neither of the east nor of the west, whose oil is well-nigh luminous, though fire scarce touched it: Light upon Light! Allah doth guide whom He will to His Light: Allah doth set forth Parables for men: and Allah doth know all things." The sense of the passage is that the light of God is veiled. It is diffused as though through glass whence it radiates into Being, but that screen forms a barrier beyond which we cannot know God directly. The light of God is self-generating: it is not fed by oil from any source but is its own source. *Holy Quran*, Surah An Nur 24:35.

what Divinity truly is. 'Looking for God' has been rather like looking for evidence of a black hole based on its gravitational effect on neighbouring suns; we never get to see the black hole itself. Similarly, Divinity exercises a gravitational pull on our hearts and minds even though we can only infer its presence. Put simply, if Divinity is the greater consciousness (or consciousness itself) it can only express itself through consciousness. Those who demand, "Prove that God exists," assume that God is seated squarely within space and time, yet if the greater part of Existence lies outside the physical universe of space and time, how is it to be proven by a methodology that only operates according to physical laws? Moreover, to prove that 'God' exists, one would first have to define God, and since one cannot define God, it follows that one cannot prove that God exists. To go further, if 'God' or 'Spirit' is the unseen creative force behind Existence, but inseparable from it, proving that 'God' exists is as pointless as proving that Existence exists. Only a fool doubts the very basis of his own existence. Truly, one who believes in nothing but what he can see and touch is like a blind man down a blind alley.

3. Ever since the Reformation and down to the American Protestant revival, Christians have uncritically understood the entire Old and New Testaments to be the 'living' word of God, even when the Jewish tradition holds that only the Law or Torah is the word of God, with the prophets being 'inspired' by God. I take the view that since God is not a person, then God is not a maker of laws; nor does God speak directly through the mouths of men but rather the Divine reveals itself through dream and vision which requires interpretation by the Reason. Succinctly, scripture is *never* literal but perforce *must* be interpreted, and the Jewish tradition has entire midrashes[260] dedicated to every passage in the Tanakh. A literal interpretation would in any case depend on the correct translation of the original ideas from Hebrew into Greek then Latin and from Latin to mother tongue, but in truth there is no such thing as a literal translation from one language

---

[260] Rabbinic commentaries on the Tanakh or Old Testament.

to another: one can only translate the *sense* of a word. The Bible, then, is for me the words of men *inspired* by an *understanding* of God, however primitively conceived, rather than the words of Divinity itself, and it reflects the views about the nature of existence of 2,500 years ago, which are understood differently today... which raises the question 'Why should we not understand Divinity through the 21st century mind?' When we read scripture, we must also understand that the writers of the gospels were not writing history as an *academic* discipline; for them, history was but the stage upon which the miraculous unveiled itself. Scripture is the meeting of myth and history as *received tradition*; no one at the time questioned what was mythic and what was historic. Further, the Scripture that has come down to us is a product of time and place and reflects the religious and cultural assumptions of the age. Every writer of every gospel interpreted the life of Jesus through their own theological understanding of his life and mission, and consequently each gospel has its own agenda. It has additionally been edited, amended and overwritten by different scribes over the centuries in line with the prevailing doctrine of the age, and some of the events in the New Testament were blatantly borrowed from the Old, such as the massacre of the innocents in Matthew 2:16-18 which was 'borrowed' from Exodus 1:8-2:4, with the intention of identifying Jesus with Moses. Similarly, the feeding of the five thousand in Luke 9: 12-17 parallels the descent of the 'manna' from heaven that fed the Israelites in Exodus 16: 1-36. Foremost, the Trinity as an essential idea in Christian religion is not even mentioned in the New Testament but was formulated by Tertullian in the second-third centuries based on earlier expositions such as the Didache. *The art of scriptural interpretation is thus not to accept everything therein as literal truth but to tease out the eternal from that which is rooted in time and culture.*

4. Scripture was written to inspire us, not to enslave us to the written word, and it can be *symbolically* true even when it is not *literally* true. The New Testament is replete with examples. Symbolically, the Nativity, set as it is in a stable, is not required to be a

literal event, but symbolically can be said to represent the birth of the spiritual principle within the animal self and the animal world. Similarly, the Virgin giving birth to Jesus can symbolically depict the soul giving birth to the Christ principle within itself. Again, it can also suggest the self-generated nature of Divinity, the Mother of Form giving suck to Existence; both are appropriate on different levels. The death and resurrection of Jesus can likewise be said to symbolise the death of the instinctual human self and its transcendence by the higher Self of the Spirit in which Jesus is Everyman; the base man dies to himself to be reborn as the man of Spirit, an event depicted in the very design of the Calvary cross whose crossbar (designating the temporal) is raised above the level of Nature on the vertical (eternal) axis.[261]

---

[261] The ratio of the horizontal to the vertical also corresponds with the measurement called the 'golden mean' set at 1.618, also said to be the 'divine proportion'. Consider also the prevalence of the number 6 in the crucifixion. Six is the number of the hexagram depicting the interpenetration of Spirit and Matter and therefore the number 6 is implicit in all aspects of the crucifixion. Thus, the letter *vav* in Hebrew has a symbolic association with the nail and its value is 6. Jesus also has six wounds inflicted (if we count the spear of Longinus). Most importantly, the simple calvary

The symbolic meanings of scripture are equally as valid as their literal interpretations, even though they are not historical events, as the Church Father Origen noted in his work *On First Principles,* when speaking of the Creation and Eden myths, and I have already referred to the Exodus as an allegorical journey of the soul in my essay on the Sacred Marriage. I like to think of the gospels as mystery plays, redolent with allegory and symbolism. One of the most beautiful metaphors in the gospels is that of Jesus healing the blind man. There are two such instances (Mark 8:22-26 and John 9), but the Mark version, however, is the more convincing as it conveys the impression of someone *gradually* seeing. Often cited as a literal example of a miracle, it can also be interpreted symbolically as the overcoming of *spiritual* blindness and the acquisition of spiritual knowledge or *gnosis.* Indeed, I tend

---

cross is the exploded form of a six-sided cube (the Cube of Saturn denoting Matter and restriction). The exploded cube is the cross of Spirit and liberation. The cube of Saturn represents the outer phenomenological aspect of form while the cross denotes the inner existential aspect of the numinous.

to the view that the story of Jesus' death and resurrection is not so much literal history as an allegorical drama of the soul (see *Discursive Essay on the Nature of the Soul*).

5. There is no contradiction between religion and science, only between biblical literalism and science. Both religion and science seek to understand our place in the universe, but science uses empirical observation while faith is the intuition of a higher order of reality through our conscious connection with it, however much it is subsequently dressed in theology. To put it another way, the reason dissects reality while faith views existence as a whole. To have faith is to understand that not everything is revealed: there is a numinous 'other' dimension beyond the phenomenological that is not observable and can only be accessed through mind. As Carl Jung rightly said, "We should not pretend to understand the world only by the intellect; we apprehend it just as much by feeling. Therefore, the judgment of the intellect is, at best, only half of the truth, and must, if it be honest, also come to an understanding of its inadequacy." As humans,

we are wired for meaning, and while science can explain how the universe works, the meaning of Existence is constructed; hence philosophy and faith provide us with models that give meaning to the universe and our place in it. While the constructs of philosophy pertain to the rational intellect, faith belongs to the intuitive, filtered through our connection to non-rational reality through the Deep Self. All that is required is that philosophy and faith enter into dialogue with science, and the contextual models we create remain open and flexible to change in accordance with understanding. Thus, we can speak of the Competency of Reason and the Competency of Faith in which the rational and intuitive are alternative ways of understanding reality: the rational from the phenomenological and the intuitive through the numinous; neither alone are complete ways of seeing. That which pertains to practical problem-solving, invention, ethics, law, and the determination of reality through the senses pertains to the Competency of Reason. That which lies outside the Competency of Reason and can only be known through the intuitive aspect of

692

Consciousness belongs to the Competency of Faith, and herein is found our comprehension of Divinity *which cannot be known through the intellect but only through the heart.*

6. Faith cannot be based on something that has a probability of being false. For this reason, faith cannot be hostage to history, since if I rest my faith on the Virgin Birth or the Resurrection and it turns out to be false, what becomes of my faith? Faith cannot be founded exclusively on the written word since scripture is the meeting of the historical and the imaginative and we cannot allow ourselves to become hostage to a worldview of people over two thousand years ago. Nor can faith rest on theology as all theology is a construct of the intellect (an interpretation of scripture that may or may not be true) and thus subject to rational dispute. Shall I place my faith in a castle of the mind? But if I say that we have our being in a reality greater than ourselves, that is incontrovertibly true. If I say that the physical universe is part of a reality that transcends it, that is incontrovertibly true. Likewise, if my faith is founded on an intuited apprehension of Divinity

or Spirit or some such metaphysical reality that proscribes definition, then no man may contest that. Faith is always provisional and ever eludes certainty. It is a series of questions, and not a set of answers. Metaphysical reality cannot be studied as though it is separate from us; it exists to be lived and experienced. It cannot be observed, it can only be intuited. We reach out to it in expectation that it will reach out to us. We can call upon it in the hope that it will answer us. Faith, in its inception and free of theological overlays, is not an idea, and the *idea* of God is not God; faith is our intuitive connection to that which cannot be compassed by the intellect. The path to faith is not reached by asking if God as some form of discrete creative entity exists; it is reached by the intuitive understanding that we are sustained by a higher order of reality within which we have our being, and our meagre consciousness is a fragment of a greater consciousness. Far from being a neat and tidy intellectual system, faith is necessarily ill-defined, belonging, as it does, to our perception of the numinous through the Deep Self. Thus, we are not required to 'prove' or justify faith because faith cannot be proven or justified and does not need to be, since it deals with realities beyond the grasp of intellect.

7. Neither scripture nor revelation can be trusted on their own terms. Scripture can be modified, and revelation may come from within one's own mind. Faith begins not with scripture or revelation but with questions. What is the meaning of Existence? Are we connected with something greater than ourselves? What is the nature of Divinity? Is Divinity a discrete creative entity or is it a consciousness and energy that moves through all things? Do we contain Divinity as Divinity also contains us? What does it mean to be saved? In short, faith, is not a solution handed to us on a plate, but something that must be struggled with. We must have faith but also a critical mind. We must ask: 'Is this passage an authentic retelling?' We must ask: 'Is this passage of scripture an expression of the prejudice of the writer or does it point to a profound truth?' We must ask, 'Is this revelation a projection of my own unconscious assumptions or does it

communicate something that is verifiable (as in an event in the future)[262] or knowledge that may help me or someone else?' In other words, is it *useful*? Is it *meaningful*? Is it *true*?

8. The contemplation of the *nature* of Divinity can draw us closer to Divinity even though we cannot *define* Divinity in intellectual terms. Our relationship with Divinity is an intuitive one in which we feel the 'presence' of the Divine, even though we cannot intellectually 'know' it. *We don't need to define Divinity in order to have a relationship with it.*

9. No idea of Man can approximate to the nature of metaphysical reality. Faith can only be provisional, and being provisional, it cannot be absolute truth. Since it is not absolute truth, faith alone will not save us. Belief alone does not change the substance of our being; we only change when we open our hearts to the Spirit, when we acquire self-awareness and

---

[262] From 1981-2, three children in a village called Kibeho in southwest Rwanda separately had visions of the Virgin Mary, calling herself the Mother of the Word, warning them that a genocidal event was about to take place, which it in fact did in 1994.

rediscover innocence, and the ability to love unconditionally. It is what we *do* with faith that changes us, not faith itself.

10. Spirituality as an idea transcends the narrow sectarianism of institutionalised religion, and I believe that one of the problems of our age is that the overriding concept of spirituality (of spiritual curiosity and openness) has been submerged beneath sectarian identity, and this is the principal reason why religion has failed humanity. *Sometimes the threat to faith comes from the faithful.* Institutional religion is too encumbered by its founding traditions, too overburdened with cultural and legal baggage, and too sectarian to reform humanity. It has become hijacked by minorities obsessed with cultural identity and by those who would see in it a unifying ideal to cement political power. In short, the enlightening principles of spirituality have been forsaken by religious chauvinism. Sectarianism is an offence against the unity that is Divinity and that transcends all religion. Faith is One, clothed in the Many.

11. Wisdom is not found in one place or received from one person. Jesus, Mohammed and

Buddha may have taught us how to live, but they did not tell us *everything*. Those who say "Bible, Bible, Bible," or "Quran, Quran, Quran," lack the advantage of a balanced education. We should seek wisdom not only from religious founders but from secular philosophers also. Everyone has something interesting to say if we listen to them. I particularly love the Sufi adage, "Seek knowledge unto China," and there you have it.

12. There is nothing so dangerous as absolute certainty in religion and politics, for it leads us down the path to tyranny. The religious mind is wired for certainty, and it views doubt as an existential threat. Truly, it is easier to believe in the certainties of theology than to arrive at a personal understanding of faith through years of doubt, questioning and mental effort. Worse, are those who assume a monopoly on the truth and rudely and patronisingly attempt to convert others to their faith. Neither scripture nor spiritual revelation can be taken at face value and do not relieve us of our struggle for the discernment of truth. Yet there are sects in Christianity today who are so alienated by the

hyper-rationalism of the age and the existential void it has created that they cling doggedly to a literalist and fundamentalist interpretation of scripture. I call it *instant soup*: take it off the shelf, add water and you have faith; there's no need to think, all you have to do is believe.

13. From its inception, Christianity was bound to an authoritarian canon of belief, at variance with the speculative nature of Greek philosophy, and the triumph of Christianity in the fifth century marked the death of the Greek philosophical tradition. Yet should not religion teach us how to think and not merely to believe? *We come to faith in the fulness of mind, not in the absence of it.* Should we abdicate our ethical and moral autonomy to the written word? Of course not! What can be said of the man who believes in God but cannot think, nor reflect upon his actions? We are thinking beings and it is beholden upon us to think! All orthodoxies stifle thought, no more so than religious orthodoxies. When worship of God as an entity external to the Self supplants the idea of connectedness with the source of our being and with each other, when blind

belief supplants the ideals of kindness and compassion, and when doctrine and orthodoxy become more important than spiritual curiosity and the pursuit of wisdom, then we have corrupt religion. Above all, religion should make us better people: if it does not make us better people, but makes us worse people, then it has failed.

14. Arguments from God are irrelevant in rational ethics, which provide a surer solution to human problems than appeals to 'God's plan'. My reason for saying this is because arguments from faith deal in absolutes: absolute moral law, absolute religious law, absolute rights, while rational ethics is more nuanced, seeking to balance competing needs and values. Ethical problems such as abortion, gay and transgender rights, and the right to terminate one's own life, fall squarely within the Competency of Reason and religion has no place in them.

15. Religion was not intended to crush the human spirit but to elevate it. Faith and sensuality are all expressions of Being and both offer us the experience of connectedness, which is not to say that sensuality should become an end in itself.

Religious austerity represses the most human and humane parts of ourselves, in which suffering becomes more important than love and kindness. *Sex without love belongs in the gutter; sex in the service of love belongs to the Spirit.* Equally, whatever one's faith, it should not take precedence over life, joy, family, and the companionable pursuits of friendship.

16. We must come to a personal understanding of our faith. Until we have made our faith our own, it will always be some else's faith. Inevitably this means that one person's faith will differ from another's and may deviate even from the 'official' doctrine of the Church (for what that is worth), but your own understanding is what will empower you as a man or woman of Spirit.

17. Faith is the path of awareness, inner discipline, compassion and respect for life. It is the enemy of all unquestioned ideas and unconsciously held assumptions. It does not – or rather should not – reflect the values of nationalism or cultural prejudice, nor the conservative values of public morality. Faith is not a badge of identity to be paraded in the street; it is not a label, nor is it a cultural statement. It is not a refuge for the

701

insecure. The reason why religion has failed Mankind is because it has become subsumed into culture and identity politics, which is nothing more than the manifestation of a deep-seated insecurity with its roots in historical experience of powerlessness, marginalisation, and diminished glory. Instead of working for the greatest good, religion instead blindly reflects the cultural assumptions of the society in which it first took root.... and so we behold forced conversion, discrimination on the basis of faith, death threats, pogroms and jihads, the repression of women, domestic abuse, female genital mutilation, bans on girls' education, girls sold off to dirty old men as soon as they can bleed and abused by ignorant husbands, rapists escaping punishment if they coerce their victims into marrying them, gay and transgender people whipped and imprisoned for being who they are... and all this is defended by religion! Rather than being a progressive reformist force in society, propelling humanity toward social enlightenment, religion has instead become a conservative force dedicated to the preservation of the existing social order, no matter how corrupt or prejudiced it is. I will say it now for all to hear: **FAITH TRANSCENDS CULTURE AND CULTURAL PREJUDICE HAS NAUGHT TO DO WITH FAITH**. Faith is not the worship of God as though we were slaves of some celestial tyrant, but the realisation of Divinity within ourselves and our dignity as children of God. If we love God but lack innocence, what can be said of us? If we love God but cannot love each other, we are damned.

18. No religious group has exclusive ownership of its founder. Jesus is not the property of Christians, the Prophet Mohammed is not the property of Muslims, nor is Buddha the property of Buddhists. As historical figures, they belong to history and all of humanity, and as human beings they are subject to the same historical criticism as all other human beings. 'Cancel culture' shuts down meaningful debate. No religious group has the right not to be offended.

19. The quality of faith depends on the quality of the one who possesses it. The faith of the ignorant is ignorance; the faith of the wise is

wisdom. It doesn't matter how enlightened a religion is: if it falls into the hands of ignorant people, it becomes a religion of ignorance. In your religion, you can be a peasant or a prince; you have this choice. What can be said of religion when a Muslim in Pakistan believes the Christian contaminates a well simply by drawing water from it? What can be said of religion when the Taliban in Afghanistan ban girls from going to school, or torture and shoot a young man for being gay? What can be said of religion when the Iranian Supreme Leader (who has never read the book) posts a 'hit job' just because a writer has 'offended' Islam, or when the same 'Supreme Leader' oversees a missile parade? What can be said of religion when an Iranian mullah casually steps over the body of a man being beaten up by guards in Evin prison? What can be said of religion when the Iranian morality police beat a young woman into a coma for not wearing her hijab correctly?[263] What can be said of religion when

---

[263] Mahsa Amini, 14th September, 2022 in Iran. Naturally, the corrupt Shiite theocracy denied it, fabricated a false autopsy

the (devoutly Muslim) Saudi secret service has a journalist dismembered in its consulate in Istanbul? When the ultimate expression of religion is an illiterate peasant with a rifle, you know faith is doomed.

20. Faith appeals to the conscience of Man. Therefore, Faith should remain apart from Power, and more, speak Truth to Power, and yet, for most of history, the Church and Mosque have been at the right arm of nationalism and power. They have never condemned the exploitation of native peoples; they have never spoken out against slavery, they have never spoken out against racial segregation, and have never interceded in unjust wars of aggression, but have themselves waged wars of religion; in the face of injustice, they have been conspicuous by their silence. What use are they? Both Christianity and Islam have acquiesced in slavery and abuse of human rights; both have initiated wars of conquest and conversion by the sword in the name of a religion of peace.

---

report and pressured the family into making a false media briefing.

The only religion that hasn't is Judaism, and for two reasons: first, Jewish society had no concept of 'state religion' and secondly, the idea of imposing Judaism on non-Jews would have been utterly irrational. What then is the point of an institution that should speak for Humanity but gets into bed with Power?

21. Spirituality always works from a position of strength and not of weakness. It is not about contemplating one's navel but showing kindness and empathy, helping those less fortunate and standing up for the good. It is not about opting out of the world but about maintaining our integrity *in* the world; it is about being true to one's own humanity which is always greater than mere personality. "For God hath not given us the spirit of fear; but of power, and of love, and of a sound mind" (2 Timothy 1:7).

We can exist passively, or we can exist actively. We can exist for the sake of existing, dodging the darts of adversity, or we can actively engage with Life and Being, in service to the higher ideal of Humanity.

22. So, in conclusion, what should be the signature attributes of faith?

Faith is our connectedness with the source of our Being and with each other.

Faith is the realisation of the presence of the Spirit within us. It is the intuitive perception of the numinous through the Deep Self that transcends Reason and Intellect.

Faith is openness to a metaphysical reality that lies beyond the phenomenological universe and can only be known through the deep mind.

Faith is the innate knowledge of a Higher Power.

Faith is spiritual curiosity.

Faith is the relentless pursuit of wisdom wherever it may lead.

Faith involves the questioning of all unconscious assumptions.

Faith is the path of awareness and self-discipline; *it is not mere belief but the way one leads one's life that saves us.*

Faith is the transformation of the Self into a consciousness that is aware, informed, disciplined, empathetic and capable of love.

Faith is a journey of inner transformation that has no end.

Faith is experiential; it is not passive belief. Faith alone, being provisional, does not of itself save us, but it does open a door to the unseen that speaks to us in dreams and visions. What we give the energy of faith to, we draw towards us.

This draws us into the question of 'what is real?' For science, that which is real is that which is verifiable, but I would argue strongly that not every dimension of existence is verifiable but can only be experienced through our mental connection with it. I may have a spiritual experience. That experience is 'real' even though it occurs in mind rather than 'out there'. The idea that something is only 'real' when it occurs in the physical world but something that occurs in mind is 'not real' is a prejudice of Scientific Materialism which theoretical physics has rendered obsolete. Is that spiritual experience merely a subconscious 'projection' of my faith (my mind reflecting back to me what it wants me to see) or has my faith itself opened a door to an acausal dimension of reality allowing me to perceive it and even communicate with it? Either may be true, but we cannot say that because the experience is unverifiable it is not 'real'. What is required, however, is that we *understand* what we have experienced, and we can relate it to the rational mind. This is the difference between revelation and madness. The insane are *mastered* by their experiences, the faithful *integrate* those experiences into their worldview.

FAITH IS NOT DOCTRINE
FAITH IS NOT CONFORMITY
FAITH CANNOT BE COMPELLED BY VIOLENCE
OR BY LAWS

FAITH IS THE INTERNALISATION OF
SPIRITUAL MEANING AND IT IS PERSONAL
TO THE SELF

Do not love Life
so much that you fear Death.

Make your peace with Death
while you live.

Accept it into your life
and greet it as an old friend when it comes.

Milton Keynes UK
Ingram Content Group UK Ltd.
UKHW041320231023
431179UK00001B/6